Food, Cuisine and Society in Prehistoric Greece

Sheffield Studies in Aegean Archaeology, 5

SHEFFIELD STUDIES IN AEGEAN ARCHAEOLOGY

SHEFFIELD STUDIES IN
AEGEAN ARCHAEOLOGY

Food, Cuisine and Society in Prehistoric Greece

Edited by

Paul Halstead and John C. Barrett

Oxbow Books

First published in the United Kingdom in 2004. Reprinted in 2016 by
OXBOW BOOKS
10 Hythe Bridge Street, Oxford OX1 2EW

and in the United States by
OXBOW BOOKS
1950 Lawrence Road, Havertown, PA 19083

Paperback Edition: ISBN 978-1-84217-167-7
Digital Edition: ISBN 978-1-78570-509-0

A CIP record for this book is available from the British Library

For a complete list of Oxbow titles, please contact:

UNITED KINGDOM
Oxbow Books
Telephone (01865) 241249, Fax (01865) 794449
Email: oxbow@oxbowbooks.com
www.oxbowbooks.com

UNITED STATES OF AMERICA
Oxbow Books
Telephone (800) 791-9354, Fax (610) 853-9146
Email: queries@casemateacademic.com
www.casemateacademic.com/oxbow

Oxbow Books is part of the Casemate Group

Front cover: Annual *Kourbáni* at church of Profitis Ilias, Assiros, N Greece

Contents

Abbreviations

AAA	*Athens Annals of Archaeology*
ADelt	*Arkhaiologiko Deltio*
AE	*Arkhaiologiki Efimeris*
AEMTh	*To Arkhaiologiko Ergo sti Makedonia kai Thraki*
AJA	*American Journal of Archaeology*
AM	*Mitteilungen des Deutschen Archäologischen Instituts, Athenische Abteilung*
AR	*Archaeological Reports*
ASA	*Annuario della Scuola Archeologica di Atene*
BAM	Beiträge zur Ur- und Frühgeschichtlichen Archäologie des Mittelmeer-Kulturraumes
BAR	British Archaeological Reports
BCH	*Bulletin de Correspondance Hellénique*
BICS	*Bulletin of the Institute of Classical Studies of the University of London*
BSA	*Annual of the British School at Athens*
CAJ	*Cambridge Archaeological Journal*
CMS	*Corpus der minoischen und mykenischen Siegeln*
CP	*Classical Philology*
CQ	*Classical Quarterly*
Ergon	*To Ergon tis Arkhaiologikis Etairias*
G&R	*Greece and Rome*
JAS	*Journal of Archaeological Science*
JHS	*Journal of Hellenic Studies*
JMA	*Journal of Mediterranean Archaeology*
Kr Chron	*Kritika Chronika*
OJA	*Oxford Journal of Archaeology*
PAE	*Praktika tis en Athinais Arkhaiologikis Etairias*
PBA	*Proceedings of the British Academy*
PCPS	*Proceedings of the Cambridge Philological Society*
SIMA	Studies in Mediterranean Archaeology
SMEA	*Studi Micenei ed Egeo-Anatolici*

Contributors

JOHN C. BARRETT
Department of Archaeology, University of Sheffield, Northgate House, West St., Sheffield S1 4ET, UK.

LISA BENDALL
Institute of Archaeology, 36 Beaumont St., Oxford OX1 2PG, UK.

ELISABETTA BORGNA
Università di Udine, Dipartimento di Storia e Tutela dei Beni Culturali, Piazza Antonini 8, 33100 Udine, Italy.

PETER DAY
Department of Archaeology, University of Sheffield, Northgate House, West St., Sheffield S1 4ET, UK.

PAUL HALSTEAD
Department of Archaeology, University of Sheffield, Northgate House, West St., Sheffield S1 4ET, UK.

VALASIA ISAAKIDOU
Institute of Archaeology, University College London, 31-34 Gordon Sq., London WC1H 0PY, UK.

JOHN KILLEN
Jesus College, Cambridge CB5 8BL.

KOSTAS KOTSAKIS
Dept. of Archaeology, Aristotle University, Thessaloniki 54006, Greece.

MARIA PAPPA
16 Eforia Proistorikon kai Klassikon Arkhaiotiton, Megalou Alexandrou enanti Posidoniou, 546 46 Thessaloniki, Greece.

JEREMY B. RUTTER
Department of Classics, Dartmouth College, Hanover, New Hampshire 03755, USA.

DUSKA UREM-KOTSOU
Dept. of Archaeology, Aristotle University, Thessaloniki 54006, Greece.

ELIA A. VARDAKI
38 Iroon Politechniou, Chania 73110, Crete, Greece.

DAVID WILSON
Department of Classical Studies, University of Western Ontario, London, Ontario N6A 3K7, Canada.

JAMES C. WRIGHT
Department of Classical and Near Eastern Archaeology, Bryn Mawr College, Bryn Mawr, PA 19010-2899, USA.

1

Introduction: Food, Drink and Society in Prehistoric Greece

Paul Halstead and John C. Barrett

The decision to devote the sixth annual Round Table of the Sheffield Centre for Aegean Archaeology, held in January 2001, to 'Food, Cuisine and Society in Prehistoric Greece' was taken for several overlapping reasons. First, a number of important recent papers had raised the profile of this topic, variously arguing that the consumption of food and drink had played a major role in shaping both material culture and social formations in the Aegean during the Neolithic (e.g., Hourmouziadis 1979; Vitelli 1989; Sherratt 1991; Halstead 1995) and Bronze Age (e.g., Moody 1987; Killen 1994; Wright 1996; Hamilakis 1996; 1999; Borgna 1997; Kiriatzi et al. 1997; Cavanagh 1998; Davis and Bennet 1999; Shelmerdine 1999). By drawing together colleagues working on consumption of food and drink in different time periods and different regions of the Aegean, we hoped to facilitate a comparative perspective. For example, was the social significance of food and drink consumption fundamentally different in the Neolithic village communities of northern Greece and in the later Bronze Age palatial societies of southern Greece?

The recent emphasis by Aegeanists on food and drink consumption is of course related to wider currents in archaeology and anthropology. Indeed, in the Sheffield Department of Archaeology alone, since this Round Table, three further conferences have focussed on similar issues but with a different chronological or geographical scope (Parker Pearson 2003 [including one paper, Valamoti 2003, of very direct relevance to Aegeanists]; Carroll et al. in press; Symonds in prep.). It is also arguable, however, that the Neolithic and Bronze Age of the Aegean exhibit, at least by European standards, a consistently striking elaboration of material culture related to food and drink consumption. A second reason for our choice of topic, therefore, was that we hoped to consider, albeit perhaps on a timescale extending beyond this particular Round Table, whether the distinctive development of material culture in the Aegean signalled a particularly important role for food and drink in the negotiation of social relationships. We return briefly to this point below.

A third consideration in choosing this subject was its unusual potential for multi-disciplinary research. To this end, contributions to this volume explore food and drink consumption in the Aegean on the basis of such diverse sources of evidence as ceramic function and style, iconography, architecture, faunal remains, Linear B texts and oral history.

Menu: the Content and Organization of this Volume

The papers that follow thus differ in terms of temporal and geographical coverage and evidential base. To facilitate comparison, they are arranged in an order that broadly respects both date and geography. Maria Pappa and colleagues integrate stratigraphic, ceramic and faunal evidence from a massive accumulation of primarily consumption debris in a large early Late Neolithic (LN) pit at the 'flat-extended' site of Makriyalos in Central Macedonia. The pit contains remains of hundreds, perhaps thousands, of domestic mammals, arguably representing communal or even regional commensality over a period of several months. Although apparently derived from collective consumption on a very large scale, the pit's contents also reveal a rich fabric of social inclusion and differentiation at smaller scales. Highly individualized cups underline the participation in consumption of individual social actors, while standardized serving vessels emphasize the existence both of groups of 'companions' or close kin, served from the same dish, and of a larger collective that shared a common material culture and etiquette of consumption. Neolithic commensal politics were evidently complex, while the overall scale of consumption represented here will certainly have offered scope for competitive hospitality.

Peter Day and David Wilson analyse ceramic 'tableware' from Early Minoan (EM) Knossos on Crete and argue for radical changes through time in the social context of food and drink consumption. The adoption of smaller cups, increasing elaboration of pouring vessels, addition of individual 'plates' to the ceramic repertoire, and emphasis on decorative fields visible from above suggest a shift from communal sharing among standing participants to ceremonial serving of food and drink to specific seated individuals. The development of standardized drinking/serving sets and imitation of metal forms strengthen the impression of uneven access to increasingly formal consumption events. In the later EM period, commensal politics had assumed an overtly assymetrical form that it is tempting to relate to wider claims to status and authority.

Jerry Rutter's chapter moves to the south coast of Crete, and forward in time, to the palatial period, focussing on the preparation and consumption of food and drink in the Late Minoan (LM) 'Civic Center' at Kommos. In successive phases of LMI-II activity, grinding installations or hearths with cooking pots attest to food preparation in this public area, while the recurrent association of these hearths with quantities of cups, jugs and vessels for the transport of liquids points to the consumption of drink as well as food. Fine drinking and pouring vessels, coupled with an abundance of functionally similar, utilitarian forms, suggest social gatherings in which both high-ranking individuals and large numbers of less privileged people participated. The cooking pots, representing only some of the shapes found in contemporary domestic contexts, imply that these gatherings were distinguished by menu or cuisine as well as scale and guest-list. The development of a local 'Floral Paneled Style' of decoration, perhaps identifying a functionally related 'set' of tableware, hints that these gatherings were also distinguished by an elaborate etiquette in which liquids were decanted from amphorae into jugs and then poured into cups. Intriguingly, at a time when imported vessels were growing in frequency and strikingly concentrated around the Civic Center, the Floral Paneled Style is only applied to selected Cretan shapes, indicating that commensality in this public area could highlight *local* identity as well as access to exotica.

The archaeological record of this period in southern mainland Greece, the early Late Helladic (LH), is dominated by rich graves rather than monumental architecture. Luxurious cups and jugs, metal and ceramic, from LHI-II graves at several sites imply that drinking ceremonies were an important arena for competition between emerging elite groups. A striking variety of often unique vessels, including both imports and elaborate fusions of exotic forms and decorative styles with local traditions, leads Jim Wright to argue that innovation was a key currency in elite competition. In LHIII, by contrast, when fortified citadels and monumental palaces were built, a more standardized drinking service appears even in rich burials. Wright links the decline of sumptuary display to the emergence of stable status positions, and the standardization of drinking vessels to the development of a common social etiquette, orchestrated by palace functionaries and practised at palace-sponsored feasts. Drinking ceremonies now served primarily as a vehicle of horizontal integration, as much as vertical differentiation, of Mycenaean society.

The theme of Mycenaean palace-sponsored feasting is further examined by Lisa Bendall. Linear B texts, from Pylos and Thebes on the mainland and from Knossos on Crete, record the supply of provisions for palace banquets by members of the elite, and palatial distribution of wine and perhaps pigs for feasts at regional centres. More modest contributions to palace banquets were also made by individuals of lower status. The texts offer no hint that these contributions were either obligatory or reciprocal, raising the question of the motivation for such 'conspicuous giving'. A possible answer is suggested by archaeological evidence for differential access to banquets. At Pylos, the distribution of drinking and eating vessels indicates a three-tier banqueting hierarchy: use of metal vessels in the central *megaron*, of finer ceramic vessels in the southwest wing of the palace and of coarser ceramics in the area in front of the entrance to the palace. A fourth tier, implied by textual evidence of banqueting supplies to regional centres, may be represented archaeologically in modest imitations of palatial architecture at sites such as Malthi. Banqueting thus encapsulated the inequalities of Mycenaean society and Bendall argues that the variable contributions of food and drink, by individuals of high and low status, effectively marked acceptance of the *status quo*.

Paul Halstead and Valasia Isaakidou consider faunal evidence for banqueting at Pylos. Ongoing analysis of a range of MH and LH deposits reveals a mixture of species, body parts and taphonomic conditions, dominated by fragmented but unburnt bones of sheep and pigs; among the cattle bones, adult females seem well represented. A few groups of bone from the area of the palace, and contemporary with its final phase, stand out in comprising selected body parts of cattle (probably including large males) and deer; the bones had been stripped of meat, but not broken open to extract marrow, and had then been burnt. The size and number of animals represented suggest the availability of, literally, tons of meat on single occasions – enough to provision the large-scale feasting implied by the textual and ceramic evidence. The careful deposition of these bone groups around the palace building, their exclusive composition of deer and large cattle, and the association of one bone group with a few miniature cups point to conspicuous elite generosity, while close parallels with Homeric and later burnt sacrifice underline the overtly religious context of feasting. The bones from Pylos thus echo the twin themes explored by Wright and Bendall, of feasting as a vehicle for promoting both horizontal social integration and vertical social differentiation.

Again in a Mycenaean palatial context, John Killen examines Linear B evidence from both Knossos and the mainland centres for consumption – not of wine or meat, but of olives, figs, and the three foodstuffs conventionally identified as 'wheat', 'barley' and 'flour'. With customary caution, Killen offers slight support for the thesis that the conventional identifications of **120* and **121*, as wheat and barley respectively, should be reversed. Arguably more important than the issue of which biological taxa are represented by these contentious ideograms, however, is Killen's clear demonstration that particular foodstuffs are associated with particular contexts of use. **120* is the only cereal listed in records of stored harvests and is normally, perhaps exclusively, issued as rations to women workers and their children. Conversely, **121* is issued as rations to male workers and as allowances to both male and female participants in religious festivals, is given as offerings to divinities, and appears on the menu of banquets. Evidently these seemingly mundane foodstuffs constituted a rich semiotic field that, together with 'luxury' foods such as meat and wine, with fine tableware, with refined etiquette and with exclusive architecture, helped to draw distinctions between different contexts of consumptions and between those who participated in them in different ways.

Elisabetta Borgna takes us to the end of the Bronze Age, to post-palatial Phaistos in southern Crete. Ceramic assemblages from two different areas of the site suggest divergent patterns of consumption in contrasting social contexts.

From the elevated 'Acropoli Mediana', a late LMIIIB-early LMIIIC group of fine pottery and figurines, lacking many elements typical of domestic material, appears to represent commensality and ritual activity in a public context. This assemblage is dominated, in terms of both numbers of vessels and decorative emphasis, by deep bowls and *kraters*, while the cups typical of earlier LM dining assemblages are few and either plain or simply decorated. The deep bowls are suited, by shape and decorative treatment, to *circulation* among several participants, in contrast to the movement between two parties seen in earlier palatial depictions of cups and *kylikes*. Hierarchical banqueting within the confines of the palaces has here given way to more equal participation in consumption in a public arena, but the elaboration of decoration on mainland-inspired deep bowls and *kraters* implies an element of competition that drew, *inter alia*, on appeals to the exotic. Borgna sees the communal drinking on the Acropoli Mediana as a possible precursor of the later classical *symposion*. The 'Casa a ovest del Piazzale I', overlooked by the Acropoli Mediana, has yielded a functionally more diverse LMIIIC ceramic assemblage, compatible with some form of household unit. A concentration of deep bowls and *kraters* again suggests ceremonial drinking, but in a more private context, and less elaborate ceramic decoration and large numbers of plain or simply decorated cups and *kylikes* perhaps reflect more restricted opportunities for competitive behaviour.

The final chapter brings us to the highlands of Crete in the latter half of the 20C AD. Elia Vardaki explores the diverse ways in which the preparation and consumption of food were perceived and manipulated by different individuals and groups in a village community over a period of considerable social and economic change. Over the last half century, as economic modernization has been accompanied by growing independence and material affluence of individual families, the consumption of meat at weddings and the like has intensified, but increasingly as a medium of competition, rather than as a means of promoting solidarity, between families. At the same time, as herding has declined in scale and economic significance, the consumption of lamb meat has assumed an increasingly prominent role in ceremonial contexts. In part, at least, the rising prominence of lamb meat must be understood in terms of masculine ideals, rooted in traditional male practices of herding and butchery. Conversely, some women seek to negotiate their identity by appeal to a wholly different set of values in the adoption of urban cuisine. Vardaki's observations are widely echoed in the preceding chapters, underlining the inevitable dependence of an archaeology of consumption on studies anchored in the present. From this perspective, the volume might profitably be read from back to front.

Food for Thought

One issue is highlighted by all the contributions to this volume. Food and drink, and the material culture and etiquette of their consumption, can signify a variety of social distinctions, identities and values. The subtleties of engendered commensal politics are, perhaps inevitably, most evident in Vardaki's participant observation of contemporary Cretans, while Killen's analysis of Linear B texts exposes an impressive range of social and situational distinctions signalled by mundane foodstuffs. A plethora of horizontal and vertical distinctions is also accentuated or masked, however, by 'mute' archaeological evidence – perhaps most strikingly by variation (or standardization) in the raw materials, shapes, sizes, placement and content of decoration, and spatial distribution of vessels used in the preparation, serving and consumption of food and drink.

In any one context, multiple identities and values may be contested or affirmed, as exemplified by the tension between individual and collective at LN Makriyalos, the apparent appeals to both local and exotic at LMI-II Kommos, or the advertising of both communality and hierarchy in the feasts sponsored by the Mycenaean palaces. The tension between horizontal integration and vertical differentiation (also Dietler 2001: 77), in particular, is widely implicit in commensality in so far as the latter replicates the vitally intimate but asymmetrically dependent nutritional relationship between child and parent. On this contradiction or ambiguity, arguably, rests the particular potential of commensality to (re)shape social relations. Thus, at EM Knossos, changes in tableware emphasized the asymmetry between host and guests, while affirming equality among the latter. Palace-sponsored feasting at Mycenaean Pylos highlighted several levels of social distinction in the context of large-scale commensality set against a physical backdrop that projected a common cultural identity in the face of uncivilized outsiders (Davis and Bennet 1999). Conversely, at post-palatial Phaistos, drinking vessels from the public arena of the Acropoli Mediana seem designed to play down inequalities between *participants* in ritual drinking ceremonies, but participation may well have been restricted; moreover, elaborate ceramic decoration may have served to enhance the status of participants and to project the values on which this was based. At EM Knossos and post-palatial Phaistos, and likewise in the elaborate drinking services of the LHI-II southern mainland, commensality arguably provided an arena for competition and so favoured social change or at least jockeying for position within an emerging hierarchy. On the other hand, at Mycenaean Pylos, palatial feasting helped to remind participants of their place in society and of both the privileges and obligations that this entailed.

As already noted, one of the questions posed in planning the Round Table was whether the social significance of food and drink consumption differed fundamentally between the Neolithic village communities of northern Greece and the later Bronze Age palatial societies of southern Greece. The wealth of evidence for 'diacritical feasting' (Dietler 2001) in the Mycenaean palaces contrasts sharply with the pattern of consumption at LN Makriyalos which, despite undoubted potential for competitive provisioning, seems more concerned with fission and fusion among relatively equal social actors. This contrast, to which we return below, is consistent with the traditional model, of marked social hierarchy first appearing in the Bronze Age, and so is unlikely to occasion surprise.

What is perhaps more unexpected is the huge scale of consumption of domestic animals at LN Makriyalos which, even allowing for the brief temporal span covered by surviving Linear B records, may well match or even significantly exceed that documented for the Mycenaean palaces (Halstead 2002). It might be argued that the large pit excavated at Makriyalos is exceptional – as yet it is unique for the Neolithic of Greece. It is worth noting, however, again subject to some uncertainties over temporal scales of analysis, that the volume of consumption documented for the southern Greek palaces may be eclipsed even more decisively by several sites in later prehistoric southern England. For example, a faunal sample from the Late Neolithic henge of Durrington Walls indicated consumption in a short space of time of over 100 pigs (Albarella and Serjeantson 2002); Early Bronze Age barrow burials at Irthlingborough (Davis and Payne 1993) and Gayhurst (Chapman et al. in prep.) were apparently accompanied by the slaughter of a few hundred cattle; and at LBA-EIA sites such as East Chisenbury (McOmish 1996), substantial mounds of feasting debris – equivalent in volume to some of the larger Neolithic 'tell' settlements of Greece – seem to have accumulated over perhaps two centuries.

While archaeologists sometimes assume that degree of vertical social hierarchy is proportional to extent of horizontal social integration (e.g., Renfrew 1972; 1973; 1977), it seems that scale of commensality and degree of diacritical elaboration need not be closely linked. This observation takes us back to Goody's provocative contrast between hierarchical societies of Eurasia, characterized by diacritical *cuisines* and *etiquettes*, and those of sub-Saharan Africa, where distinctions of rank or occasion may be marked by quantitative rather than qualitative differences in hospitality (Goody 1982; see also Dietler 2001: 85–87). For Goody, the Eurasian elaboration of cuisine is linked to the entrusting of elite-sponsored feasting to specialist male chefs rather than to high-status women (cf. Wright's discussion in this volume of the role of palace functionaries in formulating drinking etiquette). This inversion of gender roles is, in turn, to be understood in terms of the seclusion of high-status women in societies dependent on plough-agriculture because land (transmitted through marriage settlements), rather than human labour, is the limiting factor on food production.

The contributions to this volume suggest an alternative (though not necessarily contradictory) way of thinking about this issue. The quantitative strategy of competitive feasting has obvious benefits to the aspiring commensal politician. The slaughter of large numbers of domestic animals for a feast is not easily emulated by one's peers and so the risk that the grand gesture will pass unnoticed or be forgotten is low. On the other hand, such profligate destruction of finite resources is very costly and, unless the symbolic capital so accrued confers lasting material benefits, may not be repeatable. The qualitative strategy of competitive feasting offers the *possibility* of impressing one's peers or potential clients at more modest cost, but is unlikely to be effective unless the host already enjoys the high-status that enables her/him to set norms of cuisine or etiquette – in effect to create value.

How value was created in commensal contexts is an issue addressed by several of the contributors to this volume. In some cases, value might be regarded as almost intrinsic (cf. Renfrew 1986) to what is consumed, because of its relative scarcity, as in the case of the metal vessels of early and late Mycenaean date, respectively, discussed by Wright and Bendall. Similarly, the adult male cattle and deer represented in burnt sacrifice deposits at Pylos were probably valued for more than their carcass weight, especially given Linear B evidence that cattle of specific colours were selected for slaughter on some occasions (Palaima 1989; Killen 1994). The same logic of interpretation might be extended to the rare imported craft goods discussed by Rutter, Wright and Borgna.

Value is more obviously a cultural construct in the case of ceramic vessels that imitate metal prototypes, whether by skeuomorphism (Day and Wilson), tinning (Wright) or the adoption of 'metallic' surface colours (Bendall). Here, as with local imitations of exotic forms or decorative motifs (see Day and Wilson, Rutter, Wright, Borgna), value is almost certainly not founded on the illusion that locally-made ceramic vessels are actually metallic or imported, but rather on the acceptance that these 'imitations' symbolically represent their prototypes and the social contexts with which the latter are associated. Alternatively, value may appeal to local tradition, as in the emphasis on lamb meat with its masculine symbolism in contemporary highland Crete (Vardaki) or the elaboration of *Helladic* practices in the development of the Mycenaean drinking service (Wright). The construction of value can thus appeal to a variety of currencies, suggesting that prestige foods, drinking services or etiquettes are as likely to achieve their value by association with persons of high-status as *vice versa* (as stressed, in a slightly different context, by Voutsaki [1997]). This point is explored by Wright, in particular, in his contrast between early (LHI-II) and later (LHIII) Mycenaean drinking services. The former, produced in the context of acute competition for elite status among factional leaders, exhibit great variability and eclectically fuse a range of traditional and exotic forms. The latter, produced in palatial societies with established hierarchies, are highly standardized, reflecting the existence of stable models of elite behaviour and, in Wright's view, of officials who were as active in regulating standards of etiquette as in managing palatial estates. Evidence that palatial elites (or their functionaries) were implicated in assigning value to material goods and, by extension, in defining the status of their recipients, is provided by Linear B records of fine textiles produced under palace auspices and inventoried under rank-specific epithets (e.g., Killen 1985: 288 n 47). It is worth noting Killen's suggestion that these and other products of palace workshops may have been distributed at feasts (Killen 1994).

The construction of value through contextual association is particularly clear at Mycenaean Pylos, where Bendall shows how the status of banqueters was declared as much through the 'places' assigned to them as through the quality of the vessels from which they ate and drank (or the clothing given to them). This spatial ranking of banqueters was probably afforded divine sanction by *association* with burnt sacrifice, but even the survival of faunal evidence for this practice may be significant. Anatomically selective faunal deposits, such as have been found at Pylos and also at LHIII Nemea-Tsoungiza, imply that butchery was broken down into a series of discrete stages that were clearly separated in time or space or symbolically (Halstead and Isaakidou). At Pylos, the association of the biggest group of burnt bones with a few miniature cups suggests a sharp distinction between an initial stage of butchery and sacrifice, with a very restricted number of participants, and the ensuing distribution of meat, probably to a very large number of people. By contrast, the absence of evidence for selective anatomical deposition or segregation of stages of carcass reduction at LN Makriyalos is consistent with the apparent ceramic emphasis on inclusion rather than exclusion (Pappa et al.).

A wealth of contextual distinctions is also revealed by the Linear B records of 'staple' grains: cereal **120* is recorded as stored harvests and rations to women and children, while **121* is allocated to male workers, banqueters, deities and participants in religious festivals. As Killen shows, neither cereal can securely be identified as wheat or barley on the evidence of the texts themselves. In consequence, much of the argument has revolved around assumptions as to the relative value of wheat and barley. The recent resurgence in Europe of demand for brown, barley and rye breads, however, after centuries of retreat in the face of white wheaten loaves, reminds us that the relative value of cereals, like other foodstuffs, is a cultural construct. The apparent contradiction, in classical Greece, of wheat normally enjoying higher esteem than barley, although the latter was preferred in many religious contexts, underlines how complex these constructs may be. The safest conclusion is that the palaces' selective use of **120* and **121* in different contexts is likely to have played an active part in determining the value of different cereals in Mycenaean Greece.

Thus far, emphasis has been placed on the role of diacritical feasting in laying bare and legitimizing the inequalities in Aegean palatial society and in establishing the value of some of the material resources used to signal differential status (see also Wiessner 2001). It remains to point to a potentially important, related issue. As Bendall underlines, one of the intriguing features of Mycenaean palatial feasting is the role of both high- and low-ranking individuals in contributing to its provisioning. These contributions apparently were neither directly rewarded nor made in fulfilment of some prior obligation, suggesting that they must be understood in terms of social obligations of reciprocal generosity. To what extent this generosity was balanced may be a different matter. As host to large-scale commensality, the palace may have been ostentatiously pre-eminent in its largesse while overall receiving more resources than it expended. Even more significantly, however, as industrialized nations have found in trade with the thirdworld, the role of the palace in constructing value will have greatly enhanced its ability to benefit from such exchanges. Many of the resources expended by the Mycenaean palaces (including the cereal **121*) were not acquired through the forms of centrally organized or obligatory mobilization documented in Linear B (Halstead 1999), implying that they were raised by other means, such as the reciprocal generosity discussed by Bendall.

One of the most distinctive features of Mycenaean 'palatial economy' was the production of fine craft goods, involving scarce raw materials and/or highly specialized labour, and one of us has elsewhere described the Aegean palaces as 'arenas for the transformation of value' (Barrett 1998). There is little doubt that these items of value played a part in defining the status of those to whom they were given and in forging the social relationships that constituted the Mycenaean political economy (e.g., Killen 1985; Halstead 1999; Voutsaki 2001; also Friedman and Rowlands 1974). As Bendall reminds us below, status conferred obligations as well as privileges. Thus Mycenaean diacritical feasting, and the distribution of valuable craft goods that perhaps accompanied it, may *also* have been important mechanisms for palatial mobilization of resources. This was evidently the case in third millennium BC Mesopotamia, where a wealth of artistic evidence depicts the importance of feasts as means of mobilizing a wide range of resources as gifts or offerings (Schmandt-Besserat 2001: 392–97). Moreover, there is contemporary textual evidence that some major feasts were devoted to the consumption of barley (Schmandt-Besserat 2001: 397–99) – a grain normally used there for low-status rations or fodder (Charles 1998; Charles and Bogaard 2001); in effect, context-specific manipulation of value allowed surplus barley to be exchanged for livestock and other prized resources. Whether or not the complex categorization of cereals in Linear B can be interpreted in a similar fashion, it is clear that the elaboration of diacritical feasting in many hierarchical societies of the Bronze Age may partly be understood in terms of strategies of mobilization. The establishment of prestige *cuisines* and *etiquettes* allowed elites to use feasting to mobilize resources as gifts, without expending all these resources in reciprocal generosity.

Hungry for More?

In a paper that played a significant part in stimulating the holding of this Round Table, Yannis Hamilakis complained that Aegean prehistorians have adopted a narrowly nutritional approach to the consumption of food and drink (Hamilakis 1996). Following the Round Table and the papers presented here (see also Valamoti 2003; Wright 2004), this complaint would happily be rather harder to sustain. It is often said that 'food is good to think with'. The chapters that follow strongly suggest that, in the prehistoric (and indeed contemporary) Aegean, food and drink were very effective means of uniting and dividing people. To what extent the consumption of food and drink was a catalyst for social change, rather than just one of several media used by human agents to promote strategies of individual or collective advancement, is more difficult to assess and arguably depends greatly on the scale at which one seeks to understand social process. On a broad temporal and geographical scale, some sharp contrasts seem evident between societies (for example, in Neolithic Greece or Bronze Age southern England), in which large-scale commensality was marked by lavishness of provision, and those (for example, in Late Bronze Age southern Greece), in which elaborately diacritical feasting took place. Some initial thoughts on this contrast have been sketched out above.

In these respects, the Round Table proved as productive as we had hoped, or more so, but it may be useful also to focus on areas where more work is particularly needed. The papers that follow are extensively concerned with food/drink and society. Another 'key word' in our original title – cuisine – features less prominently, although it is addressed in the context of Linear B evidence for different forms of cereal product (Killen), of variation in cooking vessel forms (Rutter), of food residues in cooking pots (Pappa et al.) and of the opposition between traditional and modern recipes (Vardaki). For practical reasons (discussed by Rutter), the ways in which food was prepared for consumption may be less amenable, than the identity of the raw ingredients or the etiquette of serving, to large-scale, macroscopic investigation. Undoubtedly, chemical analysis of food residues in ceramics has an invaluable role to play here in linking raw ingredients, known from macroscopic analysis of animal bones or charred plant remains, to vessels used to store, prepare or consume food and drink. As we were clearly reminded at the Round Table, however, by Carl Heron and Maria Roumpou, such residues are by no means routinely preserved, are not cheap to analyse and can be difficult to interpret. In addition, as with conventional macroscopic techniques, residue analysis is far more sensitive to some ingredients, and to some stages of the storage-preparation-consumption cycle, than others. Contrary to some ambitious claims (Tzedakis and Martlew 1999), therefore, residue analysis is an invaluable complement to, rather than replacement for, other techniques and indeed is most effective when embedded in sampling frames shaped by faster macroscopic analyses.

A second respect in which the Round Table slightly deviated from expectations relates to the deliberate choice of 'food' rather than 'feasts' for our title. Our hope was to focus broadly on consumption, including both mundane and spectacular episodes, and several contributions do indeed contrast these two ends of the spectrum of consumption (e.g., Pappa et al.; Rutter; Killen; Halstead and Isaakidou), not least as a means of identifying the more formal feasts. Nonetheless, this volume clearly exhibits an overall bias towards the more spectacular consumption events. This may partly be attributable to modern academics being as susceptible, as were those whom they study, to the lure of a feast, but there may also be a more practical explanation. In order to focus on food and drink as signifiers of social categories or cultural values, and ultimately on the role of such signification in social change, the evidence must be analysed contextually and, as far as possible, in terms of short-term *episodes* rather than aggregate *periods* of consumption, as emphasized by Halstead and Isaakidou with reference to faunal remains. For obvious reasons, major feasts are more likely than small-scale domestic consumption to generate viable samples of distinctive debris and so are likely to be targetted for contextual analysis. Moreover, as discussed above, debris from *diacritical* feasting is particularly likely to be distinctive in composition and context, thanks to the role of material culture, space and time in marking such occasions as special and in differentiating between different groups of participants. The implication is that investigation of patterns of consumption will be a more demanding task in the Neolithic of Greece, than in the ostentatiously diacritical context of the Bronze Age palaces. Encouragingly, however, Pappa et al. comment that the LN pit described from Makriyalos is exceptional for the Neolithic of Greece, not only in the *volume* of cultural material discovered, but also in its *completeness* – hitherto matched only in destruction levels. The commensal consumption represented by this pit was differentiated, qualitatively, from 'normal' consumption practices in relatively subtle ways, but its associated debris was marked out by separate and rapid disposal.

Clearing up

We owe thanks to several colleagues who, for various reasons were unable to contribute to this volume, but whose participation in the Round Table helped make it a success: John Bennet; Despina Catapoti; Chrysanthi Gallou; Yannis Hamilakis; Carl Heron and Maria Roumpou; Vangelio Kiriatzi, Stelios Andreou and Kiki Psaraki; Angus Smith; and Karen Wright. For logistical help with organizing the Round Table, we are indebted to Eleni Nodarou and Giorgos Vavouranakis, while assistance in the production of this volume was provided by John Bennet, Rob Craigie, Cat Howarth, Rocky Hyacinth, Valasia Isaakidou and Rupert Thompson. As befits the topic of the Round Table, feasts were prepared by Nong Branigan and by Nancy Krahtopoulou, with assistance from Valasia Isaakidou, Vangelio Kiriatzi, Kiki Psaraki, Sevi Triantaphyllou and Duska Urem-Kotsou. The traditional *depas* was awarded to Jim Wright. The Round Table was, once again, made possible by the generous financial assistance of INSTAP.

Bibliography

Albarella, U. and D. Serjeantson

2002 A passion for pork: meat consumption at the British Late Neolithic site of Durrington

Walls. In P. Miracle and N. Milner (eds.), *Consuming Passions and Patterns of Consumption*: 33–48. Cambridge: McDonald Institute.

Barrett, J.C.
1998 Rethinking the Aegean palaces. Seminar to Sheffield Centre for Aegean Archaeology. Department of Archaeology, Sheffield.

Borgna, E.
1997 Kitchen-ware from LM IIIC Phaistos: cooking traditions and ritual activities in LBA Cretan societies. *SMEA* 39, 2: 189–217.

Carroll, M., D. Hadley and H. Willmott (eds.)
in press *Consuming Passions: Dining from Antiquity to the Eighteenth Century*. Stroud: Tempus.

Cavanagh, W.
1998 Innovation, conservatism and variation in Mycenaean funerary ritual. In K. Branigan (ed.), *Cemetery and Society in the Aegean Bronze Age* (SSAA 1): 103–14. Sheffield: Sheffield Academic Press.

Charles, M.
1998 Fodder from dung: the recognition and interpretation of dung-derived plant material from archaeological sites. *Environmental Archaeology* 1: 111–22.

Charles, M. and Bogaard, A.
2001 Third-millennium BC charred plant remains from Tell Brak. In D. Oates, J. Oates and H. McDonald (eds.), *Excavations at Tell Brak, 2*: 301–26. Cambridge: McDonald Institute.

Davis, J. and J. Bennet
1999 Making Mycenaeans: warfare, territorial expansion, and representations of the other in the Pylian kingdom. In R. Laffineur (ed.), *Polemos: le contexte guerrier en égeé à l'âge du bronze* (Aegaeum 19): 105–20. Liège: University of Liège.

Davis, S. and S. Payne
1993 A barrow full of cattle skulls. *Antiquity* 67: 12–22.

Dietler, M.
2001 Theorizing the feast: rituals of consumption, commensal politics, and power in African contexts. In M. Dietler and B. Hayden (eds.), *Feasts: Archaeological and Ethnographic Perspectives on Food, Politics and Power*: 65–114. Washington: Smithsonian Institution Press.

Friedman, J. and M.J. Rowlands
1977 Notes towards an epigenetic model of the evolution of 'civilisation'. In J. Friedman and M.J. Rowlands (ed.), *The Evolution of Social Systems*: 201–76. London: Duckworth.

Goody, J.
1982 *Cooking, Cuisine and Class*. Cambridge: Cambridge University Press.

Halstead, P.
1995 From sharing to hoarding: the neolithic foundations of Aegean Bronze Age society? In R. Laffineur and W.-D. Niemeier (eds.), *Politeia: Society and State in the Aegean Bronze Age* (Aegaeum 12): 11–20. Liège: University of Liège.
1999 Towards a model of Mycenaean palatial mobilization. In M.L. Galaty and W.A. Parkinson (eds.), *Rethinking Mycenaean Palaces*: 35–41. Los Angeles: Cotsen Institute of Archaeology, UCLA.
2002 Texts, bones and herders: approaches to animal husbandry in late bronze age Greece. *Minos* 33–34 [1998–99]: 149–89.

Hamilakis, Y.
1996 Wine, oil and the dialectics of power in bronze age Crete: a review of the evidence. *OJA* 15: 1–32.
1999 Food technologies/technologies of the body: the social context of wine and oil production and consumption in bronze age Crete. *World Archaeology* 31: 38–54.

Hourmouziadis, G.
1979 *To Neolithiko Dimini*. Volos: Society for Thessalian Studies.
Killen, J.T.
1985 The Linear B tablets and the Mycenaean economy. In A. Morpurgo Davies and Y. Duhoux (eds.), *Linear B: a 1984 Survey*: 241–305. Louvain: Louvain University Press.
1994 Thebes sealings, Knossos tablets and Mycenaean state banquets. *BICS* 1994: 67–84.
Kiriatzi, E., S. Andreou, S. Dimitriadis and K. Kotsakis
1997 Co-existing traditions: handmade and wheelmade pottery in Late Bronze Age Central Macedonia. In R. Laffineur and P. P. Betancourt (eds.), *TEXNH: Craftsmen, Craftswomen and Craftsmanship in the Aegean Bronze Age* (Aegaeum 16): 361–66. Liège: University of Liège.
McOmish, D.
1996 East Chisenbury: ritual and rubbish at the British Bronze Age-Iron Age transition. *Antiquity* 70: 68–76.
Moody, J.
1987 The Minoan palace as a prestige artefact. In R. Hägg and N. Marinatos (eds.), *The Function of the Minoan Palaces:* 235–41. Stockholm: Swedish Institute at Athens.
Palaima T.G.
1989 Perspectives on the Pylos oxen tablets: textual (and archaeological) evidence for the use and management of oxen in late bronze age Messenia (and Crete). In T.G. Palaima, C.W. Shelmerdine and P. Hr. Ilievski (eds.), *Studia Mycenaea 1988* (Ziva Antika Monograph 7): 85–124. Skopje: University of Texas at Austin, University of Skopje.
Parker Pearson, M. (ed.)
2003 *Food, Culture and Identity in the Neolithic and Early Bronze Age* (BAR International Series 1117). Oxford: British Archaeological Reports.
Renfrew, C.
1972 *The Emergence of Civilisation: the Cyclades and the Aegean in the Third Millennium BC.* London: Methuen.
1973 Monuments, mobilization and social organization in neolithic Wessex. In C. Renfrew (ed.), *The Explanation of Culture Change*: 539–58. London: Duckworth.
1977 Space, time and polity. In J. Friedman and M.J. Rowlands (ed.), *The Evolution of Social Systems*: 89–112. London: Duckworth.
1986 Varna and the emergence of wealth in prehistoric Europe. In A. Appadurai (ed.), *The Social Life of Things*: 141–68. Cambridge: Cambridge University Press.
Schmandt-Besserat, D.
2001 Feasting in the ancient Near East. In M. Dietler and B. Hayden (eds.), *Feasts: Archaeological and Ethnographic Perspectives on Food, Politics and Power*: 391–403. Washington: Smithsonian Institution Press.
Shelmerdine, C.W.
1999 Administration in the Mycenaean palaces: where's the chief? In M.L. Galaty and W.A. Parkinson (eds.), *Rethinking Mycenaean Palaces*: 19–24. Los Angeles: Cotsen Institute of Archaeology, UCLA.
Sherratt, A.
1991 Palaeoethnobotany: from crops to cuisine. In F. Queiroga and A.P. Dinis (eds.), *Paleoecologia e Arqueologia* 2: 221–36. Vila Nova de Famalicao.
Symonds, J. (ed.)
in prep. *Table Settings: the Material Culture and Social Context of Dining in the Early Modern Period.*
Tzedakis, Y. and H. Martlew

1999 *Minoans and Mycenaeans: Flavours of their Time*. Athens: Greek Ministry of Culture, National Archaeological Museum.

Valamoti, S.-M.

2003 Neolithic and Early Bronze Age 'food' from northern Greece: the archaeobotanical evidence. In M. Parker Pearson (ed.), *Food, Culture and Identity in the Neolithic and Early Bronze Age* (BAR International Series 1117): 97–110. Oxford: British Archaeological Reports.

Vitelli, K.D.

1989 Were pots first made for food? Doubts from Franchthi. *World Archaeology* 21: 17–29.

Voutsaki, S.

1997 The creation of value and prestige in the Aegean Late Bronze Age. *Journal of European Archaeology* 5: 34–52.

2001 Economic control, power and prestige in the Mycenaean world: the archaeological evidence. In S. Voutsaki and J. Killen (eds.), *Economy and Politics in the Mycenaean Palace States* (Cambridge Philological Society Supplementary Volume 27):195–213. Cambridge: Cambridge Philological Society.

Wiessner, P.

2001 Of feasting and value: Enga feasts in a historical perspective (Papua New Guinea). In M. Dietler and B. Hayden (eds.), *Feasts: Archaeological and Ethnographic Perspectives on Food, Politics and Power*: 115–43. Washington: Smithsonian Institution Press.

Wright, J.

1996 Empty cups and empty jugs: the social role of wine in Minoan and Mycenaean societies. In P.E. McGovern, S.J. Fleming and S.H. Katz (eds.), *The Origins and History of Wine*: 287–309. Philadelphia: Gordon and Breach.

2004 (ed.) The Mycenaean Feast. *Hesperia* 73, 2.

2

Evidence for Large-scale Feasting at Late Neolithic Makriyalos, N Greece

Maria Pappa, Paul Halstead, Kostas Kotsakis and Duska Urem-Kotsou

Perhaps the three most striking material features of the Greek Neolithic are the development of long-lived, compact 'village' settlements, the subdivision of the latter into something akin to 'households', and the early appearance of fine pottery. The existence, or gradual development, of a basic household unit is predicated not only on architectural remains of 'houses', but also on the argument that associated facilities suggest the storage and consumption of food primarily at a 'domestic' rather than communal level (Hourmouziadis 1979; Theochares 1980; Kotsakis 1981; Halstead 1995). The longevity of many village settlements, on the other hand, implies the existence of effective cultural mechanisms to ensure the economic survival and ideological reproduction of the larger community in the face of tendencies to domestic isolation and of potential conflict between competing households and individuals (Halstead 1999; Kotsakis 1999). The nature of these mechanisms may be suggested by the size and shape repertoire of Neolithic fine pottery, which seems more appropriate for the presentation and consumption, rather than storage or preparation, of food and drink (Kotsakis 1983; Vitelli 1989). The careful finishing and elaborate decoration of much early 'tableware' has widely been taken to indicate that periodic hospitality or commensality, on a scale larger than the household, was of great social importance as a cultural domain in which people pursued both economic and political goals, competed for power and renegotiated social ties and obligations (e.g., Kotsakis 1982). To date, however, this model of commensal politics has not been explored in terms of the necessary integrated and contextualized analysis of ceramic tableware and bioarchaeological food remains.

The Late Neolithic site of Makriyalos, N Greece, offers an excellent opportunity to rectify this situation. The horizontally-drifting character of Neolithic habitation, coupled with the unusually large scale of excavation, enabled clearer definition of individual depositional contexts than is often possible in deep soundings into the complex stratigraphy of compact tell sites. This chapter attempts to capitalize on this potential by interdisciplinary analysis of a single depositional context, exceptionally rich in finds, at Makriyalos. The integrated consideration of stratigraphic, ceramic and faunal evidence suggests that this context contains the debris from collective consumption on a massive scale.

The Site

The Neolithic site of Makriyalos is located on gentle hill slopes in the coastal lowlands of Pieria, C Macedonia. It forms a 'flat-extended' settlement of a type well known in the northern Balkans and now widely recognized in C Macedonia (e.g., Andreou and Kotsakis 1986). The known extent of the site is 50 ha, of which ca 6 ha were investigated during rescue excavations in the 1990s (Pappa and Besios 1999a; 1999b). Two distinct phases of late Neolithic occupation are evident: Makriyalos I, characterized by early LN (pre-Dimini in Thessalian terms) ceramics; and Makriyalos II, characterized by late LN (Dimini) ceramics.

Phase II occupation, on relatively low ground, is represented by a dense scatter of pit dwellings with encircling postholes, interspersed with storage and cooking pits, and by the foundations of at least one above-ground rectangular building. On the higher and more eroded slopes to the southwest of the late LN settlement, Phase I occupation is represented by circuit ditches and groups of pit-dwellings (Figure 2.1); large pits, mostly on the edge of the settlement, are interpreted as borrow pits where bedrock was mined - presumably for use in above ground constructions. The best preserved ditch, Alpha, was paralleled by

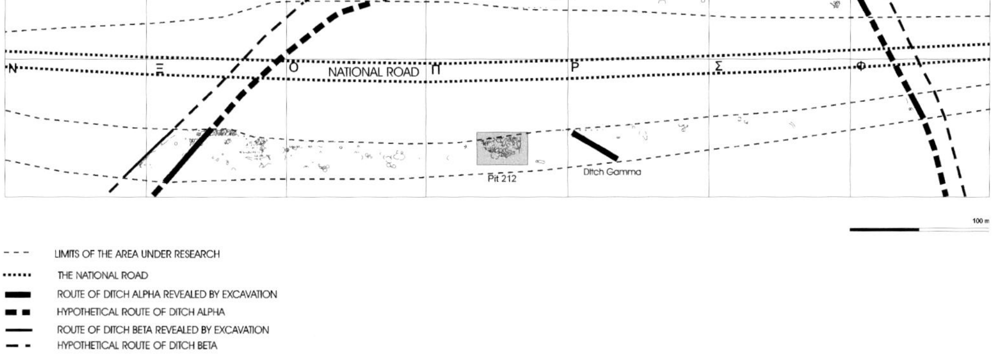

Figure 2.1. Plan of Makriyalos phase I settlement, showing location of early LN Pit 212

an external wall, suggesting an enclosing rather than excluding function. The probable role of the ditch in defining symbolically a local community is reinforced by deposition of both intact burials and scattered human remains (Triantaphyllou 1999). The phase I settlement has yielded abundant evidence, therefore, for collective activity well above the domestic level. Makriyalos I has also yielded exceptionally large artefactual and bioarchaeological assemblages, reflecting partly the unusually extensive scale of excavation, but also the discovery of some deposits very rich in finds. Phase I pottery includes a wealth of 'tableware', together with storage and cooking vessels. Phase I animal bone is dominated overwhelmingly by domesticates, as is usual in the Neolithic of Greece.

Pit 212

One phase I context proved exceptionally rich in finds. Pit 212 (or 'Pit Pi', after its location in the excavation grid) lies roughly in the middle of the area enclosed by the approximately contemporary circuit ditch Alpha (Pappa and Besios 1999a:

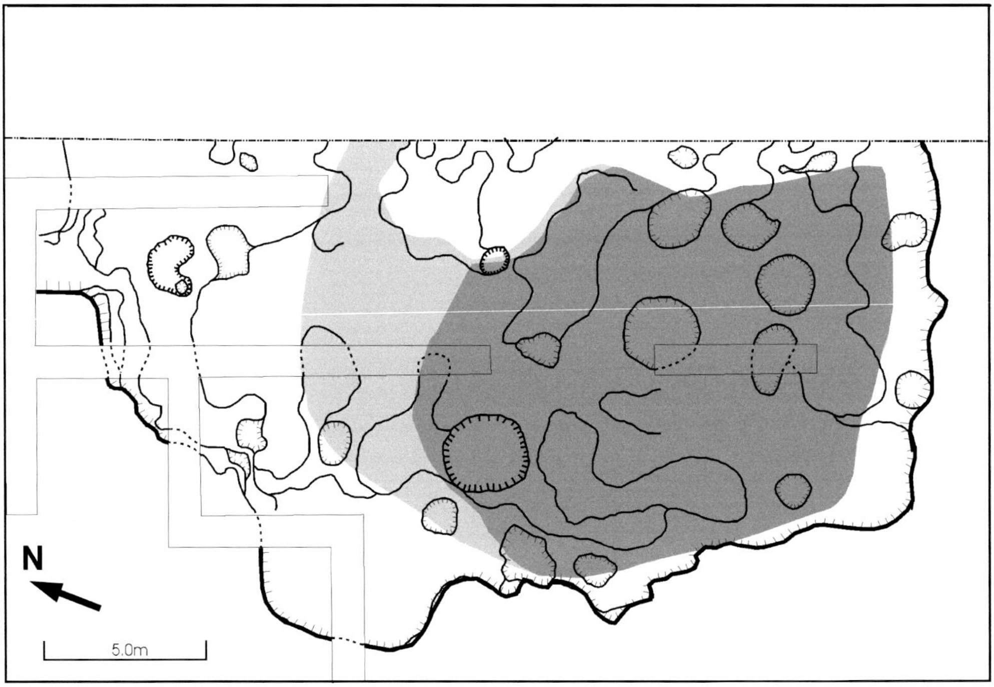

Figure 2.2. Plan of excavated part of early LN Pit 212 at Makriyalos
Key: dark shading – dense basal 'carpet' of finds
light shading – moderate density of finds
unshaded – lower density of finds

181 fig. 3, 184 fig. 7). The preserved dimensions of the pit (Figure 2.2) are 30 m N-S by 15 m E-W, but the eastern part was destroyed by motorway construction in the 1960s and the original extent is likely to have been at least 500 sq m and perhaps substantially more. The preserved depth ranged between 0.3–0.7 m on the periphery and 1.2–1.4 m in the middle, with the southern part being deeper than the northern. The bottom was marked by a mosaic of intersecting, smaller cuttings, which presumably represented the bases of pits dug during the original quarrying of this feature. Because of its large size and irregular shape, it was inferred that Pit 212 was originally dug as a borrow pit. If this interpretation is correct, the large volume of the soft bedrock removed (perhaps in excess of 500 cubic metres) must raise the possibility of quarrying for some large, collective construction project.

The stratigraphy of Pit 212 comprised three principal layers:

1. topsoil;
2. a dark brown layer rich in cockle shells, burnt clay and other finds, especially in the southern and western parts of the pit;
3. a greyish basal fill rich in ceramics, small finds, burnt clay and animal bones and, in the southern part of the pit, including a 10-cm thick 'carpet' of finds (Figure 2.2) with very little intervening soil; no lenses, such as might have indicated discontinuous deposition, were visible.

Such a large volume of finds from a single context has not previously been reported from the Neolithic of Greece and, apart from furnishing exceptionally rich assemblages of animal bones, pottery, figurines, and other artefacts, arguably offers a rare insight into the social significance of consumption. Interpretation depends greatly on the temporal scale of deposition. At one extreme, the material might have been dumped in a single episode and so would almost inevitably represent consumption at a very large social gathering. At the other extreme, it might represent long-term discard by a small social group, with repeated use of the same depositional context creating a midden as a monument, intentional or not, to a long history of consumption. The following section examines the temporal context of deposition in Pit 212, therefore, before further elucidation is attempted of the nature and aggregate scale of the activities implied by this debris. In conclusion, the possible social context and significance of these activities is considered.

The Temporal Context of Deposition

Calibrated C14 dates suggest that the phase I occupation of Makriyalos fell within the period 5300–5000/4900 BC, thus potentially spanning three to four centuries, but there are no C14 determinations from Pit 212 itself. Ceramic typology offers no greater precision. Apart from a few small, late MN sherds from a handful of excavation units, which are almost certainly residual material from earlier activity in the vicinity, the ceramic contents of Pit 212 are assignable to early LN. There is some evidence for the definition of ceramic sub-phases within early LN in Thessaly (Demoule et al. 1988), but extrapolation of the Thessalian sequence to Makriyalos would be unjustified in the present state of knowledge. Conversely, the horizontally drifting nature of occupation at Makriyalos prevents stratigraphic testing of a local relative chronology for early LN ceramic styles. Neither absolute radiocarbon nor relative ceramic dating, therefore, is of sufficiently fine resolution to discriminate between long-term accumulation of the contents of Pit 212, over a period of several decades or even several human generations, and short-term accumulation, in an episode or series of episodes perhaps lasting only days, weeks or months. Stratigraphic, ceramic and faunal evidence, however, offers complementary and more precise insights into the context of deposition of the basal fill of Pit 212.

Stratigraphic Evidence

As noted above, the uneven floor of Pit 212 is comprised of a series of cuttings into the underlying bedrock and is sealed, over much of the south and west of the feature, by the basal 'carpet' of pottery and bones. During the recent excavations, it was observed that exposed sections in this part of the site fissure deeply during hot summers and that heavy downpours then cause the sides of trenches to collapse. The apparently rapid filling in of the phase I enclosure ditches suggests that, not surprisingly, similar processes were active during the LN occupation of the site. Pit 212 is of course a broad and relatively shallow cutting, and so less easily filled in than the enclosure ditches, but the thick basal carpet of finds extends close to the southwestern edge of the feature. This suggests that the primary deposition of finds took place very soon after the initial quarrying of the pit complex and also over a relatively short period of time. How rapidly the original sides of Pit 212 collapsed will have depended on prevailing weather conditions, with cool summers and moderate rainfall favouring a longer time frame than alternating droughts and downpours. Nonetheless, recent experience suggests that this basal fill will have been deposited within months rather than years of the cessation of quarrying activity. The overlying layer 2 is less rich in finds, but these are of similar types to those found in layer 3. The contents of layer 2 may in large part represent continued rapid deposition of finds, therefore, over a further period of months during which the sides of the pit collapsed, although it must be stressed that there is no direct stratigraphical evidence for such collapse.

The Evidence of Ceramic and Faunal Taphonomy

Although the basal carpet of finds apparently accumulated rapidly, this is unlikely to represent debris from activity within Pit 212. First, the ceramic finds are well preserved, with relatively unworn fractures, and so show no sign of intensive trampling by activity within the pit. Secondly, the basal fill contains scattered fragments of burnt clay surfaces (perhaps from hearths, ovens or other burnt facilities), but no preserved trace of any *in situ* constructions. If, therefore, the pottery and bone making up the basal carpet was dumped from outside Pit 212, it might be suggested that final rapid deposition in the pit followed a lengthy period of gradual accumulation in primary discard location(s) elsewhere on the site.

As already noted, available absolute and relative dating evidence sheds no light on this issue, but analysis of ceramic fragmentation patterns strongly contradicts any suggestion that the pottery component of the fill accumulated elsewhere over a long period of time, before final deposition in Pit 212. Because of the exceptional size of this ceramic assemblage, detailed analysis has been undertaken for a 40% sample of Pit 212 excavation units. The sample included substantial parts of several vessels that have been restored from potsherds found in the same or adjacent excavation units within the basal carpet; in this respect, the basal carpet resembled a destruction deposit from the interior of a building. The time elapsed between initial discard of vessels and their deposition in Pit 212 was thus sufficiently brief for large segments to have remained intact or for adjoining fragments to have remained spatially associated; the excellent surface condition of these fragments likewise suggests only brief exposure to weathering, trampling and so on before burial.

Analysis of the surface condition of the animal bones also provides some evidence for the speed of burial of this component of the Pit 212 fill. Approximately 27% of bones bear traces of gnawing by scavengers such as domestic dogs or perhaps pigs, indicating some lapse of time between discard and burial. Among 'long bones' with old breaks, however, 'cylinders', typical of material ravaged by carnivores, are far fewer than articular ends and splinters including part of the articulation, which are fragment types characteristic of breakage for marrow extraction by humans (Binford 1981). This pattern is compatible with either the prevention of carnivore attrition by rapid burial or the discard of bone at a rate far exceeding the appetite of local populations of scavengers. Bone surfaces are by no means pristine, with frequent traces of probable mechanical damage, but do not show obvious signs of weathering and this suggests that burial took place within, at most, months of discard. Groups of articulating bones, including part skeletons of dogs, confirm the ceramic evidence that the fill of the pit was largely undisturbed after deposition. The incidence of gnawing, patterns of fragmentation and species composition vary little between layers 1, 2 and 3, supporting earlier suggestions that these represent a more or less uniform process of discard of cultural material, differentiated by changes in the rate of deposition of the sedimentary matrix.

The combined stratigraphic, ceramic and faunal evidence thus suggests that the dense basal carpet of finds (and perhaps much of the overlying fill) in Pit 212 accumulated and was deposited within a period of, at most, several months or just a few years. Whether material was initially discarded in a single event or intermittently on several occasions may potentially be clarified by considering the faunal evidence for seasons of slaughter of the four common domesticates which make up the bulk of the faunal remains in Pit 212: sheep, goat, cow and pig.

Faunal Evidence for Season(s) of Slaughter

Age at death can be assessed most accurately for young animals and so analysis focusses here principally on evidence for mortality during the first year or so of life. The most accurate, abundant and continuous record of mortality is provided by the eruption and wear of mandibular teeth, but neonatal or foetal limb bones of pig, cow and undifferentiated sheep/goat provide valuable supplementary evidence of deaths within a few weeks of birth. For each of the four common domesticates, the overall pattern of mortality in Pit 212 is broadly similar to that for Makriyalos phase I as a whole, with much higher proportions of first-year deaths in sheep (42%) and pig (45%) than in goat (10%) or cow (8% by ca 6 months, 22% by ca 18 months).

Evidence is most abundant in the case of sheep. Following a recent study of tooth eruption and wear in a large and diverse sample of modern British sheep (Jones in press), deaths of first-year lambs can be assigned to seven successive stages of dental development (Table 2.1). Deaths are heavily concentrated in the sixth stage (C6+), implying a peak of slaughter at 8–13 months or, assuming a uniform lambing date of 1st February, during the months of September-February. Given that the main lambing season in northern Greece typically lasts at least two months, this is compatible with mass slaughter over a few days in autumn-winter. The small number of mandibles assigned to the other six stages could also be accommodated to this slaughter date, by assuming appropriate combinations of early or late births, early or late tooth eruption, and fast or slow tooth wear. This apparent seasonal peak in slaughter, however, is at least partly illusory: biases of survival will have led to acute under-representation of younger jaws (Munson and Garniewicz 2003); poor retrieval of small mandibular fragments and loose

Table 2.1. Makriyalos Pit 212: attribution of first-year deaths of sheep to successive dental stages

Dental stage*	A	B	C1/2	C3/4	C5	C6+	D1/2
Age range (mths, excl. outliers)**	0–1	1–4	3–6	5–9	6–10	8–13	10–14
No. (MinAU)	1	9	8	4	5	108	8

* after Jones (in press)
** after Jones (in press)

teeth will have been compounded by greater fragmentation of fragile young jaws; and internal analysis of tooth wear at Makriyalos (cf. Deniz and Payne 1982: 194 fig. 35) shows that this was significantly faster than in recent British sheep, with the effect that stage C6+ will have been of longer duration than in the British sheep. Thus, once allowance is made for demonstrable biases in survival, retrieval and data analysis, it becomes much harder to accommodate first-year deaths in sheep to a single season. A more parsimonious interpretation is that the slaughter of lambs, although possibly concentrated in the latter part of the first year, took place more or less throughout the year. The evidence for first-year deaths among goats is sparse, but again includes a range of dental stages (Table 2.2) that requires special pleading to be accommodated within a single season.

Dental data are also abundant for pigs, but tooth wear is more variable and less precisely recorded than in sheep or goat. First year mandibles are divided in Table 2.3 into three stages of dental development. Stage A jaws are very few, but neonatal limb bones confirm that some deaths took place among newborn piglets. Stage B jaws are more numerous and, with allowance for the longer duration of stage C and for the greater size and robustness of stage C jaws, similar levels of mortality may be implied for the first and second halves of the first year. Moreover, both stage B and stage C jaws display a range of tooth eruption and wear states, suggesting that young pigs were slaughtered more or less throughout their first year of life. Sows have a short gestation period and are potentially capable of farrowing twice per year or even five times in two years. If sufficiently variable farrowing dates are assumed, the mortality data from Pit 212 could be accommodated to a seasonal cull. Analysis of enamel hypoplasia patterns in Makriyalos pigs suggests a single farrowing season (U. Albarella and K. Dobney pers. comm.), however, so that staggered slaughter through the first year is again a more parsimonious interpretation.

Table 2.2. Makriyalos Pit 212: attribution of first-year deaths of goats to successive dental stages

Dental stage*	A	B	C1/2	C3/4	C5	C6+	D1/2
Age range (mths, excl. outliers)**	0–2	2–5	5–7	6–9	6–11	11–14	11–16
No. (MinAU)	0	1	1	0	3	3	0

* after Jones (in press)

** after Jones (in press) and estimated after Deniz and Payne (1982)

Table 2.3. Makriyalos Pit 212: attribution of first-year deaths of pigs to successive dental stages

Dental stage*	A	B	C
Age range (mths)**	0–2	2–7	7–12
No. (MinAU)	2	37	92

* defined as for sheep and goat

** after Higham (1967)

Infant jaws of cow are also scarce, but deaths shortly after birth are again confirmed by neonatal limb bones. Thereafter, mandibles with erupting M1, M2 or M3 imply deaths during the first half of the first, second and third years, respectively. If calving at LN Makriyalos was concentrated in late winter-early spring, the implied deaths of cattle in spring or summer would neatly complement the possible peak of slaughter of yearling lambs in autumn-winter.

With varying degrees of special pleading, it is possible to accommodate young deaths, in all four of the common domesticates in Pit 212, to a model of slaughter in a single season. A more economical interpretation, however, particularly when the four species are considered together, is that slaughter of first-year animals was staggered through the year. It should also be noted that there is no evidence for season of death of adult animals and that, given the large carcasses and significant numbers of adults represented, any peak in slaughter of yearling lambs need not have occasioned a seasonal peak in meat consumption.

The Nature of the Activities Represented by the Fill of Pit 212

Although the combination of animal remains and ceramic fragments found in Pit 212 is immediately suggestive of the consumption, or preparation for consumption, of animal carcasses, it remains to be demonstrated that these bones and sherds have more in common than just their final depositional context. Closer examination of both assemblages sheds light on which activities each represents.

The ceramic assemblage from Pit 212 is not only exceptionally large, but also more diverse in content than the ceramic material from some other phase I contexts at Makriyalos. The majority of the Pit 212 assemblage is comprised of 'tableware' appropriate for the presentation or consumption of food and/or drink. The tableware category includes both standardized, large (ca. 20–30 cm diameter) conical or carinated 'bowls' (Figure 2.3) and non-standardized, small (up to 13 cm diameter) 'cups' (Figures 2.4–8) and so was arguably intended to cater both for the presentation (or possibly collective consumption) of food/drink and for more individual acts of consumption. Cooking (Figure 2.9) and large storage vessels are also represented in Pit 212. The ceramic assemblage thus attests to the entire sequence from bulk storage, through cooking, to presentation and consumption of food/drink. An ongoing programme of isotopic analysis of organic residues in ceramic vessels from Pit 212 further indicates that the substances prepared for consumption included the meat (or, at least, the fat) of domestic animals, as well as probable plant foods (Urem-Kotsou *et al.* 2003).

The faunal remains from Pit 212 provide two complementary forms of evidence for the preparation and consumption of food from animal carcasses: the anatomical distribution of butchery marks and body part representation. Butchery marks, the placement of which is variously characteristic of skinning, dismembering and filleting (after Binford 1981), have been recognized on bones of

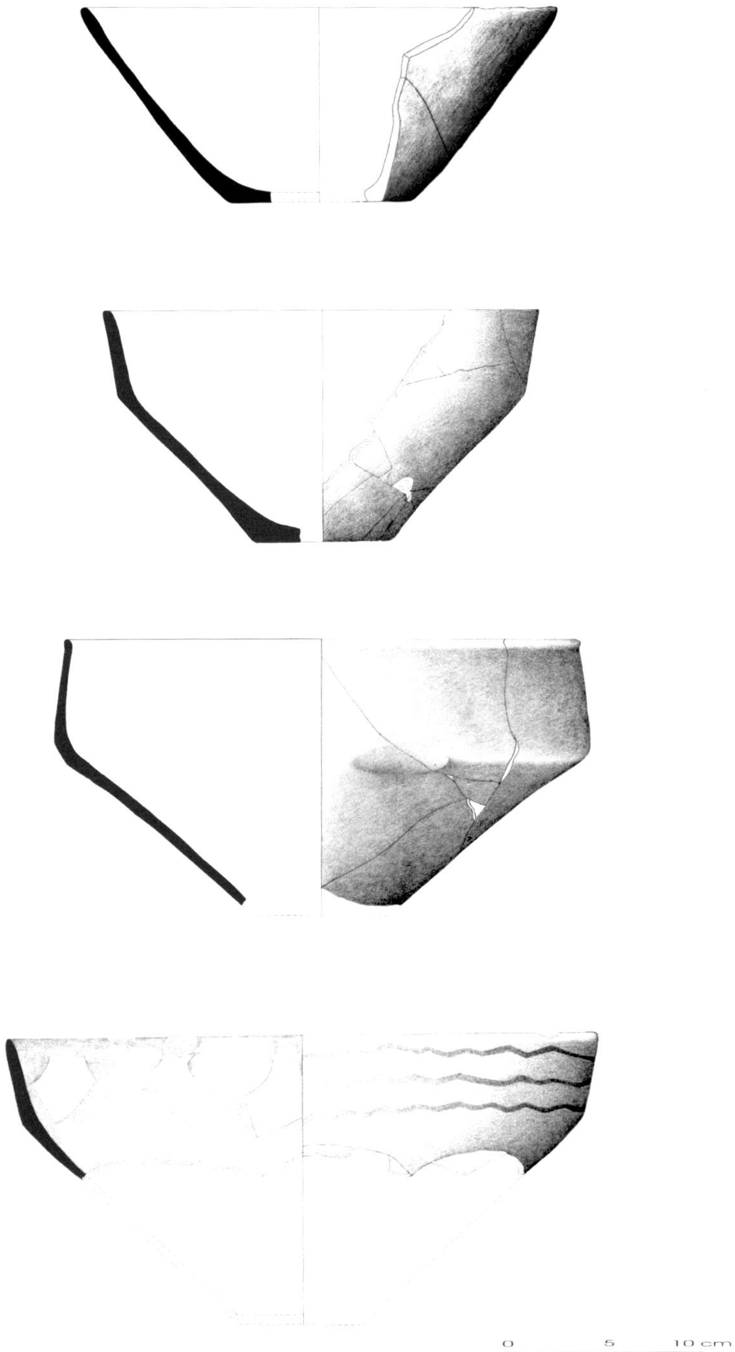

Figure 2.3. Standardized 'serving vessels' from early LN Pit 212: a representative sample of shapes and decoration

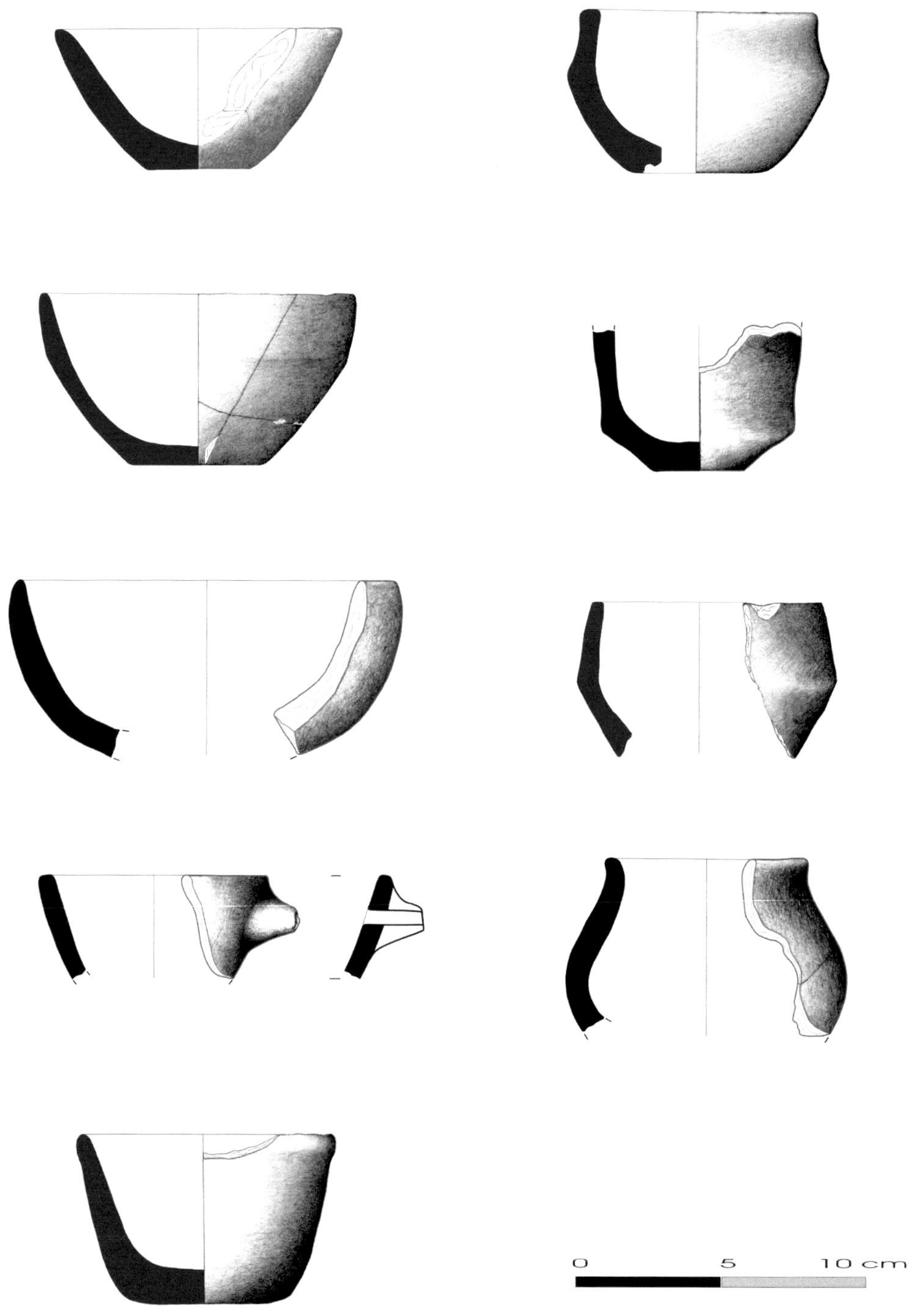

Figure 2.4. Non-standardized cups from early LN Pit 212: plain cups of varying shapes

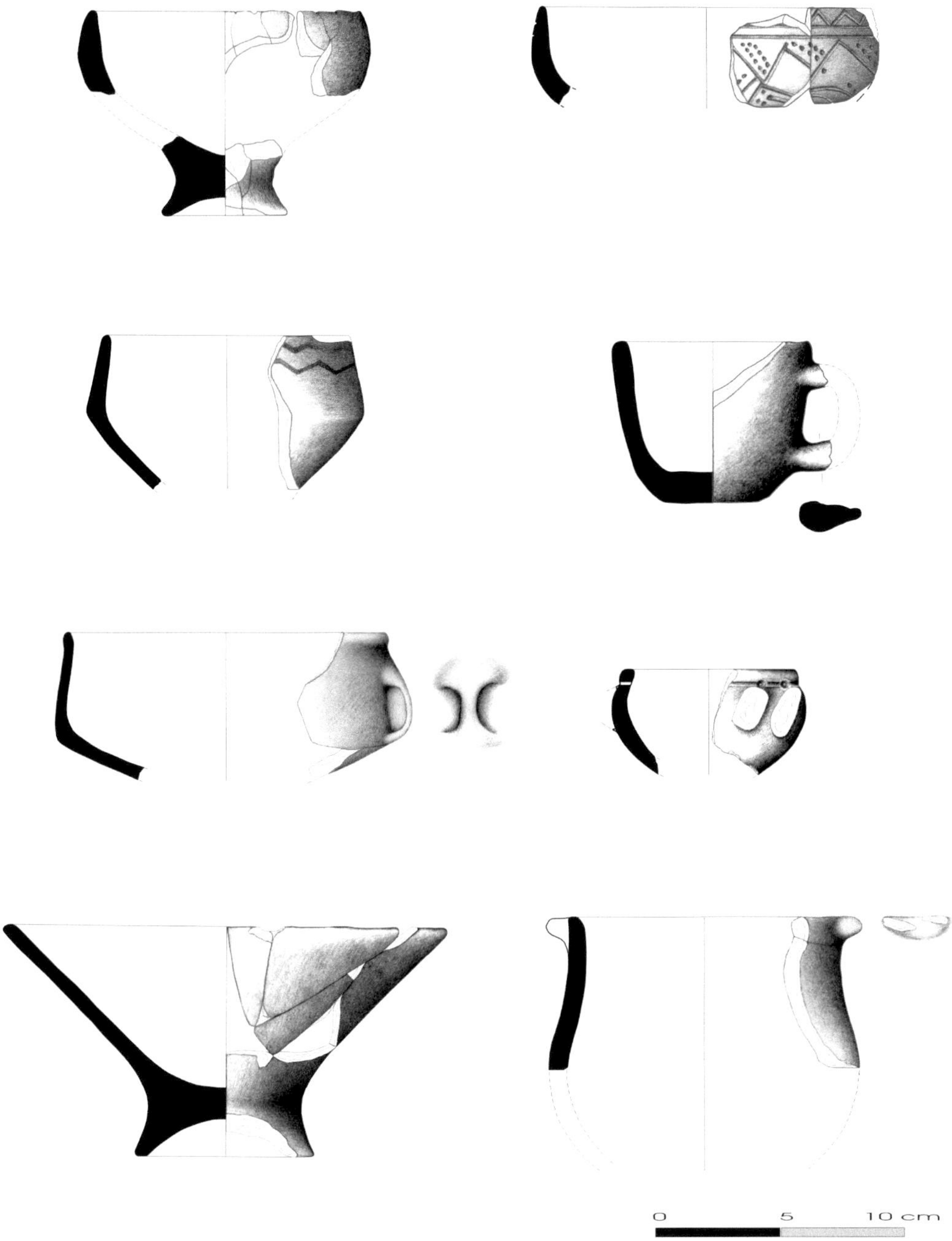

Figure 2.5. Non-standardized cups from early LN Pit 212: plain and decorated cups of varying shapes

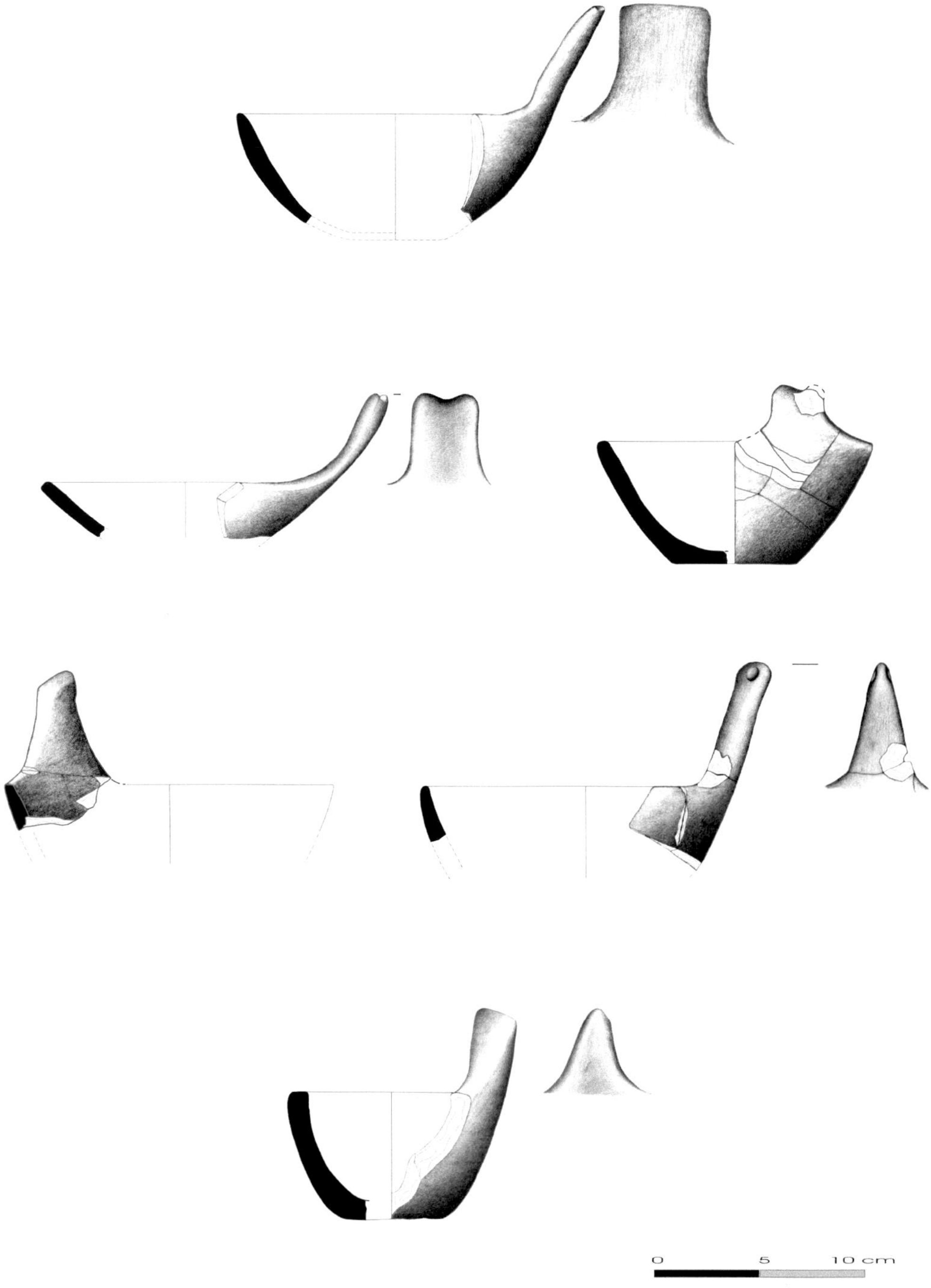

Figure 2.6. Non-standardized cups from early LN Pit 212: cups with stylized handle

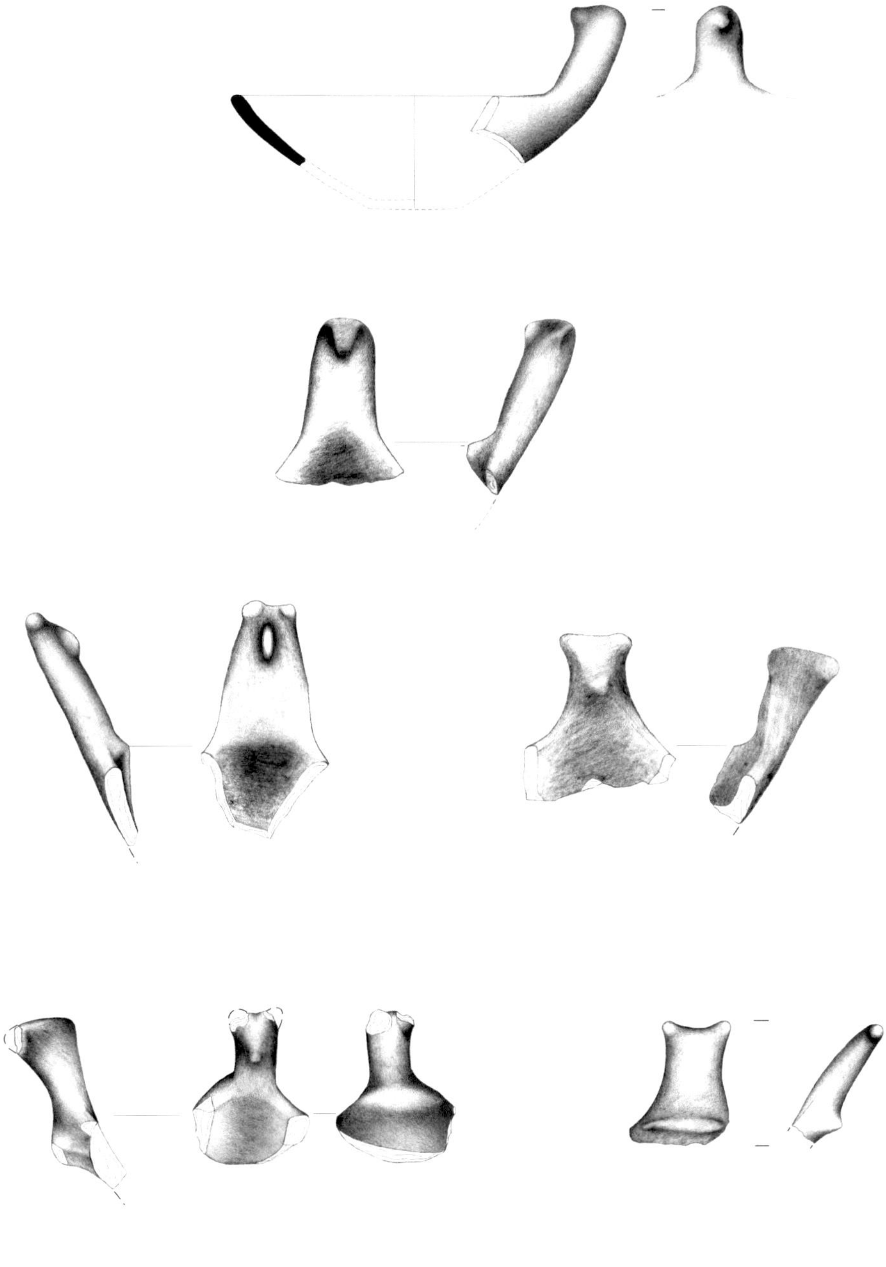

Figure 2.7. Non-standardized cups from early LN Pit 212: cups with zoomorphic handle

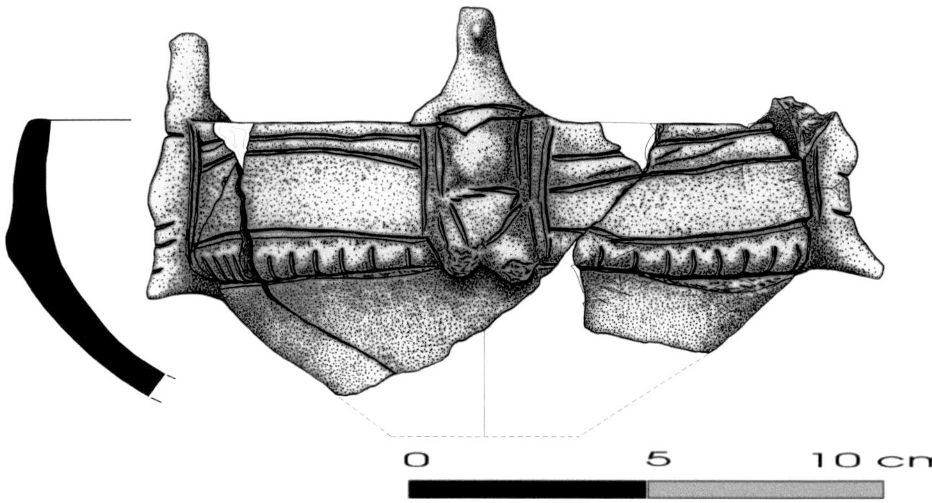

Figure 2.8. Non-standardized cups from early LN Pit 212: cup with anthropomorphic figures

cattle, pigs and sheep/goats alike. Moreover, as noted above, the pattern of long bone fragmentation strongly implies that bones were extensively broken open for the extraction of marrow. This evidence thus suggests that more or less the whole sequence of carcass processing took place in the vicinity of Pit 212, but butchery marks are (as is normally the case) only detectable on a minority of bones. Less precise, but more abundant evidence for carcass processing is provided by body part representation.

Body part representation tends to be variable for several reasons, including differential fragmentation, survival, retrieval and identifiability. To minimize the effects of differential fragmentation and identifiability, body part representation of the commonest domesticates is expressed in Figure 2.10a–c in terms of 'minimum numbers of anatomical units' (see below). The smaller foot bones of sheep/goat and pig are particularly vulnerable to incomplete retrieval (Payne 1972) and these are clearly underrepresented in Figure 2.10b–c. Body parts vulnerable to carnivore attrition (Brain 1981; Lyman 1994) are also under-represented, as is well illustrated by the broad similarity in anatomical representation between Pit 212 sheep/goats (Figure 2.10c) and modern Hottentot goats ravaged by dogs (Figure 2.10d). Anatomical representation for Pit 212 cattle is more even, probably because both larger body size and a higher proportion of adult deaths reduced vulnerability to attrition. For sheep/goat, cow and pig alike, body parts of both low meat utility (e.g., heads and feet) and high meat utility (e.g., upper limb bones) are well represented, with variation in anatomical representation plausibly attributable to incomplete retrieval and survival. This suggests that all skeletal parts were discarded with more or less equal frequency

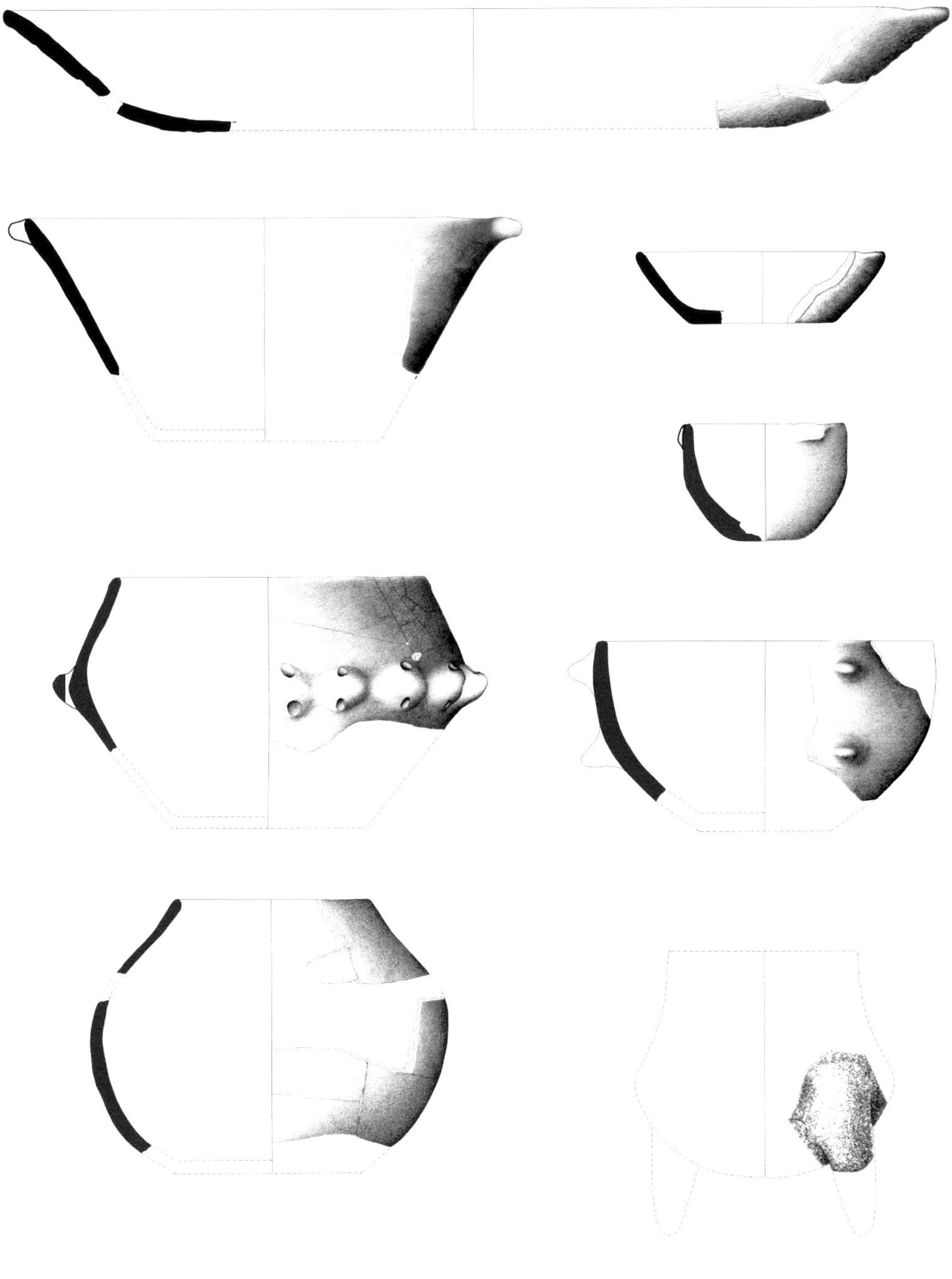

Figure 2.9. Cooking vessels from early LN Pit 212: a representative sample of vessel shapes and sizes

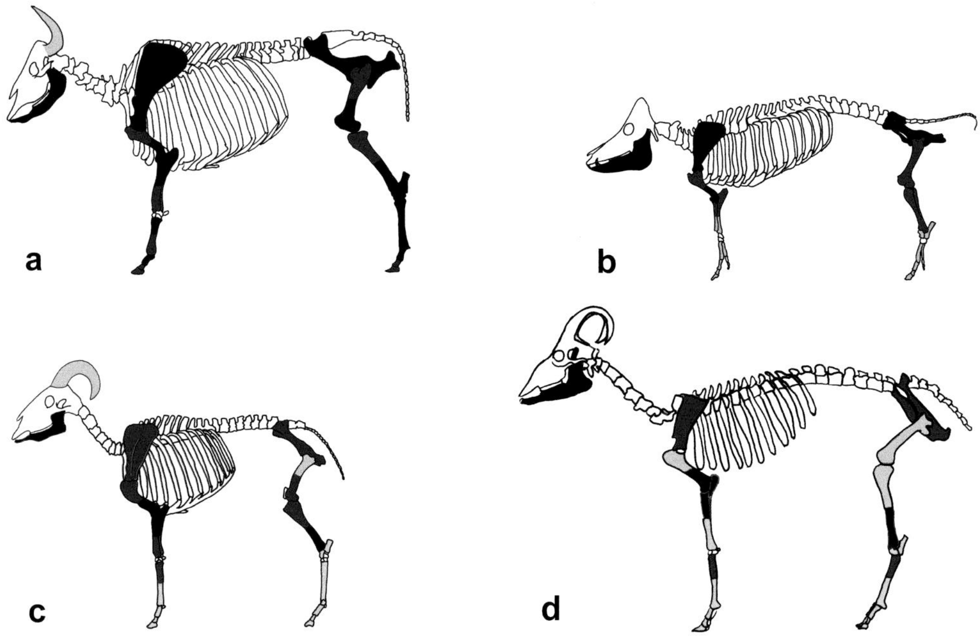

Figure 2.10. Body part representation of commonest domestic animals in early LN Pit 212, based on % survival of minimum numbers of anatomical units (treating most abundant anatomical unit as 100%). a. Pit 212 cattle; b. Pit 212 pigs; c. Pit 212 sheep/goats; d. modern Hottentot goats subjected to attrition by dogs (after Brain 1981: 277 table 5)

Key: white – body parts not analysed
light grey – 0–25% representation
dark grey – 26–50% representation
black – 51–100% representation

and supports the inference, from the minority of bones with observed butchery marks, that the entire sequence of carcass processing is represented in Pit 212.

Numerous grindstones and archaeobotanical samples rich in cereal chaff (Valamoti 2001) provide evidence that the activities represented by Pit 212 also included the processing for consumption of grain crops. Finally, the fill of Pit 212 contained concentrations of big stones and numerous fragments of burnt clay; many of the latter exhibited a smooth surface, but none bore impressions of wattle, posts or beams. These are evidently not remains of dwelling structures, therefore, but seem to be derived from built platforms or facilities, while the evidence of burning, coupled with the absence of impressions of combustible material, hints strongly at the use of fire in cooking. Thus the contents of Pit 212 include ceramic, faunal and other remains of the preparation and consumption of both plant- and animal-based foods, while organic residues of animal fats in cooking pots provide a more direct link between the ceramic and faunal components of the assemblage.

The Scale of Consumption

The assemblages of pottery vessels, animal bones and small finds from Pit 212 are unusually large. In relative terms, Pit 212 accounts for ca. 42% of the ceramic assemblage and for ca. 50% of the faunal assemblage from Makriyalos I. This concentration of finds is particularly remarkable, given the short duration of its deposition, and contrasts sharply with the relative paucity of both ceramics and animal bones in the massive and repeatedly reworked enclosure ditch Alpha. The absolute scale of consumption, represented by these assemblages of potsherds and bone fragments, is harder to assess and begs a number of intermediate questions: the number and size of ceramic vessels and animals; the use of both ceramic vessels and animals; discard practices; and post-depositional alteration of the discarded assemblages. While the use life of ceramic vessels may vary greatly, an animal carcass can only be consumed once and so the attempt to assess the absolute scale of consumption represented by Pit 212 begins with an estimate of the number of animals and quantity of meat represented by the faunal remains.

Number of Animals

Detailed recording of faunal remains was restricted to a selected group of informative anatomical units, including the mandible and most major limb bones. The abundance of each anatomical unit of each taxon was quantified in two ways: the 'maximum number of anatomical units' (MaxAU) counts each identified specimen (excluding freshly broken, adjoining fragments) and so is analogous to the widely used counts of 'numbers of identified specimens' (NISP); the 'minimum number of anatomical units' (MinAU) discounts fragments which could possibly constitute duplicate records of a single anatomical unit. MinAU figures are thus a more reliable basis for *comparison* between body parts or taxa subject to different probabilities of fragmentation, survival, retrieval and identification. It must be stressed, however, that MinAU counts are, literally, *minimum* figures. During recording of the Pit 212 assemblage, it was noted that identified fragments discounted in the estimation of MinAU were usually the most poorly preserved specimens and it is suspected that the MaxAU counts provide a much more realistic estimate of the *actual* abundance of surviving and identifiable anatomical units. The actual abundance of surviving and identifiable bone would in turn, given demonstrably incomplete preservation and the retrieval losses inevitable under rescue conditions without extensive sieving, offer a significant *under*-estimate of the animal remains originally discarded in Pit 212.

Nonetheless, the MinAU figures for the four common domesticates are very high and represent very large numbers of animal carcasses: taking account of side of body and of any evidence for age at death, the minimum number of individual animals represented is 738, including 128 domestic cattle, 238 domestic pigs, 322 sheep and goats, 36 dogs, and 14 wild animals ranging in size from aurochs down to hare. These figures have been calculated for the excavated fill of Pit 212 as a whole, because the transition between layers 2 and 3 was of variable clarity in different trenches; the MNI for layer 3 only would probably be in the region of 600. Again it must be stressed, however, that these are *minimum* figures and that, as with the estimation of MinAU from MaxAU, MNI estimates would almost certainly have been substantially higher if the assemblage had been subject to better preservation and more intensive retrieval. In addition, perhaps as little as half of Pit 212 was excavated, so the actual number of animals represented by bones discarded in the basal fill alone will almost certainly have been well in excess of one thousand and perhaps closer to two thousand.

Potential Number of Consumers

Any detailed attempt at estimating the weight of meat represented by these carcasses, taking account of the age and sex breakdown of each species and of metrical evidence for prevailing body size, would be complex and would risk creating a spurious impression of accuracy. Moreover, the condition of animals at the time of death, which could dramatically influence the weight and nutritional value of carcasses, is wholly unknown. Even on the conservative assumption of an average meat (plus offal) weight of 8 kg per sheep/goat, 40 kg per pig and 100 kg per cow (cf. Vigne 1991), however, the quantity of meat available from the animals represented in Pit 212 must be measured in tens of tons. Estimates of the duration of deposition of the basal fill of Pit 212 introduce further uncertainty into calculations, but the quantity of meat available *per year* almost certainly amounted to several tons and probably exceeded ten tons.

What evidence is there that these large quantities of meat were consumed at Makriyalos or indeed were eaten by humans? As has already been noted, the evidence of butchery marks suggests that the entire sequence of carcass processing took place in the vicinity of Pit 212. Since body parts of both low meat utility (e.g., heads and feet) and high meat utility (e.g., upper limb bones) are well represented, it seems that Pit 212 was not the locus for discard of waste from primary butchery, with meat-rich parts of the skeleton being removed for consumption elsewhere. Nor is there any evidence that meat was removed from Makriyalos off the bone: filleting marks are less common than dismembering marks in cow, pig and sheep/goat alike and this imbalance is even more marked in the very high-utility hindlimb than in the moderately high-utility forelimb (cf. Binford 1978). The ceramic repertoire, including both cooking vessels (with traces of animal fats) and tableware, leaves little doubt that at least some of the meat was consumed near Pit 212.

It might still be argued that carcasses were butchered and much of the meat then left to rot, perhaps as a deliberate display of conspicuous wastage. In social, as opposed to nutritional, terms, the distinction between conspicuous wastage and conspicuous consumption of meat may not be that significant. The occurrence of dismembering and filleting marks on both the fore- and hind-limbs of all the principal taxa, however, argues against a 'gourmet' strategy (Binford 1978: 81 fig. 2.18) of consuming just the highest-utility parts and abandoning those of only moderate meat-value. Conversely, it was argued above that human agents had broken open much of the bone discarded in Pit 212 for the extraction of marrow; this implies fairly thorough exploitation of the nutritional potential of carcasses. The most parsimonious interpretation of the faunal evidence, therefore, and likewise of the wealth of ceramic evidence for preparation, serving and consumption of food, is that the carcasses represented in Pit 212 had mostly been butchered, cooked and consumed by humans nearby.

If meat consumed over one year in association with Pit 212 amounted, for the sake of argument, to 10 tons, how many consumers might this imply? At this point, uncertainty regarding the number and size of animal carcasses butchered and the duration of deposition is compounded by the problem of estimating average levels of meat intake per person. Nonetheless, the exercise is necessary as a prelude to considering the social context of consumption represented by Pit 212. To this end, the implications of some alternative levels of meat intake may be explored.

As there is no firm faunal or ceramic evidence for the use of dairy products in LN Greece, the cautious assumption is made here that meat from butchered animals was not heavily supplemented by 'secondary products' from live animals. The evidence for plant foods in Pit 212 is relatively sparse (Valamoti 2001), but, given the climatic conditions of northern Greece and the recovery procedures of a rescue excavation, preparation for consumption of plant foods is less likely than the processing of animal carcasses to generate durable and retrievable material residues. It must be acknowledged, therefore, that food consumption associated with Pit 212 may have been dominated, in terms of both volume and nutritional value, by plant resources. Some evidence for the level of meat intake is provided by physical anthropology: dental calculus and caries rates in human remains from LN Makriyalos are consistent with higher meat consumption than in Late Bronze Age and Iron Age populations from the same area (Triantaphyllou 2001: 126–27); conversely, isotopic analysis suggests increased consumption through time of animal *protein* (potentially including dairy products – Triantaphyllou 2001: 135–40). The evidence is thus ambiguous, but is consistent with the absence of a major role for dairy products and does not indicate extreme carnivory at LN Makriyalos (Triantaphyllou 2001: 139). It might be argued that the fill of Pit 212 was deposited during a temporary period of extreme carnivory, which is not represented in the available human skeletal evidence for diet, but this is contradicted by the evidence from Pit 212 itself of grindstones, charred plant remains and probable residues of plant foods in ceramic vessels.

If pure carnivory is ruled out, recent figures for meat consumption in Crete and the United States in the late 1940s may be enlightening. For Crete, Allbaugh (1953: 111) estimated annual per caput consumption of meat and poultry at ca 14 kg, equivalent to an individual daily ration of ca 38 gr. On this basis, ten tons of meat would have been consumed in one year by about 700 people, although it should be noted that dairy products and fish play a rather important role in the traditional Cretan diet, in contrast with what has been assumed here for LN Makriyalos, and that Greece in the late 1940s was by no means nutritionally affluent. These Cretan figures might well, therefore, underestimate levels of meat intake at LN Makriyalos and thus overestimate the numbers of consumers implied by the bone remains from Pit 212. For the same period, the average daily intake of meat, fish and eggs in the USA was 0.275 kg per head (Allbaugh 1953: 131 table 15); at this far more generous rate, ten tons of meat could have been consumed in one year of sustained indulgence or periodic gluttony by about 100 persons. For the implied number of consumers to drop much below 100, therefore, meat intake at LN Makriyalos would have to rise significantly above recent levels for the USA and physical anthropological evidence from the site offers no support for such an assumption (Triantaphyllou 2001).

Consideration of a range of alternative recent figures for meat intake thus suggests that consumption of the estimated quantity of meat per year represented by Pit 212 would have required at least several dozen and perhaps several hundred long-term participants. Average figures for daily *per caput* intake are of course very problematic, not least because levels of meat consumption are likely to vary between individuals of different age, gender and status and also between different consumption events. Thus, if only young adults were involved in the Pit 212 commensality, meat intake per head may well have exceeded the recent average figures, reducing the required number of participants, although also implying that these were drawn from a larger population including young and elderly individuals. Conversely, the preceding calculations assume a stable group of consumers. Given the apparent duration of deposition in Pit 212 over at least one year, however, it may be more realistic to imagine a participating group of changing composition and, in this case, the aggregate number of consumers might well have numbered several thousand persons.

These rather speculative calculations receive some empirical support from the ceramics deposited in Pit 212. As noted above, while larger tableware vessels are very standardized in phase I Makriyalos, the smaller cups (Figures 2.4–8) are highly individualized; these cups are of a size suitable for use in individual consumption and the handle of some cups is pierced, perhaps for hanging around the neck or from the waist. Among these cups, one type has a distinctive zoomorphic handle (Figure 2.7) and so is particularly easy to quantify. Extrapolating from the ca. 120 zoomorphic handles found in the excavated part of Pit 212, more than 200 of these vessels, each perhaps representing an individual consumer, may originally have been discarded in Pit 212. The use-life of these cups is unknown and so it is possible that an individual consumer may have discarded many different cups on successive occasions, although the apparently 'personalized' form of the cups perhaps argues against this interpretation. On the other hand, it must be noted that Pit 212 also yielded fragments of numerous handleless (and so less readily quantifiable) cups, which are again highly variable in form and fabric. The numbers of individualized cups deposited in Pit 212 are thus compatible with the earlier suggestion, based on estimates of likely meat intake, that consumers numbered at least several hundred. If cups were used not by single individuals, but by groups of perhaps closely related persons, the number of consumers might, following the same logic, amount to a few thousand.

Context of Consumption

On the combined evidence of stratigraphy, faunal remains and ceramics, it has been argued that tens of tons of meat were consumed in the vicinity of Pit 212 over a period of between several months and a few years by a group probably numbering at least several dozen to a few hundred persons. What kind of social group might these persons have represented? The size and permanence of human population at flat-extended settlements is unknown, but faunal remains from Makriyalos suggest that the site should be regarded as a distinctive form of year-round settlement rather than as (only) a seasonal gathering place. If Makriyalos I contained a permanent population of the size suggested (admittedly on slender grounds) for compact tell sites, that is of up to a few hundred persons, then the bone discarded in Pit 212 could represent more or less all the meat consumed by the entire community over a period of many months. Alternatively, this bone might represent consumption by only parts of the population (e.g., adult males – but see Triantaphyllou 2001: 125) or on particular occasions (e.g., at periodic feasts to mark rites of passage or cosmological events) or by different groups of people on different occasions (e.g., in recurrent hospitality with a changing 'guest list'). In these cases, the aggregate number of implied consumers might well, over the period of deposition in Pit 212, be numbered in thousands and so commensality on a regional scale would be favoured.

If the scale of commensality implied by Pit 212 was sufficient to represent all meat consumption by the local community over a period of many months, it might be argued that this deposit merely represents a period of collectively coordinated refuse disposal rather than an unusual cycle of consumption activity. At first sight, this perhaps disappointing conclusion appears to be supported by the ceramic evidence. The ceramic material from Pit 212 is not only exceptionally abundant, but also more diverse than the rest of the Makriyalos I assemblage. Firstly, Pit 212 contains storage vessels, cooking pots and tableware, whereas some pits lack recognizable storage or cooking vessels. Secondly, Pit 212 contains a wider range of cooking vessel shapes and fabrics than other contexts, suggesting association of the former with a particularly diverse range of cooking methods. Thirdly, tableware from Pit 212 contains the full range of decorative styles and traits known from Makriyalos I, even though some of these (e.g., the distinctive cups with zoomorphic handles) are otherwise scarce or found in only certain parts of the settlement. Thus, the ceramic repertoire from Pit 212 stands out in terms of its representation of the entire culinary *chaîne opératoire* and of the full range of food preparation techniques. Taken together with the faunal evidence for large-scale consumption over a period of many months, this ceramic diversity does not suggest the association of this unusual deposit with feasting in a particular social context and is perhaps compatible with the mundane hypothesis of collective refuse disposal. On the other hand, if the ritual symbolism of feasts, defined as 'public ritual events of communal food and drink consumption', is dependent on their 'complex semiotic relationship to daily consumption patterns' (Dietler 2001: 69), then such large-scale and rapid deposition of cultural material may be precisely what should be expected of feasting debris.

In fact, several features point to somewhat restricted context(s) of consumption. First, Pit 212 stands out from other phase I contexts at Makriyalos in the absence of recognized human bone (Triantaphyllou 2001: 48). Human remains, articulated or disarticulated, are very widespread both in other pits and in the circuit ditches at Makriyalos I; their regular association with animal bone suggests that much meat consumption may have taken place in some form of mortuary or commemorative context. The absence of human bone from Pit 212 is thus striking and suggests that the meat consumption represented by its faunal contents took place in a distinctive social context with no obvious mortuary dimension. Pit 212 thus does not seem to be associated with the only rite of passage that has an obvious archaeological signal. Secondly, while the functional diversity of the ceramic assemblage perhaps suggests the mixing of debris from many different consumption contexts, the unusual stylistic variety of the Pit 212 pottery is equally compatible with consumption activity involving participants (and ceramic vessels) drawn from a wider region than is represented in other Makriyalos I deposits; the latter possibility may be clarified in the future by ongoing analyses of ceramic fabrics. Thirdly, compared with the rest of the phase I assemblage, Pit 212 has yielded a disproportionately low frequency of storage vessels and disproportionately high frequency of cups, suggesting an emphasis on the preparation, presentation and consumption rather than storage of food and hinting that either the scale or significance of consumption was unusual. Fourthly, even if discard in Pit 212 was collectively organized (a conclusion which seems almost inevitable), the volume and range of material deposited and the activities represented differ significantly from those of the Makriyalos I enclosure ditches, which have also plausibly been interpreted as the products of collective labour (Andreou *et al.* 1996). Moreover, the scale of deposition in Pit 212 is not only unusual for Makriyalos I, but is as yet unparalleled in the Neolithic archaeological record from Greece. This unusual volume and completeness of discard surely served, *inter alia*, to establish or reinforce the unusual social importance of the phase of consumption so represented.

Despite the diversity of its contents, therefore, Pit 212 seems to indicate commensality in a distinctive social context. This, in turn, increases the likelihood that the assemblage does not represent the totality of consumption at Makriyalos during the period of its deposition and thus that the participants were drawn not only from a local resident community, but also from a wider regional population. The contents of Pit 212 also reveal something of the complexity of the social identities and social relationships thus celebrated and contested. The numerous and highly individualized, small 'personal' cups have already been cited as one piece of evidence for participation in consumption by a large number of persons. Cooking pots and larger tableware vessels (bowls), however, suggest that food was prepared and presented for consumption by larger social groups, conceivably equivalent to some form of 'family' or 'household' unit. In sharp contrast with the small cups, the larger 'serving' bowls are highly standardized, underlining the importance of a still wider collective context to such consumption. This collective context is reinforced by three further considerations. Firstly, and in common with many Neolithic contexts, Pit 212 contained remains of many animals (notably at least one aurochs, numerous domestic cattle and a few boar, but also many adult sheep, goats and pigs) too large for rapid consumption by a small kin group. Such carcasses are likely to have been shared among quite extended groups of consumers, far larger than those implied by the known cooking pots and serving vessels. Secondly, concentrations of stones and burnt clay in the fill of Pit 212 have been interpreted as remains of large-scale culinary activity. The original creation of Pit 212 will have involved removal of several hundred cubic metres of earth and underlying bedrock, while the observation that the basal layer of ceramics and bone lies directly over the floor of the pit suggests that this material was essentially removed in a single operation. If Pit 212 was, as suggested, a borrow pit excavated to secure construction material, it will have yielded sufficient material for construction activity on a collective scale. It is tempting to link these observations and to suggest that Pit 212 was excavated in order to construct large platforms or facilities associated with collective food preparation and consumption and that the debris both from these structures and from the associated consumption activity was soon afterwards deposited in the pit.

Thus Pit 212 offers evidence for the playing out of commensal politics on at least three social scales, which may tentatively be equated with the individual, (family) kin group, and local community; circumstantial reasons have also been noted for distinguishing a fourth, regional scale of commensality. At each level, shared episodes of food preparation and consumption doubtless served to cement mutual obligations and to reinforce shared identities, but it is likely that consumption on this scale also entailed an element of competition. The number of animals represented in Pit 212 implies production, as well as consumption, on a notable scale. The issue is clearest in the case of cattle, which have a low birth rate and for which mortality data from Pit 212 indicate a relatively high proportion of adult deaths (cf. Halstead 1992). The slaughter of probably two hundred or more, mostly adult, cattle over a period of, at most, a handful of years would be compatible with sustainable culling from a herd of a few hundred head. In this case, the animals represented in Pit 212, as well as those who consumed them, may of necessity have been drawn from a regional rather than local population. Alternatively, unsustainable culling from a more modest herd might be envisaged, with the implication that these adult cattle were slaughtered at the end of a boom-and-bust cycle of herd growth. Sheep(/goats) and pigs were slaughtered in far larger numbers than cattle, but often at a young age; these smaller domesticates also mature more rapidly, while pig, especially, has a very high birth rate. The large numbers of sheep, goats and pigs represented in Pit 212 are less likely, therefore, to have exceeded the potential for sustainable culling from herds based at Makriyalos. On the other hand, if livestock was owned by small kin groups or households, rather than communally, then the mobilization of animals for slaughter may well have been uneven and have followed a boom-and-bust pattern for individual herds of all four common domesticates.

Discussion and Conclusions

The early LN Pit 212 at Makriyalos has yielded ceramic and faunal assemblages of a size unmatched by any other single Neolithic context (and by very few single Neolithic sites) in the Aegean. Faunal evidence for seasonality of slaughter suggests deposition over no less than several months, while stratigraphic, ceramic and faunal evidence indicates more indirectly that the duration of deposition is unlikely to have exceeded several months or just a few years. Animal bones suggest the availability for consumption in the vicinity of Pit 212 of tens of tons of meat. Although neither the removal of meat off the bone for consumption away from Makriyalos nor the conspicuous wastage of meat can be ruled out definitively, available butchery evidence is consistent with thorough carcass processing for local consumption. Comparison with recent figures for meat intake further suggests that the faunal assemblage from Pit 212 may represent the aggregate consumption of meat over several months either by a permanent gathering of from several dozen to a few hundred persons or by the periodic coming together and/or alternation of a larger population potentially numbering thousands of individuals. Large numbers of 'personalized' small cups hint strongly that participants in Pit 212 consumption numbered at least several hundred. On this basis, Pit 212 would probably represent much or all of the aggregate meat consumption by the community at Makriyalos I over a period of several months or part of the aggregate consumption of a regional population. It is not easy to choose between these two alternatives (not least because the size of any 'permanent' population at Makriyalos is unknown) and, depending on the degree of residential mobility prevailing at an inter-site level (cf. Whittle 1997), such a distinction may be somewhat academic.

It was suggested, in the introduction to this chapter, that formalized commensality may have played an important role in negotiating tensions, within Neolithic society in Greece, between the survival and ideological reproduction of the local 'village' community and tendencies to isolation on the part of its constituent 'households'. As a flat-extended form of settlement, Makriyalos I perhaps suggests less emphasis on the cohesion of the local community than do the compact tell sites and also lacks evidence for the built 'domestic' architecture known from the latter. On the other hand, the Makriyalos I enclosure ditches, including burials and disarticulated human remains, also imply significant investment in some form of collective identity, while groups of 'habitation' pits suggest that the local community was made up of smaller residential groups. The scale of consumption associated with Pit 212 is certainly consistent with a major role for commensality (in this case, in a non-mortuary context) in forging collective identity, and there are hints that this may have been reinforced by collective construction of some form of ceremonial platform or enclosure used in the same context. At the same time, the contrast between standardized serving bowls and 'personalized' cups arguably symbolized the tension between the community and its constituent kin groups or households (each perhaps represented by a male head).

This last point recalls Dietler's important observation that feasts are politically polysemous, with the capacity to 'both unite and divide at the same time' (Dietler 2001: 77). The diversity of animal species and ages represented in Pit 212, the range of culinary methods implied by surviving cooking pots and the uniformity of serving vessels are all inconsistent with Dietler's 'diacritical' feasting, as a means of symbolically naturalizing social inequality (Dietler 2001: 85–88). In a different archaeological context, with clear evidence for institutionalized social inequality, the scale of commensality represented by Pit 212 would probably be attributed to 'patron-role' feasting, in which a chief used generosity in hospitality to secure political support or labour (Dietler 2001: 82–85). By default, therefore, Pit 212 may provisionally be regarded as evidence of 'empowering' feasting, in which agricultural produce and culinary labour are invested in the acquisition of symbolic capital and maintenance of social relationships (Dietler 2001: 76–82).

As noted above, the scale of commensality represented by Pit 212 implies considerable potential for competitive inequality in the provision of animals for consumption. More particularly, the number of adult cattle slaughtered raises the possibility of the ostentatious decimation of household herds built up over a period of several years, as has been well documented with pigs in highland New Guinea (e.g., Rappaport 1968; Brown 1978: 222–33; Wiessner 2001). Moreover, the observed emphasis in Pit 212 on community solidarity in turn implies competition between settlements and it is likely that, again recalling highland New Guinea, feasting at Makriyalos was an arena for the pursuit of symbolic capital and cementing of social relationships on a regional as well as local scale. Indeed, the fact that deposits comparable with Pit 212 have not previously been recognized in the Neolithic archaeological record from Greece surely suggests that this represents a relatively rare episode or cycle of feasting – a bout of conspicuous consumption that would arguably have shaped social relations both within the local community and on a regional scale for many years.

Bibliography

Allbaugh, L.G.
1953 *Crete: a Case Study of an Underdeveloped Area*: Princeton: Princeton University Press.

Andreou, S. and K. Kotsakis
1986 Diastasis tou khorou stin kendriki Makedonia: apotiposi tis endokoinotikis kai diakoinotikis khoroorganosis. In *Amitos (Festschrift to M. Andronikos)*: 57–88. Thessaloniki: University of Thessaloniki.

Andreou, S., M. Fotiadis and K. Kotsakis
1996 Review of Aegean prehistory 5: the Neolithic and Bronze Age of northern Greece. *AJA* 100: 537–97.

Binford, L.R.
1978 *Nunamiut Ethnoarchaeology*. New York: Academic Press.
1981 *Bones: Ancient Men and Modern Myths*. New York: Academic Press.

Brain, C.K.
1981 *The Hunters or the Hunted?* Chicago: Chicago University Press.

Brown, P.
1978 *Highland Peoples of New Guinea*. Cambridge: Cambridge University Press.

Demoule, J.-P., K. Gallis and L. Manolakis
1988 Transition entre les cultures néolithiques de Sesklo et de Dimini: les catégories céramiques. *BCH* 112: 12–58.

Deniz, E. and S. Payne
1982 Eruption and wear in the mandibular dentition as a guide to ageing Turkish Angora goats. In B. Wilson, C. Grigson and S. Payne (eds.), *Ageing and Sexing Animal Bones from Archaeological Sites* (BAR British Series 109): 155–205. Oxford: British Archaeological Reports.

Dietler, M.
2001 Theorizing the feast: rituals of consumption, commensal politics, and power in African contexts. In M. Dietler and B. Hayden (eds.), *Feasts: Archaeological and Ethnographic Perspectives on Food, Politics and Power*: 65–114. Washington: Smithsonian Institution Press.

Halstead, P.
1992 From reciprocity to redistribution: modelling the exchange of livestock in Neolithic Greece. *Anthropozoologica* 16: 19–30.
1995 From sharing to hoarding: the neolithic foundations of Aegean Bronze Age society? In R. Laffineur and W.-D. Niemeier (eds.), *Politeia: Society and State in the Aegean Bronze Age* (Aegaeum 12): 11–20. Liège: University of Liège.
1999 Neighbours from hell: the household in Neolithic Greece. In P. Halstead (ed.), *Neolithic Society in Greece* (SSAA 2): 77–95. Sheffield: Sheffield Academic Press.

Higham, C.F.W.
1967 Stock rearing as a cultural factor in prehistoric Europe. *Proceedings of the Prehistoric Society* 33: 84–106.

Hourmouziadis, G.
1979 *To Neolithiko Dimini*. Volos: Society for Thessalian Studies.
Jones, G.
in press Tooth eruption and wear observed in live sheep from Butser Hill, the Cotswold Farm Park and five farms in the Pentland Hills, UK. In D. Ruscillo (ed.), *Advances in Methods of Ageing and Sexing Animal Remains*. Oxford: Oxbow Books.
Kotsakis, K.
1981 Tria oikimata tou oikismou tou Sesklou: anaskafiki erevna. *Anthropologika* 2: 87–108.
1982 Recent research at Seskło. In *Symposia Thracica 1982*: 265–69.
1983 *Keramiki Tekhnologia kai Keramiki Diaforopoiisi: Provlimata tis Graptis Keramikis tis Mesis Neolithikis Epokhis tou Sesklou*: PhD thesis, University of Thessaloniki.
1999 What tells can tell: social space and settlement in the Greek Neolithic. In P. Halstead (ed.), *Neolithic Society in Greece* (SSAA 2): 66–76. Sheffield: Sheffield Academic Press.
Lyman, R.L.
1994 *Vertebrate Taphonomy*. Cambridge: Cambridge University Press.
Munson, P.J. and R.C. Garniewicz
2003 Age-mediated survivorship of ungulate mandibles and teeth in canid-ravaged faunal assemblages. *JAS* 30: 405–16.
Pappa, M. and M. Besios
1999 The Neolithic settlement at Makriyalos, northern Greece: preliminary report on the 1993–1995 excavations. *Journal of Field Archaeology* 26: 177–95.
1999 The Makriyalos project: rescue excavations at the Neolithic site of Makriyalos, Pieria, northern Greece. In P. Halstead (ed.), *Neolithic Society in Greece* (SSAA 2): 108–20. Sheffield: Sheffield Academic Press.
Payne, S.
1972 Partial recovery and sample bias: the results of some sieving experiments. In E.S. Higgs (ed.), *Papers in Economic Prehistory*: 49–64. London: Cambridge University Press.
Rappaport, R.A.
1968 *Pigs for the Ancestors*. London: Yale University Press.
Theocharis, D.R.
1980 To neolithiko spiti. *Anthropologika* 1: 12–14.
Triantaphyllou, S.
1999 Prehistoric Makriyalos: a story from the fragments. In P. Halstead (ed.), *Neolithic Society in Greece* (SSAA 2): 128–35. Sheffield: Sheffield Academic Press.
2001 *A Bioarchaeological Approach to Prehistoric Cemetery Populations from Central and Western Greek Macedonia* (BAR International Series 976). Oxford: British Archaeological Reports.
Urem-Kotsou, D., K. Kotsakis, C. Beck and E.C. Stout
2003 Organic residues from Late Neolithic Makriyalos cooking pots. Paper to 4th Conference of the Greek Archaeometric Society, Athens.
Valamoti, S.-M.
2001 *Archaeobotanical Investigation of Late Neolithic and Early Bronze Age Agriculture and Plant Exploitation in Northern Greece*: PhD dissertation, University of Sheffield.
Vigne, J.-D.
1991 The meat and offal weight (MOW) method and the relative proportion of ovicaprines in some ancient meat diets of the north-western Mediterranean. *Rivista di Studi Liguri* 57: 21–47.
Vitelli, K.D.
1989 Were pots first made for food? Doubts from Franchthi. *World Archaeology* 21: 17–29.

Whittle, A.

1997 Moving on and moving around: neolithic settlement mobility. In P. Topping (ed.), *Neolithic Landscapes*: 15–22. Oxford: Oxbow Books.

Wiessner, P.

2001 Of feasting and value: Enga feasts in a historical perspective (Papua New Guinea). In M. Dietler and B. Hayden (eds.), *Feasts: Archaeological and Ethnographic Perspectives on Food, Politics and Power*: 115–43. Washington: Smithsonian Institution Press.

3

Ceramic Change and the Practice of Eating and Drinking in Early Bronze Age Crete

Peter M. Day and David E. Wilson

Material and Social Dimensions of Food and Drink Consumption

Any one of us challenged to justify our choice of vessels for a specific occasion involving the consumption of food and drink would be able to provide a wide array of reasons for the suitability, preference or desirability of one type of receptacle over another. Our reluctance to serve a Sunday roast on plastic plates comes from an awareness of the 'correctness' of certain choices, something accentuated when guests are present: a link between material culture and the meal as occasion. Similarly, the sharing of the chalice in Christian communion is central to the meaning of the religious rite; this affects the choices regarding the materials from which the chalice is made as well as its size. Greek 'meze' comprises a markedly communal way of eating; the size, number and placement of the plates structure and reinforce the act of sharing within the confines of a single delimited space: the table. In this case, the role of the host is important in offering food and keeping drink glasses topped up.

Observations, evaluations and interpretations of social acts involving food and drink consumption often are strongly materially based. Not only do we have a sense of which is the right vessel, but also what is the correct way to use it. It is on such bases that social inclusion and exclusion are developed.

Social dimensions of food and especially of the meal have been given prominence recently in considering the past. Emphasis has been placed on the way in which the consumption of food and drink as a practice can be pivotal in social reproduction, in the maintenance of cohesion and even of inequality. Seen from the perspective of agency, it can be used both to bolster and to challenge power structures within society (Barrett 2000). Perhaps the most prominence has been given to feasting (e.g. Dietler and Hayden 2001), but acts of consumption do not need to be large scale, special occasions to have meaning, the material remains of everyday commensal activity may be just as informative.

In studies of prehistory the material correlates of such different behaviours have still to be exploited to the full, although there are some notable exceptions. Sherratt has argued that broad patterns of ceramic design reflect the increased importance of formalized eating at a table in the Neolithic of Europe and the Near East (Sherratt 1987), while Hayden has emphasized the social importance of highly decorated cooking vessels in early hospitality and display (Hayden 1995).

More frequently, drinking vessels have been the focus of study, emphasizing the nature of drinking rituals and actions (Wright 1995; Palmer 1995; Hamilakis 1996: 24–25; Day and Wilson 1998: 357), and the identification of locations of ceremonial activity (Day and Wilson 2002). At times our own modern, culturally-induced reactions to drinking vessels are even crystallized in the names we give to some ancient shapes: hence ouzo cups, tankards, teapots, etc..

This paper offers a discussion of the marked changes that took place in the ceramic repertoire of Crete during Early Minoan I-IIB and primarily during EMIIA. In considering basic criteria of vessel size, form, decoration and function, it is hoped to present and interpret fundamental changes in the contexts of food and drink consumption during the third millennium BC, generally considered a period of marked social change.

Variability in Prepalatial Ceramic Assemblages

We will concentrate on the pottery assemblage of Knossos, which at present offers an unrivaled sequence for the periods of EMI-IIB in Crete. This assemblage, however, has to be put into perspective with contemporary non-funerary assemblages from around the island.

Variability within Phases

Although mostly derived from fills, the EMI pottery groups at Knossos are clear in their ceramic composition and bear comparison with the few other contemporary sites on Crete that have been published. At Knossos, the differences between the EMI Well deposit (Hood 1990a, 1990b) and that of other fills have been argued to be indicative of ceremonial activities evidenced by the well deposit, rather than defining sub-phases of EMI (Wilson and Day 2000). Although it contains a substantial proportion of 'Cycladic-style pottery' that is absent from Knossos, the 'Minoan' portion of the EMI pottery assemblage at Poros-Katsambas is comparable in terms of the pottery types present, if not in the exact proportions of those different types (Wilson *et al.* in press). The pottery of the EMI settlement of Kalo Khorio in east Crete shows significant similarities to the EMI Well deposit at Knossos, with the shapes and ware groups almost identical to those from Knossos considered here (Haggis 1996).

Aside from the deposits of early EMIIA in the West Court House at Knossos, there remain few studied and published contemporary assemblages. Those at the harbour town of Poros-Katsambas are similar in the nature of their 'Minoan-style' pottery, which often shares the same provenance as that from Knossos (Wilson *et al.* in press). Besides the small amount of material in the first phase of occupation at Myrtos Fournou Korifi (Warren 1972), there remain only the EMIIA levels at Debla (Warren and Tzedakis 1974) and Nopigeia (Karantzali 1992–93) which provide some information on pottery types in the West of the island.

The later EMIIA deposits present at Knossos have no published counterparts in settlements in other parts of the island. At Knossos they are represented by fills found in various tests beneath the palace including the northern quarter (Wilson 1994: 32 n. 61; forthcoming; Wilson and Day 1999: 40–41). This is a key period of change in the nature of the pottery assemblage at this site.

Besides the EMIIB at Knossos (Wilson and Day 1999) there exists a large destruction deposit from Myrtos Fournou Korifi (Warren 1972), which offers the best resource for understanding ceramic function and associated architecture for the Prepalatial period (Whitelaw *et al.* 1997).

Ceramic Variability over Time

For the purposes of this diachronic comparison, the assemblage at Knossos is our only available sequence that can provide a perspective from EMI through EMIIB.

There is a number of differences between the latest deposits of the Neolithic at Knossos and those of EMI, notably the introduction of large ceramic storage jars, the appearance of a clear set of fabrics and shapes for cooking, and also a marked increase in the number of vessels associated with the pouring of liquids. There are very rare beaked jugs in the latest Neolithic deposits at Knossos (Evans 1971: 113–14), but the large number of jugs in EMI levels stands in stark contrast. We should keep in mind, however, that if the jugs of EMI indeed imitate gourds (Hood 1971: 30; Betancourt 1985: 23, 30), then we may be missing an organic component of the Neolithic vessel assemblage which has not survived in the archaeological record.

In general, the EMI and EMII assemblages at Knossos are comparable, indeed they share many shapes and wares, with burnished finishes being used for drinking vessels and wiped, scored or dark-on-light paint effects being used for pouring vessels. The major change takes place during EMII, when the later phase of EMIIA shows substantial innovation, with the introduction of the shallow bowl/plate, the first appearance of the individual footed goblet, and the development of the long-spouted jar or 'teapot'. There exist at this time a variety of types of drinking sets, with red/black slipped ware and dark-on-light drinking sets occurring alongside the last of the dark grey burnished goblets. Not only are the new groups clearly produced as drinking/serving sets, but they are also the start of a trend that continues in the polychrome sets of the First Palace period (MacGillivray 1987: 274).

The increasing emphasis on pouring and drinking sets in EMI-IIB and the change in their size, design and decoration is what this paper addresses, and for this reason we deal almost exclusively with fine table ware.

Evidence of Change in the Prepalatial Ceramic Assemblage.

We have chosen to highlight a number of sometimes inter-related aspects of the ceramic assemblage: the size of vessels, the introduction of the individual drinking cup and shallow bowls, the development of the spouted jar, the quantity and standardization of pottery, the nature of different drinking /eating sets, the placement of decoration on the vessel, and the imitation of different materials in ceramic finishes.

Size of Vessels/Introduction of Footed Goblet

One of the most striking aspects of the EMI Well assemblage at Knossos, which tends also to be mirrored in other assemblages of the period, is the size of many of the pottery vessels (Figure 3.1). The large pedestalled bowls can be over 40 cm in height (about twice the size of the chalice or more), while some of the large wiped and washed ware, round-based jugs may have been roughly of the same height. The drinking vessels of this period are also large, essentially comprising chalices in dark grey burnished ware (rim diameters of about 20 cm compared to 40 cm or more for the pedestalled bowls), usually with pattern burnishing comparable to that on the pedestalled bowls (Wilson and Day 2000: 27–30). Although still in dark grey burnished ware, the stemmed goblets and pedestalled goblets, which largely replace the chalices in the early phase of EMIIA, show a distinct reduction in size (rim diameters of 11 cm, on average, compared to 20 cm for the chalice) (Figure 3.1). Drinking vessels are further diminished in size in the later phase of EMIIA, with the introduction of the smaller footed goblet (= 'eggcup'), in either dark-on-light painted or red/black slipped ware (Figure 3.1). Although not present in east Crete, the footed goblet became the standard drinking vessel in many Central Cretan assemblages by the early Middle Minoan period.

Introduction of Shallow Bowls

Shallow bowls first appear in Crete during the late phase of EMIIA at Knossos and from the start are produced and used in large numbers; they continue to be frequent in EMIIB as part of drinking/eating sets (e.g. Myrtos: Warren 1972: 114–7; Knossos: Wilson and Day 1999: 9; Figure 3.1). This is not an isolated phenomenon in the Aegean. The appearance of the shallow bowl at this time in the Mainland, Cyclades and the Troad has been noted by others (e.g. Wilson 1999: 121–22; Wiencke 2000: 596, 601).

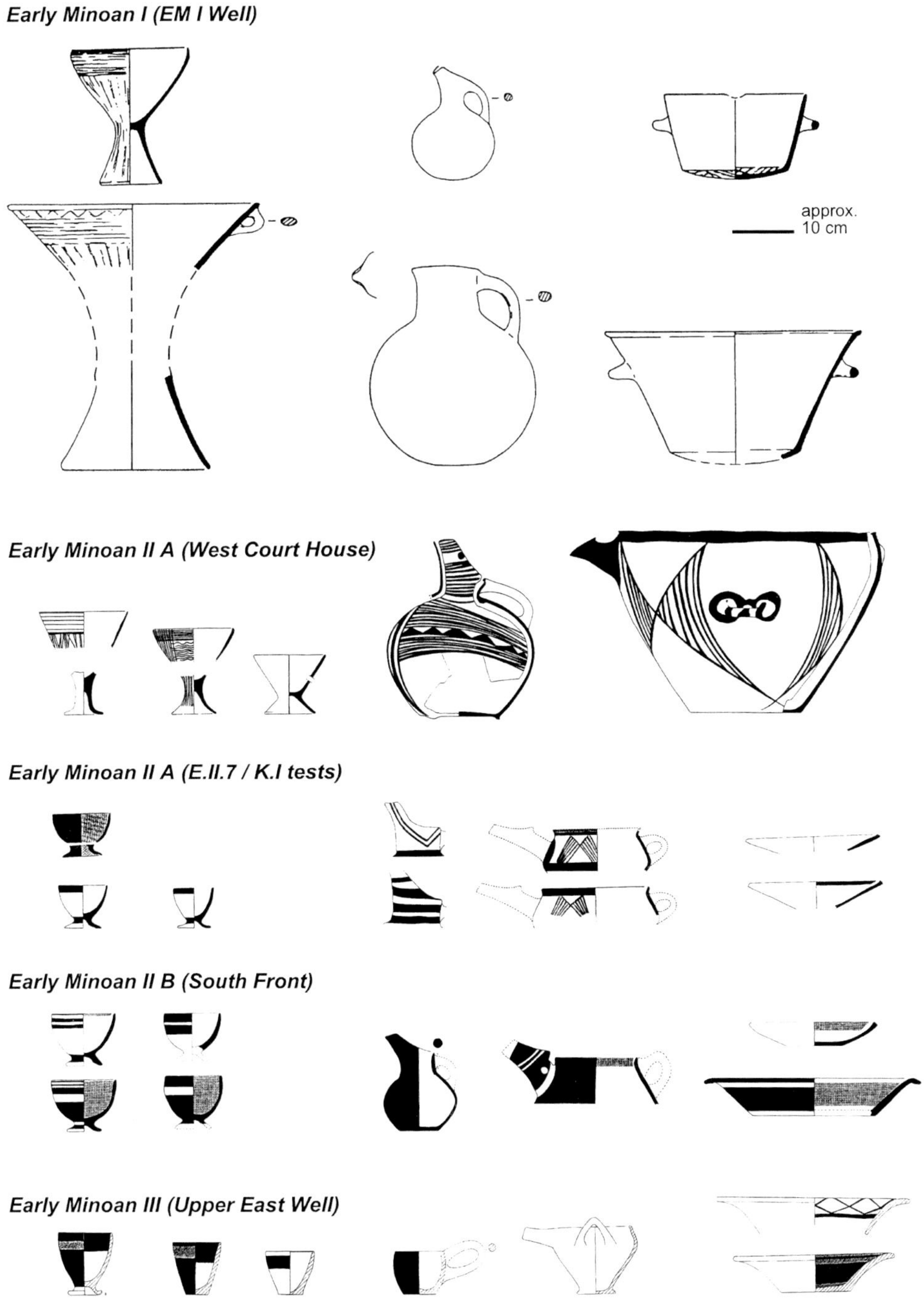

Figure 3.1. Pottery shape charts for drinking, pouring and serving vessels from deposits dated to EMI, EMIIA, EMIIB and EMIII at Knossos (after Hood 1990a; Wilson 1995, Wilson and Day 1999; and Momigliano 1991)

Change in Pouring Vessels

The introduction of common pouring vessels in the first phase of the Early Bronze Age on Crete was not accompanied immediately by a proliferation in their morphological types. In EMI there are essentially two forms: 1) large, wiped and washed, or scored, one-handled jugs with a wide-mouthed spout, and a rounded or flat base; and 2) small dark-on-light painted jugs, which at Knossos are probably mostly flat-based, with a cut-away spout (Figure 3.1).

In early EMIIA, in addition to the above two jug shapes continuing from EMI, other new pouring vessels are introduced. A range of spouted deep bowls/ basins are present in a variety of shapes. Perhaps the largest of these is the strikingly decorated dark-on-light painted, spouted deep bowl/krater from the West Court House (Figures 3.1, 3.2; Wilson 1985: P93 fig. 14). High quality, small, side-spouted bowls, many originating in the Mesara (Wilson and Day 1994: 25–30), also occur in the same early EMIIA deposits at Knossos. Their open nature and frequently small size might suggest their use to mix liquids and pour them in small quantities, perhaps in acts of libation.

The most notable introduction of a new pouring vessel shape occurs in the later phase of EMIIA at Knossos, and continues in EMIIB: the long-spouted jar or 'teapot' (Figure 3.1). The length of the spouts in late EMIIA is relatively modest, but becomes more extended in the EMIIB period (Figure 3.3). Perhaps the most exaggerated examples occur in EMIIB Vasilike Ware (e.g. Myrtos: Warren 1972: 150) and in EMIII-MMI East Cretan White-on-Dark ware (Betancourt 1984: 46–47, shape 10).

During EMII in some Cretan assemblages, there appear alternative pouring vessels, although the different types might not be present always in equal numbers. In early EMIIA at Knossos there exists a single, common pouring vessel: the beak-spouted jug (Wilson 1985), while later EMIIA and EMIIB deposits have a variety of common pouring vessels, including the new long-spouted jar. While the explanation of the possible roles of these different vessels would benefit from more contextualized data and further publication of primary material, the appearance of the long-spouted jar, which quite clearly puts emphasis on the act of pouring and serving, is taken here to be of primary social significance.

Correlation of Drinking Sets to Ware Types

It is noteworthy that during EMI and early EMIIA, drinking vessels have very different surface treatment than pouring vessels. The former are made exclusively in dark burnished finishes, while the latter are either wiped/scored and slipped or are dark-on-light painted. This pattern changes from late EMIIA, when drinking/eating sets comprising long- and side-spouted jars, jugs, footed goblets and shallow bowls appear in dark-on-light painted, red/black slipped, and red slipped and burnished wares. The exception to this is that shallow bowls occur only very rarely in red/black slipped ware. This increased variety of alternative

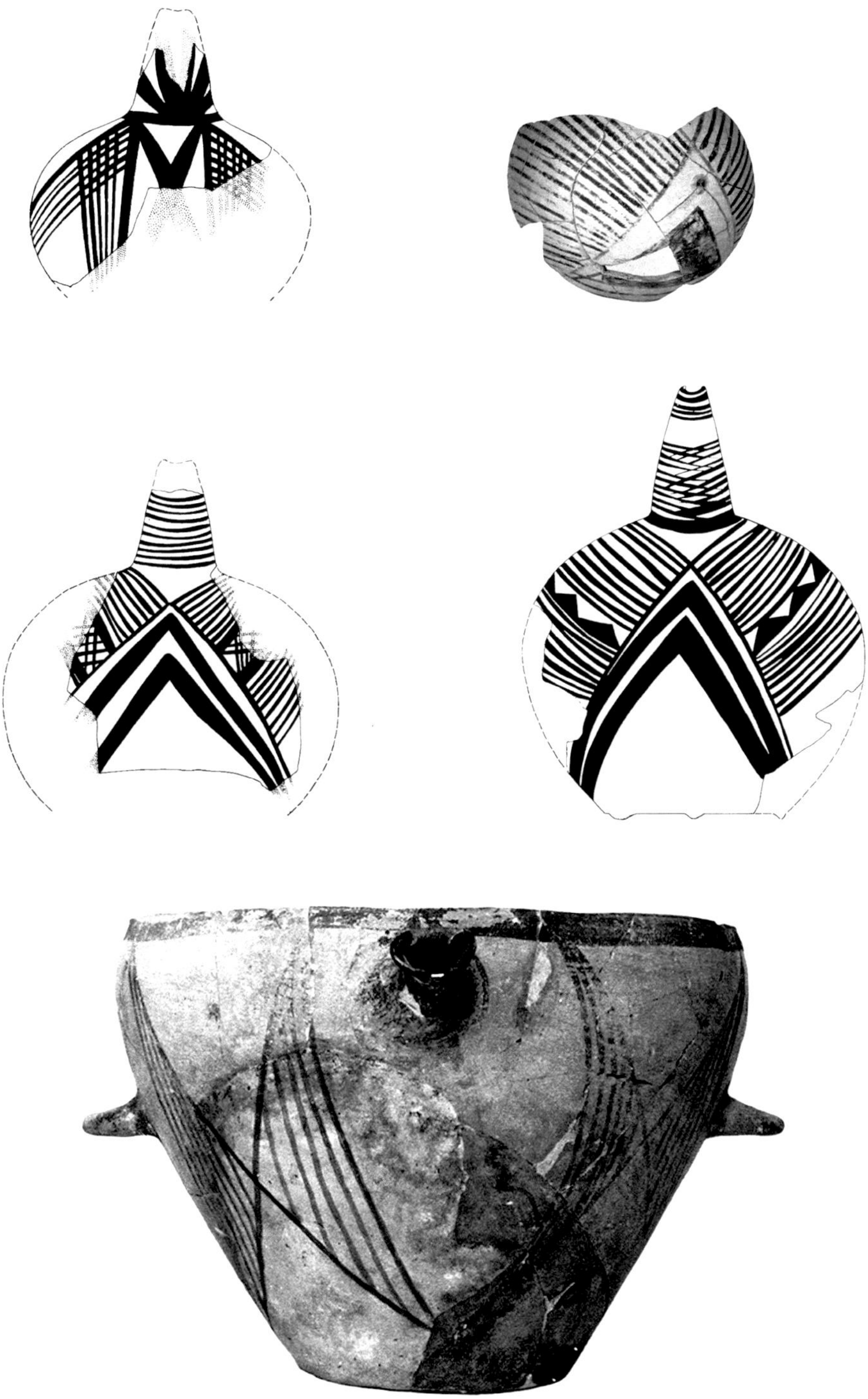

Figure 3.2. Early EMIIA jugs and krater from the West Court House, Knossos (from Wilson 1985)

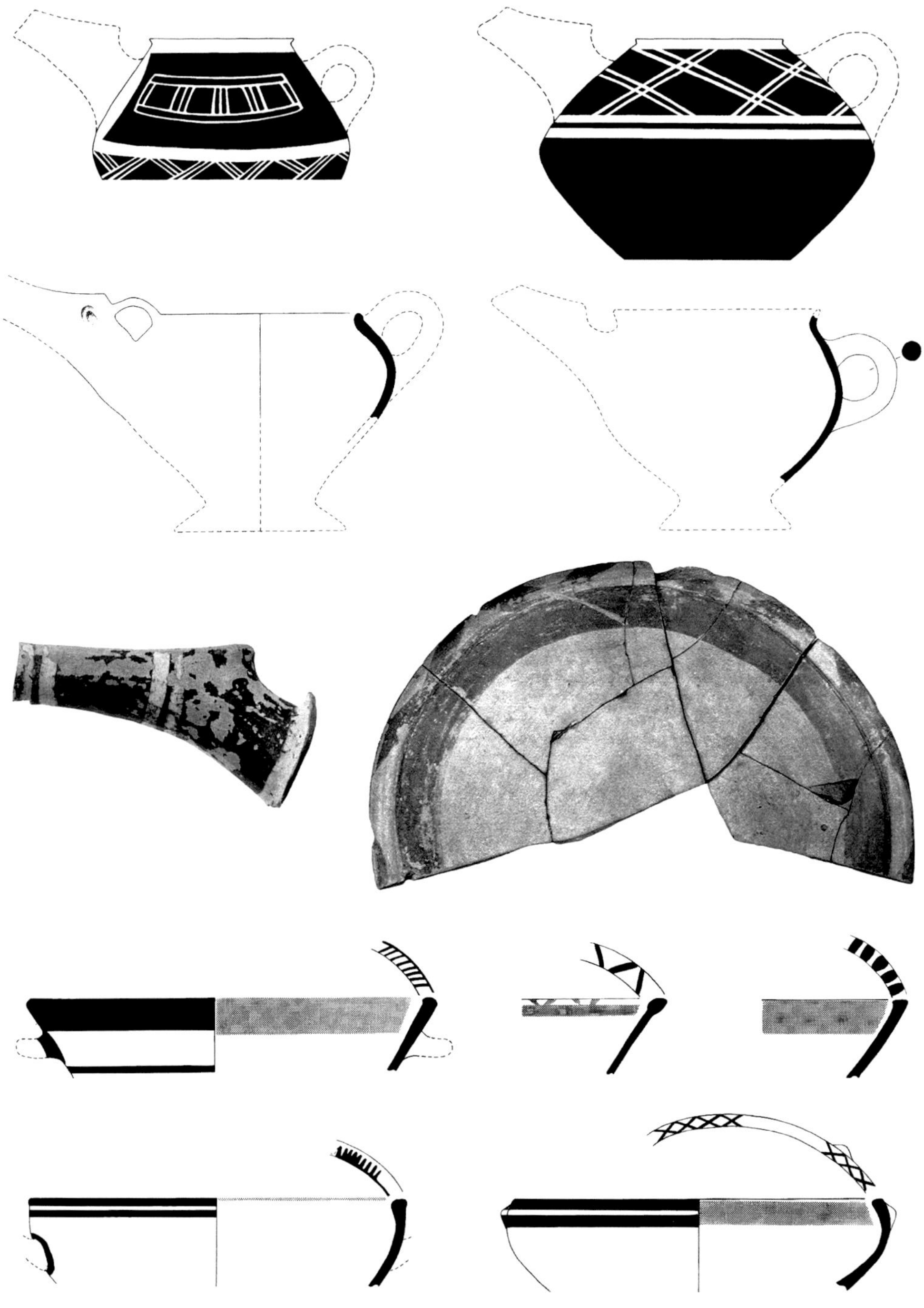

Figure 3.3. EMIIB long-spouted jars ('teapots') and eating/serving bowls; most from the South Front deposits, Knossos (from Wilson 1985; Momigliano and Wilson 1996; and Wilson and Day 1999)

drinking sets, in a number of different wares, during late EMIIA is followed by a more standardized picture in EMIIB, with the disappearance of dark grey burnished goblets and the red slipped and burnished ware drinking assemblages which had occurred in EMIIA.

Skeuomorphism/Imitation of Different Materials

Many of the ceramic drinking, mixing and serving vessels of the Prepalatial period seem to imitate other materials, a trend which is seen elsewhere in the Aegean in this same period (Renfrew 1972: 335–37). Rambach has shown convincingly the probable origins in basketry of a range of Early Cycladic incised motifs (Rambach 2000: vol. 2 figs. 27, 28) and we may identify references made to other materials in these ceramic forms. In EMI at least some materials imitated appear to be organic, whereas in EMIIB most of the fine pottery assemblage would seem to be made in imitation of metal prototypes. Certainly the footed goblet, long-spouted jar and shallow bowl, introduced in late EMIIA, appear to imitate metal, a comment that also pertains to the familiar sets of the Kastri Group. This latter trend continues into the first palatial period of Crete, where fine decorated pottery, especially Kamares Ware, exhibits marked metallising features (MacGillivray 1987: 277–8; Walberg 1976: 34–9; 1983: 24–5).

It has been suggested elsewhere that the EMI cut-away spout jug is derived from gourds (Hood 1971: 30), that dark pattern burnished pottery may deliberately resemble wood graining (Evans 1921: 59–60), and that some painted decoration of this period may imitate string net patterns (Hood 1971: 30). It is notable that the candidates for the imitation of metal in EMI are the rare drinking goblets in fine grey ware, which may mimic silver vessels (Wilson and Day 1994: 79), and the dark grey burnished / pattern burnished ware chalices. A number of features of these chalices suggest that they skeuomorph metal: their overall biconical profile, the bulbous swelling at the join of pedestal to chalice bowl, and the incised banding on the upper part of the pedestal.

During EMIIA a number of pottery traits at Knossos suggests the increasing influence of metal prototypes; these include sharply out-turned rims and carinations in red slipped and burnished wares, with their lustrous, mottled surface reminiscent of metals. The new pottery drinking and serving sets introduced in late EMIIA also imitate metal, with the appearance of fine, in-turned rims on shallow bowls and the joining of individually crafted parts of the vessels, such as the rounded goblet foot with the upper body (Figure 3.1). Perhaps the best documented case of effective imitation of metals exists in Vasilike Ware pottery (Branigan 1970: 129–30; Betancourt *et al.* 1979: 24–25). The marked increase in metal-imitating drinking and pouring shapes at Knossos in EMIIA may reflect the probable increase in metal vase production in the Aegean as a whole during EBII.

Standardisation of Ceramic Assemblages and 'Alternative Sets'

From late EMIIA onwards, there exists a trend towards the standardization of pottery types, which appear to be produced in increasingly large numbers. Painted wares (dark-on-light painted and red/black slipped) at EMIIB Knossos seem to be of poorer quality than earlier, perhaps with less labour investment in each individual vessel. There seem to be alternative sets of pottery of a higher quality, such as Vasilike Ware, which is much less common outside of East Crete, and therefore may have a greater social value in Central and West Crete.

Changes in the Scheme of Decoration

A marked change in the overall decorative scheme of pottery occurs in EMIIA, going from a tendency to treat the whole of the pot as one field of decoration, to a concentration on decorating the upper body. Almost without exception, vessels of Early Minoan I are decorated with the entire body treated as a single field. Additionally, the stark visual contrasts between dark, pattern burnished pedestalled bowls, scored or wiped jugs and jars, and dark-on-light painted collared jars or jugs, mask a certain unity of decoration, with a scheme of horizontal bands and vertical stripes covering the whole body, which can be found in all three wares (Wilson and Day 2000: 57).

In early EMIIA the patterns covering the whole vessel body are more elaborate, with large ornate motifs on dark-on-light painted jugs and spouted basins which seem to be intended to be viewed as striking, whole vessels (Figure 3.2; Wilson 1985: P93 fig. 14, P218 figs. 22–23).

From late EMIIA, the decoration of pottery becomes much more restricted and focused in its placement on the vessel. Upper bodies, rims, and the interior of bowls receive the most attention in painted wares (Figure 3.1; Wilson and Day 2000; Wilson forthcoming). It seems that, in these cases, vessels are designed to be viewed from above, an observation emphasized by the placement and orientation of the decorative scheme.

Meanings of Changes in the Ceramic Repertoire of EMI-IIB

We have described a number of physical changes in the ceramic repertoire of EMI-IIB Knossos and elsewhere. Clearly their meanings do not lie in the examination of the pottery in isolation, but in relation to the individual or group that uses it and the environment or context in which it is used. For example, the size of the pot matters in its relationship to the scale of the human body and to the elements of the built environment in which it exists. Equally the placement of the decoration leads to meaning only when viewed with the role/s of the individual or group as observers of that decoration. The same pot or set of pottery would have had different meanings in relation to the different performers and observers at the same occasion. In the same vein, vessels would have a variety of emphases depending on their context of use, for example within a public or private forum.

Communal and Individual Uses of Vessels

The burnished chalice and large pedestalled bowl are most common at Knossos in EMI. Along with the large, carinated, round based mixing bowls (Figure 3.1; Hood 1990a : fig. 1 nos. 1–2, 9) they appear to demonstrate the communal serving and consumption of food and drink. Standing to a height of over 20 cm, the chalice itself clearly is not intended for the use of an individual; rather it invites us to think of the sharing of drink between a number of people. The context of the EMI Well at Knossos, where large numbers of such vessels were recovered from what seems to represent a single occasion, or a succession of similar events in the same location, might indicate just how important such an act of sharing might be, with the vessel passed from hand to hand. Of course, if we are correct in suggesting a communal use for these large vessels, they may not reflect a real 'egalitarian' practice of drink consumption. Rather they might be used in a way that promotes the image of equality, in order to ward off challenges to the existing social order and authority.

From late EMIIA onwards, the pottery assemblage at Knossos is of quite a different nature (Figure 3.1). The flat-bottomed, smaller vessels are now of a scale which might feasibly be used on a table. They comprise sets of pottery that even bring to mind the accoutrements of a dinner service, now matching each other in decoration. Whatever the case, there can be no doubt about the emphasis on the serving of drink, and possibly food, on an individual level. While the EMI communal chalices would have to be held with both hands due to their size, the EMII stemmed and footed goblets could be easily handled by the individual user in one hand. This marks a significant change in the actual physical practice of drinking and how participants in drinking may have interacted with one another. The goblets hold drink for one person, while the spouts on bowls/jars provide emphasis to the act of pouring. The observer is drawn by this vessel extension to concentrate on the spout and presumably on the valued liquid content that emerged from it. The focus on pouring, which is even more marked in the extended spouts of the EMIIB phase, seems to have *serving* as its central concept (Figure 3.3). It is the act of serving someone that has perhaps the most potential in defining the relationship between those serving and those served (Catapoti forthcoming).

Object-Viewer Relations

Pottery vessels of EMI and early IIA have a decorative composition that exploits the whole of the vessel as its field. Perhaps most noticeable in the West Court House phase of EMIIA are the dark-on-light painted jugs that often have the central part of their painted composition under the spout itself, drawing the attention of the viewer to the front of the pot and the pouring spout (Figure 3.1). The most effective visual presentation of these jugs, then, is for them to be held with their fronts directly facing the viewer/s, with both the presenter and viewer/s standing. A similar focus of decoration on the frontal display exists on large spouted kraters such as that from the West Court House (Figure 3.2).

The jugs of late EMIIA to EMIIB, have a painted decoration which is either an overall effect as in the case of 'Myrtos Ware' jugs in east Crete (Warren 1972: P443–444 fig. 69), or is confined to the shoulder of the pot in one or two bands as is the norm at Knossos (Warren 1972: P459 fig. 69; Wilson forthcoming; Wilson and Day 1999: fig. 8). This decorative focus on the shoulder and spout of jugs is also seen in the new long-spouted jars that appear in late EMIIA and become common in EMIIB (Figures 3.1 and 3.3; Momigliano and Wilson 1996: fig. 22; Wilson and Day 1999: figs. 11–12). In addition, the new shallow bowls have a simple decorative scheme comprising painted bands on the rim and interior (Figure 3.3; Wilson and Day 1999: fig. 2), while larger serving bowls, often with broad everted rims, have their decorative focus on the upper rim surface and interior (Figures 3.1 and 3.3; Wilson and Day 1999: figs. 5 and 9).

These decorative schemes in the later periods place emphasis on the upper parts of vessel bodies, which are often incurving and carinated for the first time, and even on the interior. This leads to the conclusion that they are meant to be observed at a shorter distance than pots of the earlier period, either from an observation position above the pot, or at an oblique angle to it. We suggest that this is because the vessels now are used by participants sitting around a table or positioned in a fashion such that the vessels were viewed from above. One is reminded in this instance of much later Archaic and Classical red-figure hydriai used at *symposia* on which the figured decoration is often restricted to the shoulder of the pot since these vessels were placed on the floor of the *andron* and meant to be viewed by the banqueters from their dining couches above.

Serving/Consuming Liquids

We have suggested that the pouring vessels of late EMIIA and EMIIB emphasize pouring by their shape and decoration, the latter viewed most effectively from a short distance, possibly when displayed on a table. Their size also reflects such a change in their use. Rather than seeing the long-spouted jars only as serving vessels, it is possible to suggest that they might have held a place in the preparation of drink formerly taken by some of the large spouted bowls (Hood 1990a: fig. 1 no.9 for carinated bowls in the EMI Well; Wilson 1985: fig. 14 for large spouted deep bowl/ krater in EMIIA). In other words they may have been a receptacle in which the ingredients of the drink were mixed before being served. The class of vessels into which the drink or drinks was poured demonstrates perhaps the greatest changes in the pottery assemblage. From being essentially vessels of communal drinking in EMI, as with the chalice, the introduction of the small, footed goblet in late EMIIA marks a quite different relationship between the consumer and the drink. That each individual has been given their share would imply that there is someone giving out the portion of drink. We have suggested elsewhere (Day and Wilson 2002) that this reflects a marked change in social practice.

Serving/Consuming Food

The appearance in late EMIIA of shallow bowls, which are effectively the first ceramic plates, is of great importance. It is part of a wider phenomenon observed throughout the Aegean in late EBII comprising a new group of drinking and eating shapes dubbed the Kastri or Lefkandi I Group in the Cyclades and mainland (principally Attica, Euboea and Boiotia).

As with the case of the long-spouted jars, the shallow bowls seem to place an emphasis on serving. Many are small enough to be for individual use, as with the footed goblets. In this case they might be considered together with goblets and pouring vessels to comprise a set of table-ware: a repeated set of vessels for use around the table. The larger shallow bowls seem to be more concerned with the display or presentation of different types of food. As with the relationship of the long-spouted jar to the goblet, one would have to serve/be served from the larger bowls to individual receptacles, an act which at once includes and divides, emphasizing the position of the individual within the social milieu.

Contexts of Use

These comments are not meant to assume that pottery has a set meaning and mode of use, regardless of context. Indeed much of the above is based upon the assemblages at Knossos, where indeed there may have been a special emphasis on ceremonial aspects of food and drink consumption. But Knossos is certainly not alone in the drinking emphasis of its fine wares in the EBII Aegean. The House of Tiles at Lerna on the Greek mainland also may have provided a forum for some type of ceremonial drinking/feasting practice (Wiencke 2000: 651).

Yet this does not diminish the importance of these vessels in what might be considered more 'domestic' contexts. In substantial assemblages of the EMIIB period, such as those at Myrtos Fournou Korifi (Warren 1972), the same drinking and eating sets clearly are important in the social relations within such communities, with an emphasis on acts of hospitality. Indeed such acts, in all communities, may serve as referents to practices carried out elsewhere, either by the same actors or by others.

Social Referents of Food/Cuisine/Etiquette

This range of serving vessels, and the introduction of shapes suggesting the increased importance of a formalized meal, has a broader Aegean context. Drinking vessels, elaborate pouring shapes and individual plates are features emphasized not only by the Minoan assemblage, but also by the Kastri Group in the later phase of EB2 in Western Anatolia, the Cyclades and areas of coastal mainland Greece (Wilson 1999: 94–101). This makes us aware that each occasion of their use refers to others previously observed, imagined or heard about. The very number of vessels which seem, according to their decoration, to belong together as sets means that a range of actions can be made with them and in different sequences. Therein lies the potential for knowledge to be demonstrated, for conformity, for the correct performance. In the case of individual sets, this puts certain emphases on the person as an actor to perform his/her part correctly. Yet serving vessels also hint at a key role for one or more individuals, in the context of distributing key components of food and drink in the act of consumption. Their emulation or interpretation of such specific actions allows the reproduction and redefinition of social relationships (Catapoti forthcoming).

In this context, the imitation of metal by these ceramic assemblages suggests that they existed with reference to perhaps more valuable, homologous sets made of metal (see Bendall, this volume, for a hierarchy of different vessels of consumption in the later Palace of Nestor at Pylos). That certain sets of vessels may be more desirable and more exclusive indicates the possible sources of the practices mimicked or followed in the consumption of food and drink. The sets may therefore epitomise identity, hierarchical or horizontal social divisions, aspirations and emulation. At Knossos we might suggest that such social divisions may be reflected in the categories of pottery. While in EMI and early EMIIA there is essentially only one type of drinking cup (the chalice or pedestaled goblet respectively) restricted largely to a single broadly local ware (dark grey burnished), in late EMIIA the options in both wares and shapes increase significantly and include at least some non-local drinking cups and jugs (red slipped and burnished and early Vasilike Ware). This trend continues in EMIIB, when drinking and eating sets exist in Vasilike Ware, dark-on-light painted ware, and also in red/black slipped wares, the latter without the shallow bowls. Vasilike Ware may be non-local in provenance and much of it manufactured in east Crete (Day *et al.* 1999: 1032–3). We might suggest that Vasilike Ware, with its close imitation of metal and its scarcity and distant provenance might have been of higher value than some of the other more local ceramic sets. The prevalence of Vasilike Ware vessels at Myrtos only about 25 km from its source (Whitelaw *et al.* 1997) may suggest that it carried with it a rather different social message in that settlement than it did for example in North-Central Crete.

If, as we have observed, this change in the ceramic assemblage represents evidence for a transformation in the practice and *mores* of food and drink consumption, then such changes or fashions are visible well beyond the coast of Crete. Hence, just as the individual using the pottery set may consume drink in a manner that refers to the practice of others, perhaps differentiated by social or geographical distance, so those knowledgeable of these practices, and able to obtain materials from a distance, would refer to the practices of similar groups elsewhere in the Aegean.

The explosion of drinking sets, of small-scale, flat-based tableware, in late EMIIA perhaps exemplifies the intense social competition at this time. It has been argued recently for the Mesara that EMII witnesses a contraction in regions, and expansion in the importance of place, of collective structures which highlight solidarity and boundaries (Relaki 2003). Drinking ceremonies may have moved away from the funerary arena and the small scale acts of consumption may have provided the possibility of simultaneous integration and negotiation. Hosting certainly provides the opportunity to emphasize the local community, even to bolster the structure of families, but it also offers an arena for conflict and competition, kept controlled within the boundary of community. Although we have less spatial definition for north-central Crete at this time, many of these processes clearly were important in later Prepalatial Knossos.

Regardless of whether ceremonies were carried out at a ritual centre or in more domestic circumstances, the use of this pottery in the consumption of drink can be used to define roles, position and identity. This may happen on a variety of levels and much the same practice might be used to define the roles of host and guest as might be used to differentiate those in a position of authority. Yet this definition of roles might in itself be dynamic, not only confirming social roles, but challenging them (Catapoti forthcoming). Whatever the case, this is surely fertile ground for the definition of different social roles, for the promotion of cohesion in the face of instability and for the confirmation or challenging of power.

Comment

In this paper we have referred to distinct changes in the ceramic assemblage of Minoan Crete during EMII, with an emphasis on Knossos. The introduction of individual drinking sets and the shallow bowl follow similar developments in other areas of the Aegean. The smaller size of the vessels and the change in their decorative scheme is argued to represent a move from vessels of communal use in feasting and drinking ceremonies with the participants standing, to individual sets which may also have been used in formal consumption acts or meals but with the participants now seated at a table/s. Ultimately, with such changes in material culture and human action, we suggest an increase during EMII of drinking/eating practices that form the arena for social competition; the social acts which signal divisions, differentiation, identity and power in the EBII Aegean.

Acknowledgements

For discussions on this and related themes, we would like to thank Despina Catapoti, Yannis Hamilakis and Maria Relaki. For access to material discussed specifically we have benefited from the generosity of Gerald Cadogan, Sinclair Hood and the Council of the British School at Athens.

Bibliography

Barrett, J.
2000 A thesis of agency. In M-A. Dobres and J. Robb (eds.), *Agency in Archaeology*: 61–68. London: Routledge.

Betancourt, P.P.
1984 *East Cretan White-on-Dark Ware*. Philadelphia: University Museum, University of Pennsylvania.
1985 *The History of Minoan Pottery*. Princeton: Princeton University Press.

Betancourt, P. P., T. K. Gaisser, F. R. Matson, G. H. Myer, and C. P. Swann
1979 *Vasilike Ware. An Early Bronze Age Pottery Style in Crete* (SIMA 56). Göteborg: Paul Åströms Forlag.

Branigan, K.
1970 *The Foundations of Palatial Crete*. London: Routledge.

Catapoti, D.
forthcoming *Rise to the Occasion: Rethinking the Emergence of the 'Palatial Phenomenon' in Minoan Crete*. PhD dissertation, University of Sheffield.

Day, P.M. and D.E. Wilson
1998 Consuming power: Kamares ware in Protopalatial Knossos. *Antiquity* 72: 350–58.
2002 Landscapes of memory, craft and power in Prepalatial and Protopalatial Knossos. In Y. Hamilakis (ed.), *Labyrinth Revisited: Rethinking 'Minoan' Archaeology*: 143–66. Oxford: Oxbow.

Day, P.M., E. Kiriatzi, A. Tsolakidou and V. Kilikoglou
1999 Group therapy in Crete: a comparison between analyses by NAA and thin section petrography of Early Minoan pottery. *JAS* 26: 1025–36.

Dietler, M. and B. Hayden (eds.)
2001 *Feasts: Archaeological and Ethnographic Perspectives on Food, Politics, and Power*. Washington: Smithsonian Institute.

Evans, A.J.
1921 *The Palace of Minos at Knossos, 1*. London: Macmillan.

Evans, J.D.
1971 Neolithic Knossos: the growth of a settlement. *Proceedings of the Prehistoric Society* 37,2: 81–117.

Haggis, D.C.
1996 Excavations at Kalo Khorio, East Crete. *AJA* 100: 645–81.

Hamilakis, Y.
1996 Wine, oil and the dialectics of power in Bronze Age Crete: a review of the evidence. *OJA* 15: 1–31.

Hayden, B.

1995 The emergence of prestige technologies and pottery. In W. Barnett and J.W. Hoopes (eds.), *Emergence of Pottery*: 257–66. Washington: Smithsonian Institute.

Hood, M.S.F.

1971 *The Minoans*. London: Thames and Hudson.

1990a Autochthons or settlers? Evidence for immigration at the beginning of the Early Bronze Age in Crete. In *Proceedings of the 6th International Cretological Congress,* A1: 367–75. Chania.

1990b Settlers in Crete c.3000 B.C. *Cretan Studies* 2: 151–58.

Karantzali, E.

1993 Stoikhia Protominoikis katoikisis sta Nopigeia Kisamou. *ADelt. 47–48, A*: 65–82.

MacGillivray, J.A.

1987 Pottery workshops and the old palaces in Crete. In R. Hägg and N. Marinatos (eds.), *The Function of the Minoan Palaces*: 273–79. Stockholm: Swedish Institute at Athens.

Momigliano, N.

1991 MMIA pottery from Evans' excavations at Knossos. *BSA* 86: 149–271.

Momigliano, N. and D.E. Wilson

1996 Knossos 1993: excavations outside the South Front of the Palace. *BSA* 91: 1–57.

Palmer, R.

1995 Wine and viticulture in the Linear A and B texts of the Bronze Age Aegean. In P.E. McGovern, S.J. Fleming and S.H. Katz (eds.), *The Origins and Ancient History of Wine*: 269–85. Philadelphia: University of Pennsylvania.

Rambach, J.

2000 *KYKLADEN I-II. Die Frühe Bronzezeit Grab- und Siedlungsbefunde*. Bonn: R. Habelt.

Relaki, M.

2003 *Social Arenas in Minoan Crete: a Regional History of the Mesara from the Final Neolithic to the End of the Protopalatial Period*. PhD dissertation, University of Sheffield.

Renfrew, C.

1972 *The Emergence of Civilisation*. London: Methuen.

Sherratt, A.

1987 Cups that cheered: the introduction of alcohol to prehistoric Europe. In W. Waldren and R. Kennard (eds.), *Bell Beakers of the Western Mediterranean: the Oxford International Conference 1986* (BAR International Series 331): 81–106. Oxford: British Archaeological Reports.

Walberg, G.

1976 *Kamares. A Study of the Character of Palatial Middle Minoan Pottery* (Boreas 8). Uppsala: Academia Upsaliensis.

1983 *Provincial Middle Minoan Pottery*. Mainz: Philipp von Zabern.

Warren, P.

1972 *Myrtos. An Early Bronze Age Settlement in Crete*. London: British School at Athens.

Warren, P. and Y. Tzedakhis

1974 Debla, an Early Minoan settlement in Western Crete. *BSA* 69: 299–342.

Whitelaw, T., P.M. Day, E. Kiriatzi, V. Kilikoglou and D.E. Wilson

1997 Ceramic traditions at EMIIB Myrtos, Fournou Korifi. In R. Laffineur and P.P. Betancourt (eds.), *TEXNH. Craftsmen, Craftswomen and Craftsmanship in the Aegean Bronze Age* (Aegaeum 16). Liège: University of Liège: 265–74.

Wiencke, M.H.

2000 *Lerna, 4. The Architecture, Stratification, and Pottery of Lerna III*. Princeton: American School of Classical Studies at Athens.

Wilson, D.E.
1985 The pottery and architecture of the Early Minoan IIA West Court House at Knossos. *BSA* 80: 281–364.
1994 Knossos before the palaces: an overview of the Early Bronze Age (EMI-EMIII). In D. Evely, H. Hughes-Brock and N. Momigliano (eds.), *Knossos: A Labyrinth of History. Papers Presented to Sinclair Hood*: 23–44. London: British School at Athens.
1995 The pottery and architecture of the EMIIA West Court house at Knossos. *BSA* 80: 281–364.
1999 *Keos IX, 1. Ayia Irini: Periods I–III. The Neolithic and Early Bronze Age Settlements.* Mainz: Philipp von Zabern.
forthcoming Early Minoan I–II. In N. Momigliano (ed.), *Knossos Pottery Handbook, 1: Neolithic and Minoan* (BSA Studies). London: British School at Athens.
Wilson, D.E. and P.M. Day
1994 Ceramic regionalism in Prepalatial central Crete: the Mesara imports at EMI to EMIIA Knossos. *BSA* 89: 1–87.
1999 EMIIB ware groups at Knossos: the 1907–08 South Front tests. *BSA* 94: 1–62.
2000 EMI chronology and social practice: pottery from the early palace tests at Knossos. *BSA* 95: 21–63.
Wilson, D.E., P.M. Day and N. Dimopoulou-Rethemiotaki
in press The pottery from EMI-IIB Knossos and its relations with the harbour site of Poros-Katsambas. In G. Cadogan, E. Hatzaki and A. Vasilakis (eds.), *Knossos: Palace, City, State* (BSA Studies). London: British School at Athens.
Wright, J.
1995 Empty cups and empty jugs: the social role of wine in Minoan and Mycenaean societies. In P.E. McGovern, S.J. Fleming and S.H. Katz (eds.), *The Origins and Ancient History of Wine*: 287–309. Philadelphia: University of Pennsylvania.

4

Ceramic Sets in Context: One Dimension of Food Preparation and Consumption in a Minoan Palatial Setting

Jeremy Rutter

For the past decade, I have been charged with the sorting, dating, and contextual evaluation of the prehistoric pottery recovered at the Middle and Late Bronze Age centre of Kommos on Crete. Excavations at this harbour town situated at the western end of the Mesara plain, less than 5 km south of the ridge at the east and west ends of which lie the better known inland centres of Phaistos and Ayia Triadha, have uncovered a wide range of find contexts of considerable interest for anyone investigating the social implications of prehistoric Aegean cuisine and diet. In view of my own particular interest in the history and function of Minoan ceramics, the following paper will focus on the implications of selected food containers found at Kommos (Betancourt 1990; Watrous 1992; Van de Moortel 1997: 21–274, 689–746, 865–927; 2001) rather than on food remains *per se* (Shay and Shay 1995; Reese et al. 1995; 2000; Ruscillo n.d.). I will also concentrate on aspects of food preparation and consumption in the public spaces of the so-called Civic Center at Minoan Kommos (Shaw and Shaw n.d.) at the expense of domestic contexts within the adjacent town (Shaw 1995; Shaw and Nixon 1996; Wright and McEnroe 1996; Shaw and Shaw 1993).

Prologue: a Brief Introduction to Recent Work at Kommos

The focus of attention at Kommos during the decade when I have served as a member of the excavation team has been the so-called Southern Area (Shaw and Shaw 1993). Positioned at and just above sea level, and extending between thirty and a hundred metres inland from the hypothesized location of the Bronze Age shoreline, this portion of the site represents the southernmost extent of the Minoan settlement, separated from steeply sloping terrain to the south by an east-west gully and lying at the foot of higher ground to the north, across which latter the Minoan town spread for several hundred metres to the north and possibly another hundred metres or more to the east as well (Shaw 1995: 12; Hope Simpson 1995:

Figure 4.1. MMIII–LMIII period plan of Southern Area at Kommos.

396; J.W. Shaw 1996: 5–7, 13 n.11). A broad, handsomely paved road (Figure 4.1: 17) runs east-west across the northern portion of this Southern Area and neatly divides the town, with its quite densely packed residential structures on the sloping hillside to the north, from a relatively flat expanse to the south that was occupied from the Middle Minoan (henceforth MM) IIB phase (18th century BC) down to the time of the site's abandonment for one or two centuries beginning in the Late Minoan (henceforth LM) IIIB phase (13th century BC) by a stratified series of monumental buildings which we have collectively termed the site's 'Civic Center' (M.C. Shaw 1996; Shaw 2001: 8–9). Thus far, only small portions of an enormous court-centred structure laid out in this area in the late Protopalatial era have been exposed (the building we call AA; Shaw 2001: 8 and n.9). Both built and destroyed in MMIIB, this structure was immediately replaced, in the local MMIII ceramic phase that represents the beginning of the Neopalatial era in the

Mesara, by a second court-centred building occupying virtually the same architectural 'footprint' as its predecessor. We feel confident that this Neopalatial structure (designated T – Figure 4.1) belongs to the same functional category as the monumental complexes that have long been identified at the Minoan centres of Knossos, Phaistos, Mallia, Zakro, and Gournia – and now Galatas, Petras, and probably Archanes and Chania as well (Rehak and Younger 2001: 394–96, 467–68) – as 'palaces' (Shaw et al. 2001: 1; Shaw 2001: 5–8, fig. 1).[1] Badly damaged very early in its history of use, and as a consequence partially abandoned and also repeatedly remodeled in significant ways, Building T (Figure 4.2) continued to be used throughout the Neopalatial era and into the LMII phase of the succeeding Monopalatial period.[2] In this last phase, the impressive residence directly across the great east-west road from Building T's northeast corner, our House X (Figures 4.1–2), was refurbished so as to become a seemingly public 'house shrine' (in Room X7) provided with some auxiliary storage space (in Rooms X4 and X5) (Shaw and Shaw 1993: 131–61). Throughout the relatively brief Monopalatial era encompassing LMII to the time of the great destruction at Knossos in early LMIIIA2, or a little over a century (Manning 1995: 217–29; Rehak and Younger 2001: 391 table 1; Manning 1999: 335–40, fig. 62), the shrine complex in House X provides by far the richest evidence for human activity of any locale within the Southern Area. But at the beginning of the ensuing Final Palatial period, the shrine appears to have collapsed and been built over, while the huge space occupied by the ruined 'palace' to the south and southwest was likewise remodeled (Shaw 2001: 9). Initially, two large galleries plausibly identified as monumental shipsheds were constructed from cannibalized materials over the northern end of Building T's east wing (Figure 4.1: P1 and P2), while the westernmost surviving portions of T's north wing were converted into an independent structure we have called N (Figure 4.1). Subsequent building during the later 14th and perhaps also early 13th centuries BC resulted in the addition of four more galleries (P3 through P6) to the gigantic ship-storage facility P, as well as a secondary courtyard in the angle between P and N (Figure 4.1: 15) and some minor alterations to Building N. This group of buildings was in turn abandoned at some point during LMIIIB, after which only scant traces of human activity are attested in this region of the site prior to the construction of the earliest temple over the eastern portion of Building N in the later 11th century (Shaw 2000a: 2 table 1.1, 8–10, 90 ns. 6–8; 2000b: 698–700; Callaghan and Johnston 2000: 212–14, pls. 4.1, 4.6, 4.40 [Deposit 1]).

Food Preparation and Consumption in a Palatial Setting at Kommos

The MMIIB court-centred Building AA appears to have been demolished to below its original floor levels during subsequent building operations, so that very little evidence survives for how the various spaces within it functioned. But its

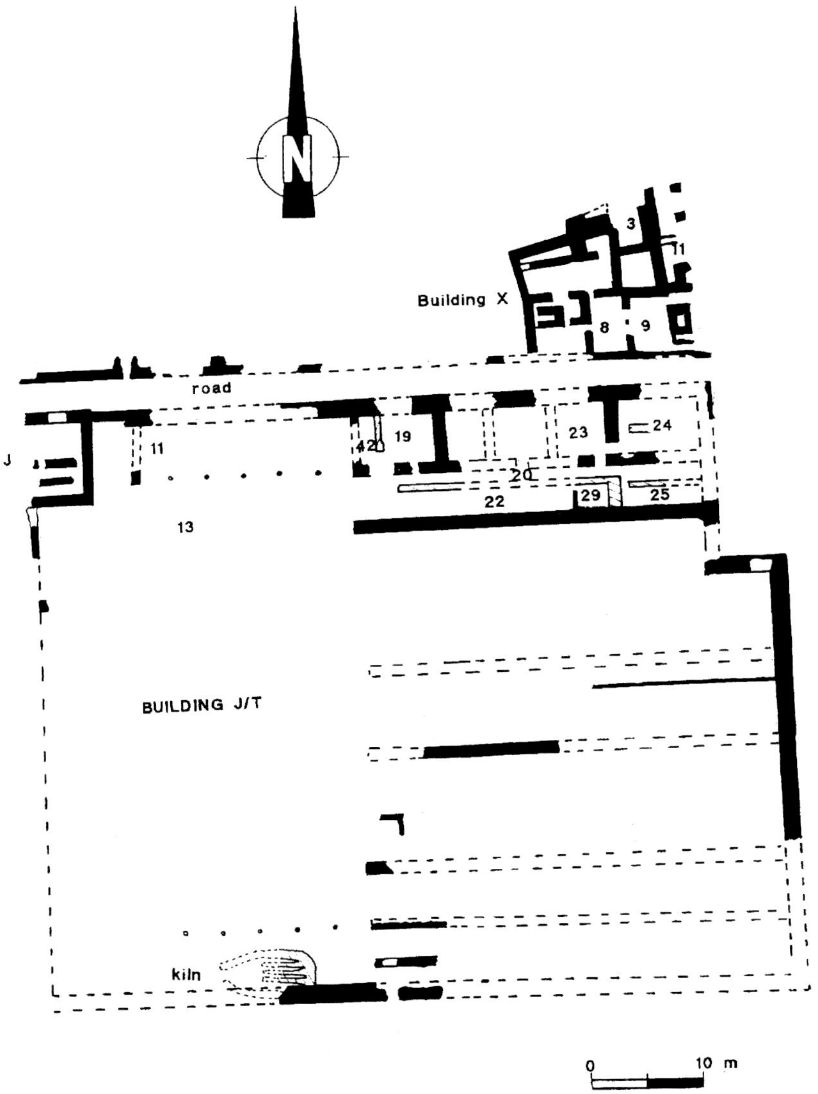

Figure 4.2. Plan of Building T at Kommos (after Driessen and Macdonald 1997: 208, fig. 7.63).

Neopalatial successor, Building T, has fared somewhat better, and we can identify a number of different functions within particular spaces on its ground floor with the help of either specific architectural features or ceramic contents or both. Thus several rooms in the building's northeast corner (Figure 4.1: 23–25) can be confidently identified by concentrations of pithos fragments accompanied by lamps as storage areas, or magazines, during the initial stages of the building's use. The construction of a multiply flued kiln (Figure 4.1: 47) within the space of the south stoa (Figure 4.1: 48), and the discovery of massive quantities of misfired and broken pottery accompanied by wasters in the debris immediately surrounding the kiln on the east, north, and west, have revealed that this portion of the building for a time served an industrial function (Shaw et al. 2001). This must have occurred when the space in question was unroofed, and consequently when it looked very different from its elegant, original state as a roofed portico with frescoed walls. The eastern end of the north stoa at the opposite side of T's central court (Figure 4.1: 16, east half) was likewise refurbished to accommodate a distinctly different and chronologically secondary function, in this case the grinding of grain in a series of plaster-lined bins each provided with its own grinding slab. The ceramic assemblage associated with this phase of the space's use (Rutter n.d.: Groups 26 and 33) includes two decidedly unusual shapes – a large, plain, coarse basin (Kommos inv.no. C8342) and a small, decorated, fine tubular-spouted jar (Kommos inv.no. C8337) – that it shares with a contemporary usage of some of the annexes attached to the nearby tholos tomb at Kamilari (Levi 1961–2: 55–76, figs. 83a–d, 90). From this same context at Kamilari comes a relatively well-preserved terracotta model illustrating either grain-grinding or, possibly, bread-making (Levi 1961–2: 145–47, figs. 177a–c; Novaro 1999).[3] So in this case an unsuspected connection between a particular kind of food-processing (i.e. the grinding of grain) and an odd pair of ceramic types not previously associated with this activity can be suggested.

Indicators of a food-preparation area can also, of course, take other forms, such as hearths (Metaxa-Muhly 1984; Shaw 1990; M.C. Shaw 1996: 357–59; Rethemiotakis 1999). Several discrete locations of fixed hearths, each accompanied by largely restorable cooking pots, are an interesting feature of palatial structure T. Significantly, no more than one of these locations was in use at any given time in the building's two or three centuries of use. Moreover, these various locales and their associated cooking equipment exhibit some interesting commonalities. The earliest hearth is situated near the central court's southeast corner, against the south wall of space 36 near its western end (Figure 4.1). Lying broken in and immediately adjacent to this hearth were found two large tripod cooking pots (Figure 4.3: C9436, C9430), which differ appreciably in the details of their shapes. The context in which they were found dates to LMIA Early (Van de Moortel 1997: 235–44; 2001: 89–91; Rutter n.d.: Group 9b), probably contemporary with the fire that put T's northeast wing out of use as well as with the destruction of the south stoa. Whether this first cooking site was replaced immediately or not is uncertain; excavation of Building T has thus far not produced a hearth anywhere within it that can be attributed to the next local ceramic phase that we call LMIA Advanced (Table 4.1), the time during which the kiln was constructed and first used within the ruins of the south stoa (Van de Moortel 1997: 245–58; 2001: 91). We can, however, be sure that no cooking pots were produced in the kiln at any time during its one to two generations of active use (Van de Moortel 2001: 43 table 4, 67 fig. 39, 102). In the following LMIA Final phase (Van de Moortel 1997: 258–67;

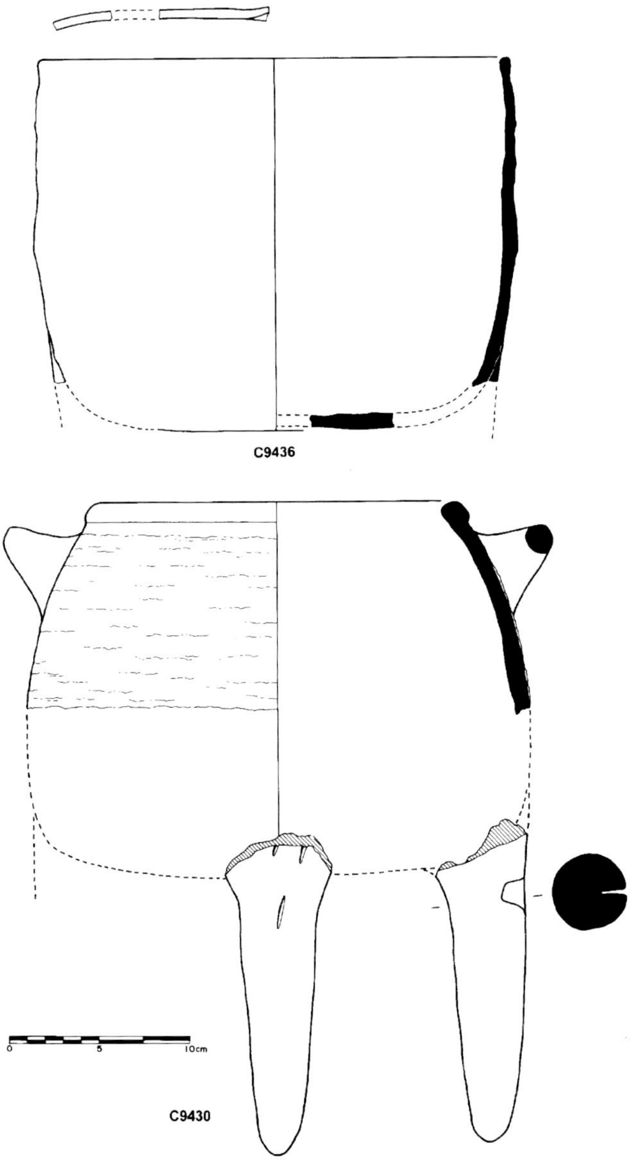

Figure 4.3. Kommos Building T, space 36, LMIA Early: tripod cooking pots C9436 and C9430.

2001: 91–92), a new cooking locale that features two adjacent hearths built up against the south wall of space 22 near its western end (Figure 4.1) shows that such activity had been relocated close to the northeast corner of the central court by this time, with roughly the same spatial relationship relative to the building's other former stoa at the court's north end as the earlier cooking site had had with respect to the now ruinous and partially overbuilt remains of the south stoa

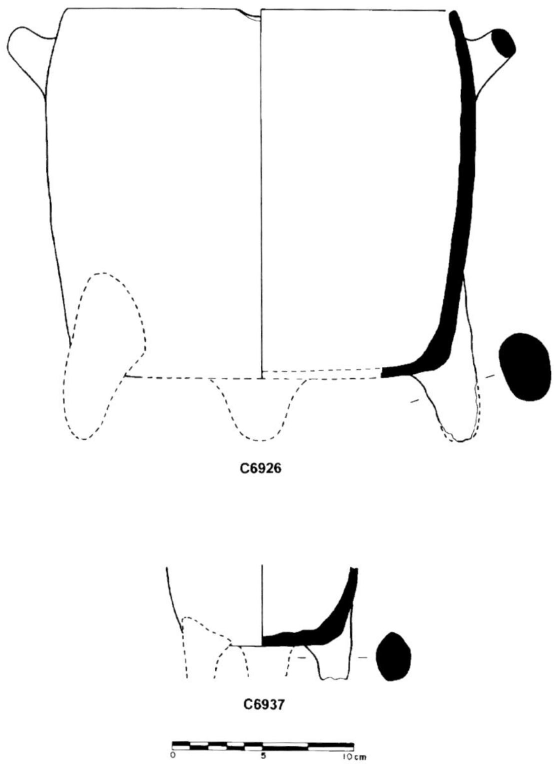

Figure 4.4. Kommos Building T, space 22, LMIA Final: tripod cooking pots C6926 and C6937.

(Figures 4.1–2). Once again, we are fortunate enough to have found restorable cooking pots in and immediately around these later LMIA hearths, and once again they are tripod cooking pots of different sorts, but in this case one large one and one small (Figure 4.4: C6926, C6937). Like the earlier LMIA cooking context some 35 m to the south, this one also contained a fair number of mendable drinking cups and jugs (Rutter n.d.: Group 24). Unlike that earlier context, however, this one, broadly contemporary with the grain-grinding horizon in the nearby space 16 just to the northwest, contains a number of fragments from imported vessels including Cypriot Proto Base Ring jugs (Kommos inv. nos. C10777 – C10779), a Late Helladic I Vapheio cup (Kommos inv. no. C6912), and a large transport vessel from an unidentified source (Kommos inv. no. C7626).

The next location for a hearth in Building T is in the northwest corner of its court, built up against the north wall of the court underneath the broad corridor numbered 7 that belongs to the later LMIII Building N (Figures 4.1–2). The datable periods of use of several architecturally and stratigraphically discrete phases of this hearth are LMIB Late and LMII, but only from the latest phase of its use do we have a cooking jar that was probably used in it (Figure 4.5: C2563; Rutter n.d.:

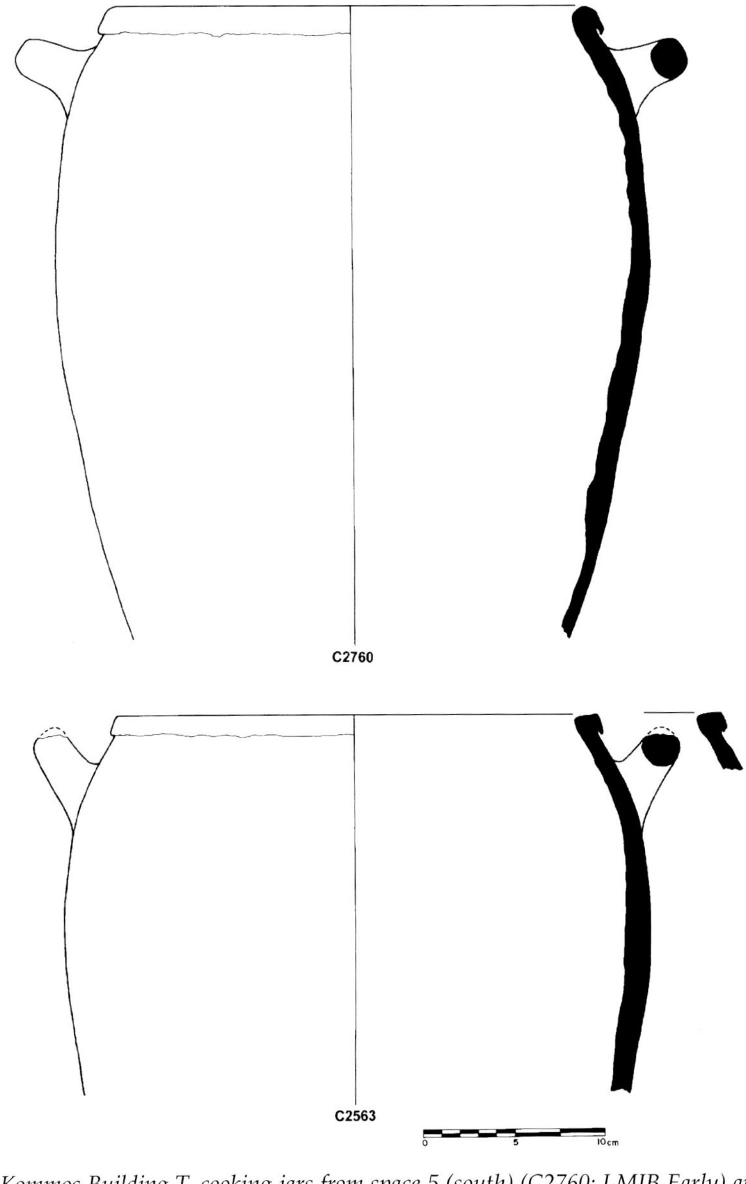

Figure 4.5. Kommos Building T, cooking jars from space 5 (south) (C2760: LMIB Early) and northwest corner of central court (C2563: LMII).

Group 45). The discovery of several largely restorable cooking pots – one of them (Figure 4.5: C2760; Watrous 1992: 15 no. 273, pl. 7) a virtual twin of the jar just mentioned – in a LMIB Early dumped fill in the staircase area at the south end of space 5 just to the north (Figure 4.1; Watrous 1992: 14–16 Deposit 7, figs. 17–18, pls. 5–7; Rutter n.d.: Group 40) suggests that either this hearth or else another

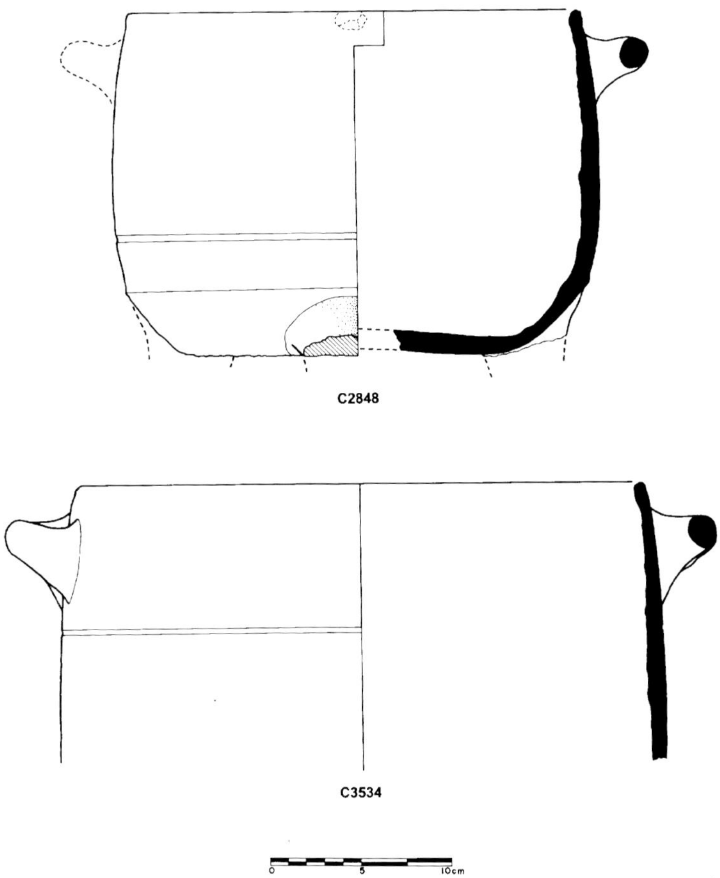

Figure 4.6. Kommos Building T, space 5 (south), LMIB Early: tripod cooking pots C2848 and C3534.

one somewhere nearby that has yet to be located was already in use at or near the court's northwest corner shortly after the abandonment of the LMIA Final hearths in space 22. The shape range of these mendable cooking pots has now become slightly more diversified – large tripod vessels (Figure 4.6) are joined by deeper-bodied, horizontal-handled, but legless jars (Figure 4.5). Furthermore, one of the two tripod vessels (Figure 4.6: C3534; Watrous 1992: 16 no. 275, pl. 7) lacks any traces of burning and has an applied reddish yellow slip on the interior, indications that this vase probably had a significantly different function from its somewhat smaller look-alike (Figure 4.6: C2848; Watrous 1992: 15–16 no. 274, pl. 7; Van de Moortel 1997: 201–2, 207–8, 210). Once again, the contexts from which these LMIB and LMII cooking pots come contain copious quantities of drinking cups, jugs, and transport vessels, a substantial number of which are imports. By the time of the LMIB Late and LMII usage of the hearth at the northwest corner of T's court, most of the interior spaces of Building T that have so far been excavated had gone out of use, a fact which might explain why cooking in the building was now being done in the unroofed court itself.

To summarize, cooking activity in Kommos' palatial Building T was always located in relatively well-ventilated spaces either directly adjacent to or actually within the central court. The restorable cooking pots found in direct association with hearths in three different locales represent only two different shapes, tripod cooking vessels and deeper as well as substantially larger jars.[4] In all the relevant contexts are found substantial quantities of ceramic types associated with drinking – namely, cups and jugs – and usually also vessel types employed for the transport of liquids in bulk (either oval-mouthed amphoras or large stirrup jars), but not pithoi or large open shapes such as tubs and basins. It is difficult not to conclude that these cooking facilities were in every case connected with large-scale feasting and drinking ceremonies that took place either in the central court or in spaces easily accessible to large numbers of people that opened directly off of it (such as the north and south stoas in the early history of Building T). The often very high quality and exotic nature of the pouring and drinking vessels in question further suggest that these festive occasions were attended by the elite members of the society, although the far greater frequencies of more utilitarian versions of these same functional types indicate that the hypothetically higher-ranking users of these exotic vessels were heavily outnumbered at these social gatherings by less privileged members of the society (Moody 1987; Hamilakis 1996: 24–26; 1999: 48–50; Rupp and Tsipopoulou 1999).

A closer examination of the fine wares and readily identifiable imports associated with this hypothesized feasting behaviour provides some additional insights into its nature and evolution through time. For example, in the earliest stages of Building T's use – MMIII and LMIA Early (Table 4.1) – when the entire structure was in service and the cooking facility was positioned in space 36 adjacent to the south stoa, imports are relatively rare, especially insofar as vessels from outside of Crete are concerned. Locally produced tablewares are still decorated in a light-on-dark mode which is stylistically rather crude as well as decoratively impoverished. By far the most common single pattern is a thick and clumsy retorted running spiral, and polychromy is rare. By comparison with pottery of either the preceding MMIIB phase or later LMIA and IB phases, ceramics are at a low ebb artistically (Betancourt 1990: 37–48, 96–129 [Contexts 15–21], 166–90 nos. 1410–2036; Van de Moortel 1997: 225–44).

In contrast, the pottery of the subsequent LMIA Final and LMIB Early phases is far richer in every way. Imports have become quite common and take the form of Cypriot black- and red-slipped (or Proto Base Ring) jugs (Rutter 1999: 167–70 table 1), Mycenaean Vapheio cups (Rutter 1999: 180–83 table 6), and semiglobular cups, straight-sided cups, and jugs from several different regions within Crete (Watrous 1992: 149–53, 170–73). Moreover, the imports from regions outside of Crete are markedly concentrated in, if not absolutely restricted to, the Southern Area of the site; that is, they are found principally in the site's Civic Center rather

Palatial Era	Kommos Ceramic Phase	Building Events and Destructions in 'Civic Center' at Kommos	Building Events and Destructions in House X at Kommos
Protopalatial	Middle Minoan IIB	Construction and use of Building AA	
Neopalatial	Middle Minoan III	Construction and initial use of Building T	
	Late Minoan IA Early	Destruction by fire of northeastern wing (spaces 23-25); destruction of south stoa; abandonment of cooking facility in space 36	Construction of House X (?)
	Late Minoan IA Advanced	Construction and initial use of kiln within former south stoa of Building T	Initial use deposits within House X
	Late Minoan IA Final	Construction of walls subdividing former north stoa; grain-grinding in space 16; cooking at west end of space 22; abandonment of south stoa kiln before end of phase	
	Late Minoan IB Early	Deep fills dumped in staircase in south part of space 5 and in spaces 10-11; final floor in space 16 at high level above buried grinding bins	Up to four LMIB floors preserved in some rooms (e.g. Room X2)
	Late Minoan IB Late	Cooking in northwest corner of central court and gradual accumulation of feasting debris above this portion of pebbled surface of court; no significant break in activity between LMIB Late and LMII	
Monopalatial	Late Minoan II		Initial use of shrine in Room X7
	Late Minoan IIIA1		Floruit of shrine in Room X7
Final Palatial	Late Minoan IIIA2	Construction of Galleries P1 – P2; refurbishment of Building T's NW corner as Building N	Collapse and abandonment of shrine (Room X7) and associated storage areas (Rooms X4 – X5) early in phase
	Late Minoan IIIB	Construction of Galleries P3 – P6; minor remodelling of Building N; final floor deposits in Galleries P1 – P6 and Building N date from near end of phase	Only patches of higher-lying floors survive belonging to renovated building constructed directly over House X

Table 4.1. Chronological table of ceramic phases identified at Kommos and correlation of these with the major era of Minoan palatial culture and with significant episodes of construction or destruction in Kommos' Southern Area.

than in those portions of the town's residential neighbourhoods so far excavated. The later of these two phases witnesses the appearance of an occasional exotic unguent container from Cyprus (e.g. Watrous 1992: 156 no. 278, fig. 70, pl. 51) or elsewhere on Crete (Watrous 1992: 15 no. 270, fig. 18, pl. 6), and also of the earliest Egyptian transport vessel to have been found anywhere on the site (Watrous 1992: 162 no. 277). It is during these two phases that locally produced fine wares decorated in a dark-on-light mode, often combined with light-on-dark accents, first become prominent (Van de Moortel 1997: 258–74), although these were *not* produced in the south stoa kiln, which in fact went out of use at some point during the LMIA Final phase (Van de Moortel 2001: 94–110). Among the fine wares manufactured at Kommos or in its immediate vicinity are a substantial number decorated with a homogeneous range of patterns in a recurring syntax that suggest an intentional effort on the part of their producers to promote a group of shapes as sets decorated in a single style that I have christened the Floral Paneled Style. The shapes so decorated, in decreasing order of popularity,

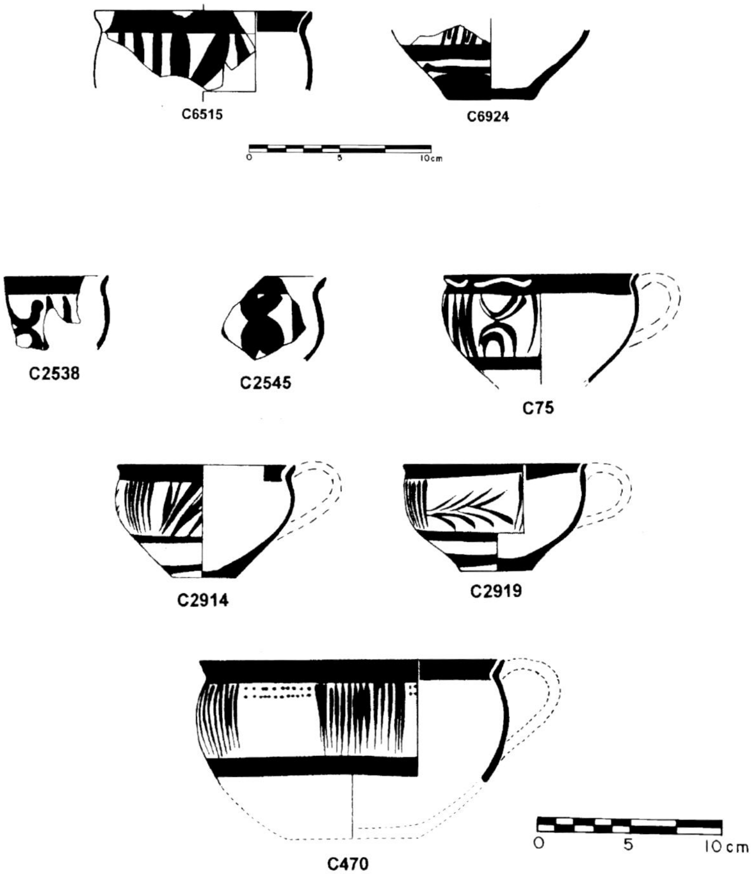

Figure 4.7. Floral Paneled Style: semiglobular cups from Kommos.

are: the semiglobular cup (Figure 4.7); the in-and-out (or horizontal-handled) bowl (Figure 4.8); the collar-necked jug (Figure 4.9); and the oval-mouthed amphora (Figure 4.10). Conspicuously absent from this list are standard Neopalatial shapes such as the straight-sided cup, the bridge-spouted jar, and the beaked jug that are common at other sites (Van de Moortel 1997: 111–14, 146–48, 159–62). The decorative fingerprint of this style is a frieze consisting of alternating groups of six to twelve or more vertically aligned stripes or leaves framing panels in which appear single floral motifs of various kinds – three-petalled buds (Figure 4.11), horizontal (Figure 4.7: C2919) or diagonal (Figure 4.7: C2914) reed sprays – or alternatively single floating or antithetical upright and pendent semicircles, either single (Figures 4.7: C2545, C2538, 4.8: C10820) or double (Figures 4.7: C75, 4.9: C4132). Friezes of this kind occupy the shoulders of collar-necked jugs and the exterior handle zones of semiglobular cups and bowls. The interiors of the horizontal-handled bowls decorated in this style (Figure 4.8) have, by the LMIB

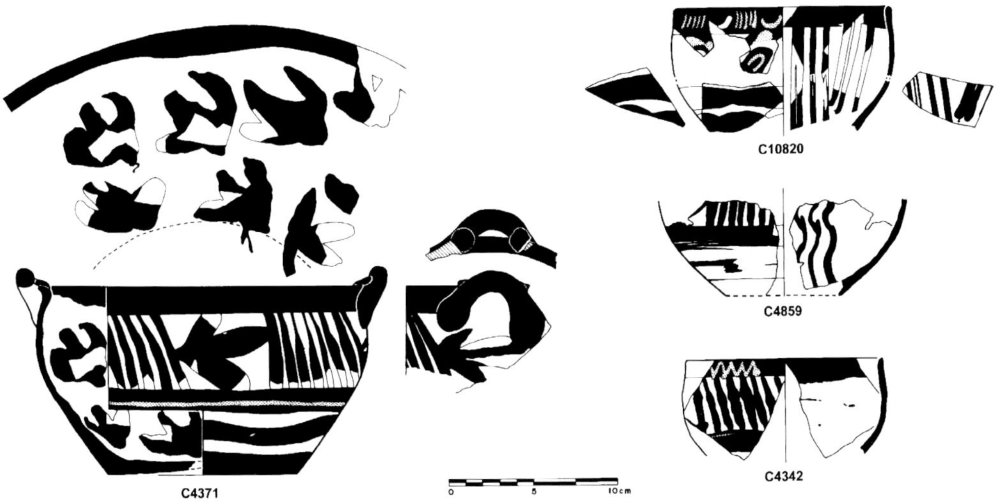

Figure 4.8. Floral Paneled Style: in-and-out (or horizontal-handled) bowls from Kommos.

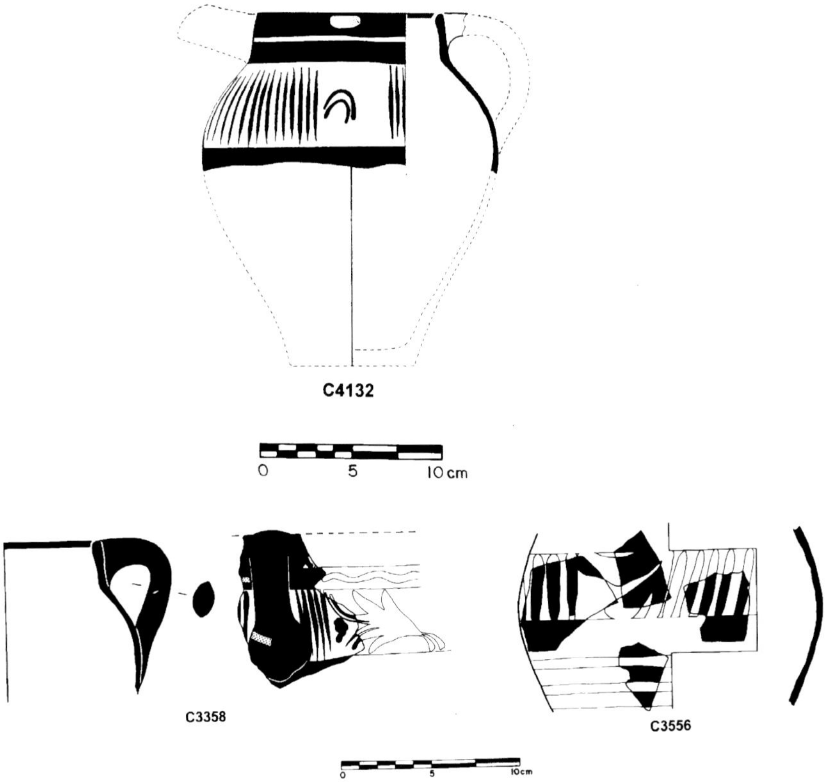

Figure 4.9. Floral Paneled Style: collar-necked jugs from Kommos

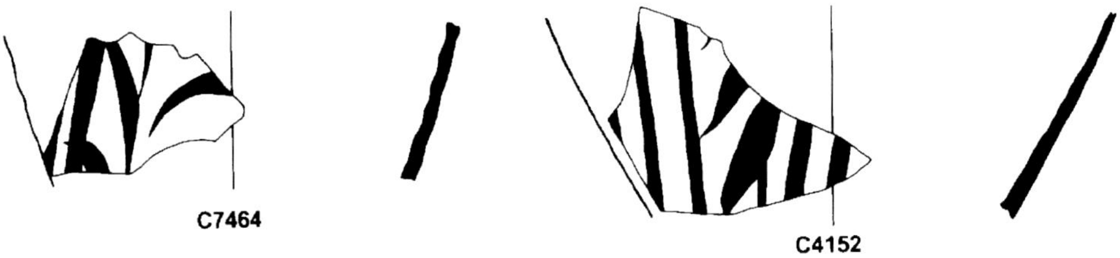

Figure 4.10. Floral Paneled Style: oval-mouthed amphoras from Kommos.

Figure 4.11. Possible LMIA Final set of shapes decorated in Floral Paneled Style from Kommos, Building T.

Early phase, developed a characteristic interior treatment which features groups of three vertical lines, either straight or wavy, alternating with a second motif organized in threes, either shorter vertical lines (Figure 4.8: C10820) or plump diagonal leaves (Figure 4.12: C2755). It is this scheme of triple verticals fringed or alternating with diagonal leaves that then makes up the characteristic ornament of the entire exterior body of the oval-mouthed amphoras decorated in this style (Figure 4.10: C4152, C7464). Examples of this style have been found in comparably dated deposits in the Chalara houses (Levi 1967–8: 110 and n.3 [F.3841], fig. 73a [collar-necked jug]; 110 and n.1 [F.3960], fig. 74a [oval-mouthed amphora]) as well as the palace at Phaistos (Levi 1976: 471, fig. 720, bottom right [semiglobular cup]), and also in one of the houses at Selì (Cucuzza 1993: 31 XXVII-14, pls. 12, 34a = La Rosa and Cucuzza 2001: 108 XXVII-12, figs. 169a, 352 [collar-necked jug]), but they are nowhere nearly as common at either one of these other sites in the Mesara as they are at Kommos.[5] The evidence from Kommos so far suggests that cups and bowls, and probably jugs as well, were the first shapes to be decorated in this way, during LMIA Final (Figure 4.11), with the oval-mouthed amphoras possibly being a somewhat later development of the LMIB Early phase. The shape of the reed sprays on some of the teacups from Kommos (Figure 4.7: C2919, perhaps also C2914) indicates that the style persisted into LMIB Late, and a few other teacups from a LMII context include at least one that must have been produced as late as this phase (Figure 4.7: C470). Whether bowls, jugs, and amphoras continued to be decorated in this way by local potters after LMIB Early, however, is uncertain; that is, as an approach to decoration spanning multiple shapes, this Floral Paneled Style may belong exclusively to the LMIA Final and LMIB Early phases.

The evidence in favour of a local centre of production at or near Kommos for this distinctive and easily recognizable style appears to be solid enough, but the same unfortunately cannot yet be said for the notion that different shapes decorated in this way were intended as sets (Wright 1995: 287, 300, 308 n.11), to be used on special occasions in the same way as symposiastic services were in Archaic Athens or silver tea services have been in Europe and North America since the 18th century. Only unusual contextual circumstances could possibly prove this point, and our chances of stumbling across such a context are slim at a site that has been as subject to continuous disturbances as has the settlement at Kommos. For what it may be worth, I would simply note that the teacup C2749 and the bowl C2755 both come from the same context (Rutter n.d.: Group 40), while the jug fragment C3358 comes from a context some five metres away to the southeast (Rutter n.d.: Group 37e) that could have been deposited at precisely the same date in LMIB Early (Figure 4.12); that is, these three vessels may have been part or even all of a functionally related group of vessels that it may have been one purpose of the Floral Paneled Style to set apart. In the case of three other vessels representing the same triad of shapes (Figure 4.11: C6515, C4371, C3556), again very closely related in terms of their ornament but in this case featuring thicker stripes and stubby three-petalled buds rather than the thinner stripes and more complex six-petalled sprays of the LMIB Early group, two come from adjacent LMIA Final contexts (Rutter n.d.: Groups 24 and 26), while the jug fragment comes from a later LMIB context (Rutter n.d.: Group 37c) several tens of metres away. So we have surviving physical evidence for at least two possible sets, even if we cannot yet be sure that they were actually intended as such.

Let us for a minute accept the notion that ceramic sets of this kind were indeed being manufactured at or near Kommos for use on particular occasions at the site. The following hypothetical consequences of such a notion merit future testing:

1. The shape range of the set suggests that the principal forms of activity which it served was the serving of something in bowls attractively decorated on both interior and exterior, accompanied by the drinking of a liquid decanted

from medium-sized amphoras into jugs, and then poured from those into cups. That is, it does not seem possible to identify all the shapes produced in the Floral Paneled Style as marking a single activity such as drinking, in contrast, for example, to the somewhat later Ephyraean Style of the LHIIB Greek Mainland (Mountjoy 1983; 1986: 37, 44, 46–49, fig. 47: 1, 5 [FS 143 jugs], 54 [FS 254 goblets]; 1999: 25, 100 nos. 83–84, figs. 17–18 [FS 118 and FS 135 jugs], 103 and n.418 [FS 262 high-handled goblet or dipper] 264 no. 75, fig.87 [FS 279 krater]) or earlier Protopalatial sets comprising cups and bridge–spouted jars (MacGillivray 1987). It is, I suppose, just conceivable that the bowls were designed to hold some kind of additive to the beverage being served in the cups (compare modern sugar bowls, cream pitchers, and ice buckets). But if the beverage being consumed was wine, as most authorities imagine was the case (e.g. Hamilakis 1996; 1999; Wright 1995), I cannot think of what an appropriate additive might be.

The absence of a large bowl form from the Floral Paneled Style that might be considered functionally comparable to the Mycenaean through Hellenistic krater may be evidence for a fundamentally different approach to ceremonial drinking on the part of the Minoans in which the primary beverage (wine?) was consumed in undiluted form (Van de Moortel, pers. com.). Whether or not this practice is in turn connected with the generally smaller capacity of Minoan drinking vessels in Protopalatial and Neopalatial times in comparison to, for example, contemporary Middle Helladic and Mycenaean goblets and even kantharoi is another question that may be worth pursuing.

2. The items served in the small to medium-sized bowls of the Floral Paneled style are, in my opinion, likely to have been one or more foodstuffs that had been prepared for consumption at the various cooking installations surveyed earlier. The absence of mendable cooking dishes and trays from the groups of cooking pots found in and around these cooking facilities suggests that the items to be eaten did not take the form of a flatbread of some sort. A better candidate for what was eaten, in view of the palace's location, might be some form of seafood, such as the limpets (*Patella*) consumed in such enormous quantities at the later sanctuary of Kommos during the early Archaic period (Reese et al. 1995: 204–73; 2000: 495–560, 571–642).
3. The sets are indicative of an interest in establishing a sense of local identity during the periods when we have some confidence that they were produced; the choice of specific shapes implies a conscious rejection of types popular at the same time elsewhere. The ratios of drinking cups to jugs, and the maximum number of cups or jugs belonging to a particular set, may independently provide some indication of how large the group was that made use of a single service, or set of vases. At present, for example, it is unclear whether a given set was designed to serve an individual or a group – neither of the two hypothetical sets so far identified consists of two or more cups or jugs (Figures 4.11–12).[6]

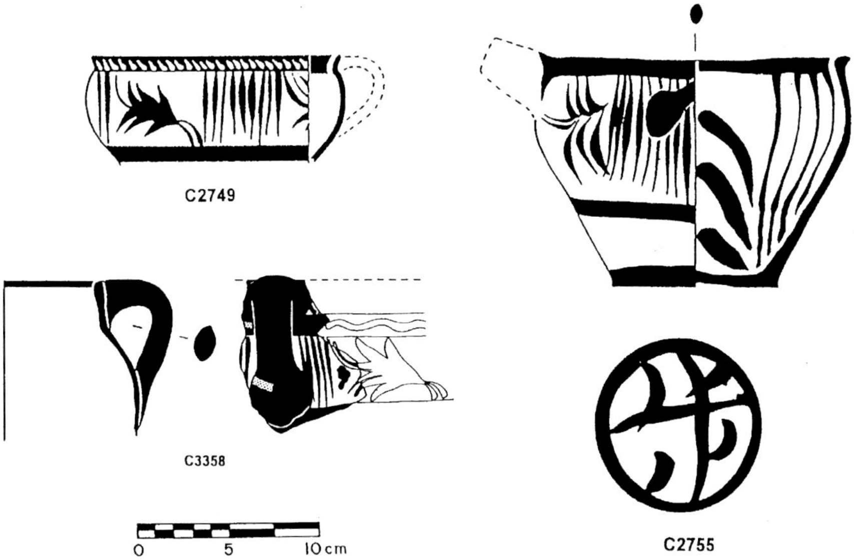

Figure 4.12. Possible LMIB Early set of shapes decorated in Floral Paneled Style from Kommos, Building T.

4. Usage of a distinctively decorated Kommian set for the activities just hypothesized would set individuals and/or groups apart from those using different types for the same purposes. Such formally discrete yet functionally equivalent types were definitely in use at Kommos during LMIA Final and LMIB Early, whether in the form of locally made vessels such as conical cups, ewers (or bridge-spouted jars), and kalathoi on the one hand, or of exotic imports such as Cypriot jugs and fancily decorated Mycenaean or non-local Minoan cups on the other. Whether or not a social hierarchy was expressed by individuals' choices of drinking vessels used at communal celebrations in Building T is an intriguing question, but unfortunately one that the limited nature of the contextual information that survives has simply not allowed us as yet to address in any systematic fashion.
5. What if any relationship there may be between the Floral Paneled Style and the later styles of the so-called 'Special Palatial Tradition', that flourished during the later LMIB period (Betancourt 1985: 140–48; Müller 1997), is a question which it might be rewarding to explore. Syntactically closest to the Floral Paneled Style of Kommos would appear to be the Alternating Style of the very end of the LMIB phase. But the range of decorative motifs that characterizes the Alternating Style is quite different from the uniformly floral decorative content of the Kommian predecessor. The Alternating Style also lacks the neatly defined rectangular panels of the Floral Paneled Style. Furthermore, Müller's exhaustive treatment of the shapes exploited in the

four 'styles' that together constitute Betancourt's 'Special Palatial Tradition' (viz. Marine, Floral, Abstract and Geometric, and Alternating) shows clearly how different these are from the earlier Floral Paneled Style of Kommos: collar-necked jugs and in-and-out bowls are relatively rare in the later LMIB styles, for example, and oval-mouthed amphoras are altogether absent.

6. Finally, although the identification and interpretation of sets of fine decorated vases has often enough been a focus of scholarly attention in Aegean prehistory, I am not aware of a comparable interest in the identification of cooking or kitchen sets. One reason for this is no doubt the lack of some means of identifying a cooking set as such, a coarse ware equivalent of the decorative features that I have used above to define what I have termed the Floral Paneled Style. In the absence of distinctive modes of decoration, production techniques, or surface finishes applied to Minoan cooking pots, perhaps we should simply rely upon spatial contexts – that is, hearths, ovens, and other cooking facilities – to establish a series of Minoan cooking sets. Already published evidence from Kommos makes clear that some hearths are associated with dishes and trays, others with tripod pots alone or else with tripod pots accompanied by deeper-bodied jars.[7] As noted above, the cooking installations in palatial Building T never feature the first two shapes, and this must surely reflect the nature of the food being prepared. But what does the regular pairing of tripod cooking vessels signify, and is anything in particular to be read into the fact that the two vessels in question in the Building T contexts routinely differ significantly, although in different ways (Figures 4.3, 4.4, and 4.6)?

A Final Palatial Epilogue

During at least the first half of the ensuing Monopalatial era, the phase termed LMII, feasting continued to take place in the central court of Building T at Kommos, but this may have been discontinued toward the end of the 15th century. In the meantime, exchanges with Egypt and Cyprus had increased markedly (Watrous 1992: 173–83; Rutter 1999), while substantial numbers of transport vessels from the Syro-Palestinian region and a reasonably full suite of Western Anatolian tablewares (e.g. Rutter 1999: 143, 175–76 table 4, figs. 1–2; Günel 1999: Lev. 156: 2, 162: 1–2, 174: 1–3) are further evidence of Kommos' rapidly expanding participation in eastern Mediterranean intercultural exchanges following the dramatic and relatively sudden collapse of Minoan Neopalatial culture around mid-century.

At about the time of the great destruction at Knossos ca. 1380 BC or very shortly thereafter, Kommos' Civic Center underwent a thoroughgoing architectural transformation that appears to have reflected a notable shift in the principal functions that this area of the site served. As either a natural prelude to

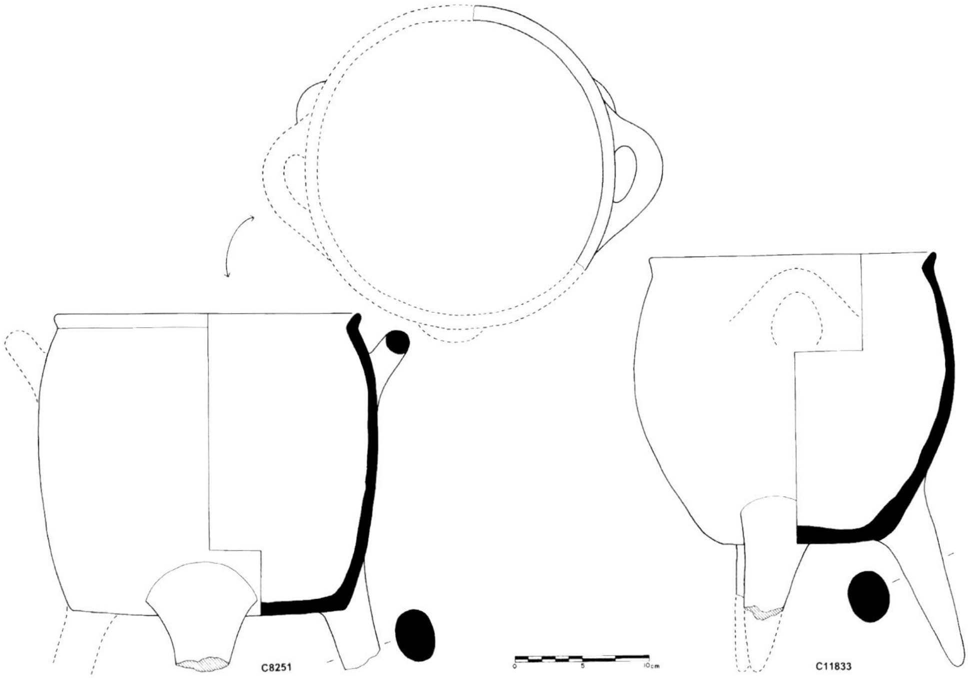

Figure 4.13. Kommos, northeast corner of court fronting Building N on south and Galleries P1 – P2 on west, LMIIIA2: tripod cooking pots C8251 and C11833.

or an artificial part of this massive reconstruction effort, the west wing of Building T was entirely removed, and its formerly enclosed court became readily accessible from the sea to the west and perhaps from the south as well. Cooking continued to take place in the new Buildings P and N, but the social context of this cooking appears to have been quite different. Toward the east end of Gallery P2 was found a LMIIIA2 hearth not far from a possible oven located in the gallery's southeast corner. A small floor deposit that included a large fragment of a tripod cooking pot (Kommos inv. no. C10466), a couple of plain conical cups, a pattern-decorated collar-necked amphora, and a large fragment of a possible second, all of these probably local, also featured a Cypriot Base Ring II cup, a plain, dark-surfaced Cypriot lamp, and a plain Mycenaean kylix (Rutter n.d.: Group 56b). Just outside the western end of Gallery P1 in the northeastern part of the court was found a contemporary LMIIIA2 floor deposit that included two tripod cooking pots (Figure 4.13: C8251, C11833), two cooking jars (Figure 4.14: C8205, C11836), single examples of pattern-decorated specimens of a teacup, a collar-necked jug, and a horizontal-handled bowl, three conical cups, a Cypriot bucchero juglet, a Western Anatolian reddish-brown burnished jug, a Canaanite jar bearing a possibly Cypriot post-firing incised mark on one handle, and an East Cretan amphora or jug (Rutter n.d.: Group 56e). The location of the hearth to be connected

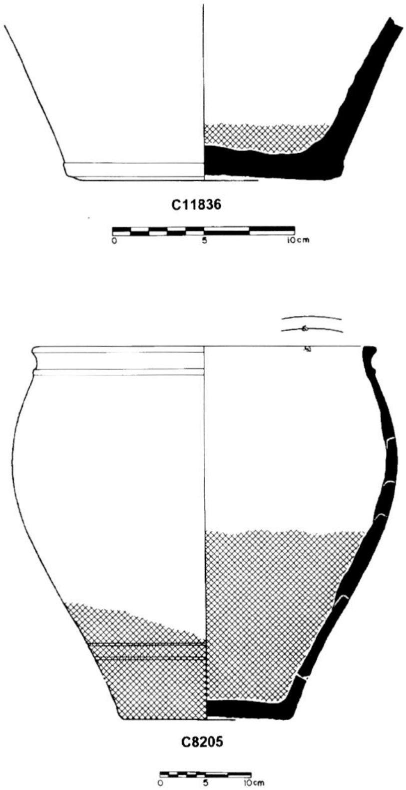

Figure 4.14. Kommos, northeast corner of court fronting Building N on south and Galleries P1 – P2 on west, LMIIIA2: cooking jars C8205 and C11836.

with the cooking pots in this second LMIIIA2 group is uncertain, but the overall character of this assemblage is similar to that from Gallery P2 in its international flavour and its relatively broad range of shapes, many of them distinctly utilitarian. Might these two multicultural but aesthetically rather unremarkable ceramic assemblages have been left behind by international groups of seamen who worked in and around shipsheds P1 and P2 during the first generation or two of their use?

A final pair of LMIIIB floor deposits marking the sudden abandonment of Building N once again includes a mix of tripod cooking pots (Figure 4.15: C2497 = Watrous 1992: 79 no. 1362, pl.34; C2494 = Watrous 1992: 78 no. 1346, fig. 50. pl. 32) and cooking jars (Figure 4.15: C2496 = Watrous 1992: 78 no. 1352, pl. 78; Figure 4.16: C6403 = Watrous 1992: 77 nos. 1332+1334, pl. 32; Figure 4.16: C6402 = Watrous 1992: 77 no. 1336, pl. 31; C6442 = Watrous 1992: 77 no. 1335, fig. 49, pl. 32). The cooking facility where these pots were presumably used was a large hearth occupying a roughly central position in Room 5 at the building's northwest

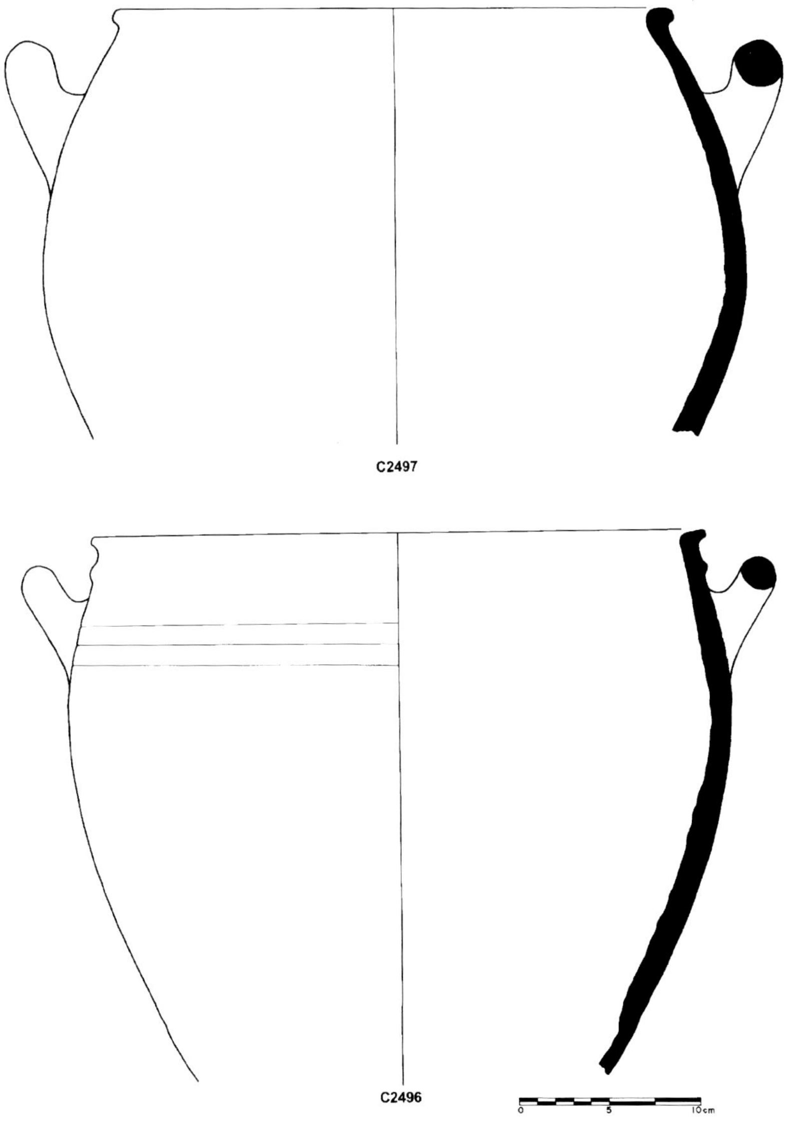

Figure 4.15. Kommos, Building N, LMIIIB: tripod cooking pot C2497 and cooking jar C2496.

corner. The remaining vessels in these large deposits include a wide range of pattern-decorated and plain vases that were locally manufactured – feeding bottles, semiglobular cups, kylikes, deep bowls, an amphoroid krater, a basin, a lid, and transport stirrup jars among the former, conical cups, champagne cups, kylikes, ladles, shallow rounded bowls, basins, deep two-handled jars, and pithoi among the latter – as well as Chaniote, East Cretan, and Sardinian imports

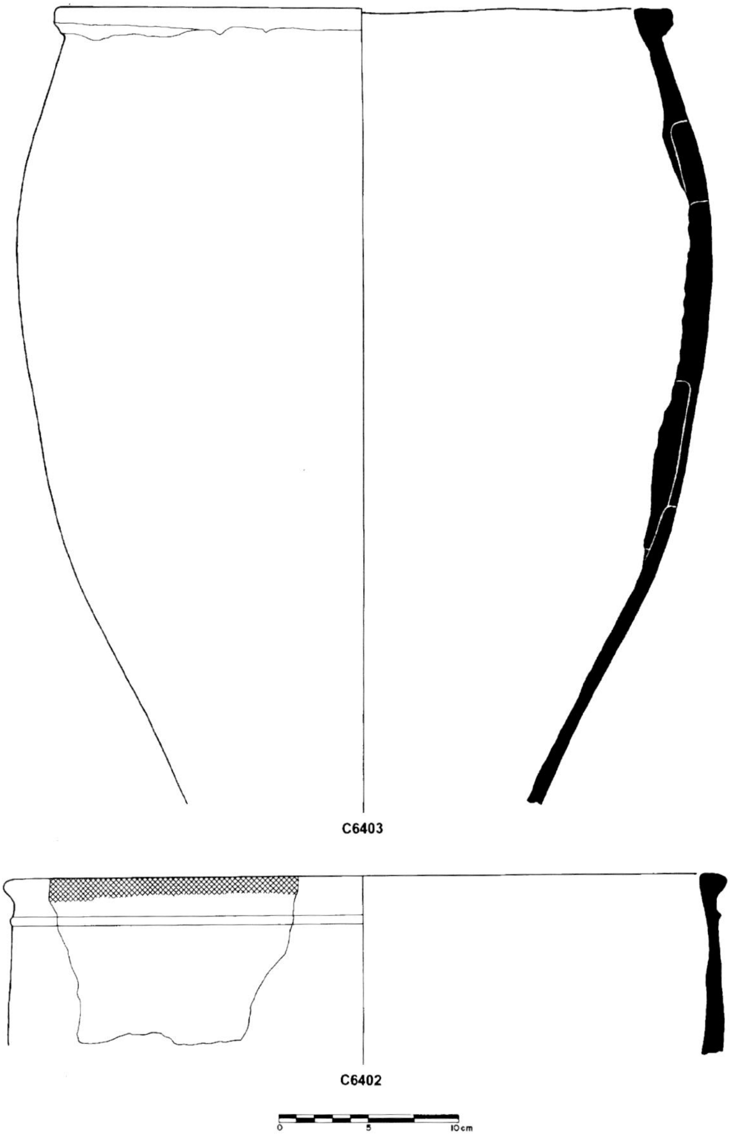

Figure 4.16. Kommos, Building N, LMIIIB: cooking jars C6403 and C6402.

(Watrous 1992: 76–79 Deposits 77–78, figs. 49–51, pls. 30–34; Rutter n.d.: Groups 59–60). These look like normal household floor deposits, closely comparable to those from houses excavated on the hillside and hilltop to the north of the road. They encompass the full range of storage, cooking, eating, and drinking functions typical of ordinary household debris. In other words, there is no ceramic evidence from Final Palatial levels in Kommos' Southern Area for the kind of periodic mass-feasting that is such a pronounced feature of the Neopalatial and early Monopalatial deposits in and around the court of Building T.

Acknowledgements

I would like to thank J.W. and M.C. Shaw for their initial invitation to join the excavation team, as well as for all the support and encouragement with which they have provided me during my ten years of participation in excavations (1991–95) and study (1996–2000) at the site. I am particularly grateful to them for permission to use here the year 2000 edition of the Kommos Southern Area, Period Plan as the basis for Figure 4.1, as well as for their comments on an earlier draft of this paper. The line drawings of pottery from Kommos presented here are the work of Julia E. Pfaff, chief illustrator of the Kommos Excavations since 1992, for whose keen eye, superior organizational skills, and consummate abilities as an archaeological illustrator I have been thankful for more than fifteen years. For teaching me much of what I know about the Neopalatial pottery of Kommos, as well as for useful comments on an earlier version of this paper, I am also very grateful to A. Van de Moortel. The principal publications of prehistoric pottery recovered at Kommos since excavations began there in 1976 are: Betancourt 1990; Watrous 1992; Van de Moortel 1997: 21–274, 689–746, 865–927; 2001. The principal publications of prehistoric find contexts at Kommos are: Shaw 1995; Shaw and Nixon 1996; Wright and McEnroe 1996; Shaw and Shaw 1993; Shaw et al. 2001.

Endnotes

1 For a fairly comprehensive bibliography through 1999 on the Minoan architectural form conventionally identified as a 'palace', see http://projects.dartmouth.edu/history/bronze_age/lessons/bib/12bib.html (1 December 2001). The monumental Protopalatial building at Monastiraki in the Amari valley is probably also 'palatial', and is omitted from the list of names in the text simply because the building in question is not of Neopalatial date.

2 For the terms 'Monopalatial' and 'Final Palatial', Rehak and Younger 2001: 384-85 and n.5, 441-42; Rutter 1999: 139, 148-149 and ns. 1 and 3. Unlike the 'palaces' of the Neopalatial era which conform in most respects to a single architectural form (supra n.1), those of the 'Monopalatial' (LMII – IIIA1) and 'Final Palatial' (LMIIIA2 – [mid-?]LMIIIB) eras are as yet poorly defined in architectural terms. The 'palaces' to which these terms refer might thus more appropriately be conceived of as 'administrative centres' represented by Linear B documents (Knossos, Chania) or, in the case of the later era, sometimes merely by monumental building programs (Ayia Triadha, Tylissos).

3 The well-dated and close parallels from Kommos' Building T make a somewhat earlier dating toward the end of LMIA for the Kamilari miniature coarse basins and fine tubular-spouted jar, as well as the four terracotta models, preferable to Novaro's suggested date for these in LMIB. The tubular spouted jar from Building T space 16 at Kommos (C8337) is

sufficiently similar to that from Kamilari to suggest that the two may have been products of the same workshop or even individual potter.

4 Recent publications focussing on Middle and Late Minoan cooking pottery include: Betancourt 1980; Borgna 1997; Tzedakis and Martlew 1999: 85-92 (A. Tsigounaki on Protopalatial Apodoulou), 93-97 (A. Kanta on Protopalatial Monastiraki), 98-109 (M. Andreadaki-Vlasaki on Neopalatial and Postpalatial Chania), and 110-116 (Y. Tzedakis on Neopalatial through Final Palatial Armenoi); Hallager 2000: 158-63, fig. 32.

5 Many of the examples of the style illustrated here have already been published by Watrous 1992: 5 no. 85, fig. 13 (= Figure 4.7: C2538), 6 no. 91, pl. 2, fig. 13 (= Figure 4.7: C2545), 15 no. 267, pl. 6, fig. 18 (= Figure 4.12: C2755), 18 no. 305 (= Figure 4.9: C4859), 21 no. 346, pl. 9, fig. 18 (= Figure 4.7: C75), 21 no. 354, pl. 9, fig. 19 (=Figure 4.8: C470), 29 no. 494 (=Figure 4.10: C7464), 103 nos. 1781 and 1783, pls. 45-46, fig. 65 (=Figure 4.7: C2919 and C2914, respectively), 104 no. 1801, pl. 45, fig. 65 (=Figure 4.9: C4132). Additional examples of the following shapes have also been published by Watrous: teacups: 3 no. 36, pl. 1 (C5539), 10 nos. 174 and 173, pl. 4 (C3033 and C5203, respectively), 13 no. 229, pl. 5 (C5471), 22 no. 371, pl. 9 (C2250), 103 no. 1782, pl. 46 (C2915); oval-mouthed amphora: 104 no. 1804, pl. 45 (C5814).

6 A fragment published by Watrous (1992: 3 no. 36, pl. 1 [C5539]) appears to have belonged to a semiglobular cup decorated identically to the set illustrated here in Figure 4.11. The context from which this fragment comes lies well outside Building T on the sloping hillside to the north and was probably refuse from the Neopalatial occupation of the House of the Snake Tube. It is uncertain whether the vessel represented by this fragment was part of a larger set (several other constituents of which come from Building T) or belonged to another small set decorated indistinguishably from the small set identified in Building T.

7 At least three different kinds of cooking sets can be identified within the town of Kommos alone on the basis of specific cooking assemblages associated with hearths: (a) cooking dishes and trays but no tripod vessels or jars: Hilltop Room O12, LMIIIA (Shaw and Nixon 1996: 65; Watrous 1992: 50-53 Deposit 46, nos. 872, 884, 916, 918; note also the lid no. 871); (b) tripod vessels only: Central Hillside, House of the Snake Tube, Room 5, LMIIIB (Wright and McEnroe 1996: 230-32, pls. 3.114, 3.151; Watrous 1992: 96 Deposit 93 nos. 1663-1664, pl. 43, fig. 63); (c) a tripod vessel and a horizontal-handled jar: Central Hillside, House of the Snake Tube, Room 4, LMIIIB (Wright and McEnroe 1996: 226-29, pls. 3.113, 3.115; Watrous 1992: 95-96 Deposit 92, nos. 1654-1655, pl. 42, fig. 62). In the case of the last example, a second hearth in the same room contained a single brazier (Watrous 1992: 95 no. 1653, pl. 42, fig, 62), presumably indicative of another kind of cooking-related activity.

Bibliography

Betancourt, P.P.

1980 *Cooking Vessels from Minoan Kommos: a Preliminary Report* (Occasional Paper 7). Los Angeles: University of California at Los Angeles, Institute of Archaeology.

1985 *The History of Minoan Pottery*. Princeton: Princeton University Press.

1990 *Kommos 2: the Final Neolithic through Middle Minoan III Pottery*. Princeton: Princeton University Press.

Borgna, E.

1997 Kitchen-ware from LM IIIC Phaistos: cooking traditions and ritual activities in LBA Cretan societies. *SMEA* 39: 189–217.

Callaghan, P.J. and A.W. Johnston
2000 The pottery from the Greek Temples at Kommos. In J.W. and M.C. Shaw (eds.), *Kommos 4,1–2: The Greek Sanctuary*: 212–301. Princeton: Princeton University Press.
Cucuzza, N.
1993 *Materiali dell'insediamento neopalaziale di Selì*. PhD dissertation, Università di Catania.
Driessen, J. and C.F. Macdonald
1997 *The Troubled Island: Minoan Crete before and after the Santorini Eruption* (Aegaeum 17). Liège: Université de Liège.
Günel, S.
1999 *Panaztepe 2: die Keramik von Panaztepe und ihre Bedeutung für Westkleinasien und die Agäis im 2. Jahrtausend*. Ankara: Türk Tarih Kurumu Basimevi.
Hallager, B.P.
2000 The Late Minoan IIIC pottery. In E. and B.P. Hallager (eds.), *The Greek-Swedish Excavations at the Agia Aikaterini Square, Kastelli, Khania, 1970–1987, 2: the Late Minoan IIIC Settlement*: 135–74. Jonsered: Paul Åströms Forlag.
Hamilakis, Y.
1996 Wine, oil and the dialectics of power in Bronze Age Crete: a review of the evidence. *OJA* 15: 1–32.
1999 Food technologies/technologies of the body: the social context of wine and oil production and consumption in Bronze Age Crete. *World Archaeology* 31: 38–54.
Hope Simpson, R.
1995 The archaeological survey of the Kommos area. In J.W. and M.C. Shaw (eds.), *Kommos 1,1: the Kommos Region, Ecology, and Minoan Industries*: 325–402. Princeton: Princeton University Press.
La Rosa, V. and N. Cucuzza
2001 *L'insediamento di Selì di Kamilari nel territorio di Festòs* (Studi di Archeologia Cretese 1). Padua: Bottega d'Erasmo.
Levi, D.
1962 La tomba a tholos di Kamilari presso a Festòs. *ASA* 39–40: 7–148.
1968 L'abitato di Festòs in località Chálara. *ASA* 45–46: 55–166.
1976 *Festòs e la Civiltà Minoica 1*. Rome: Edizioni dell'Ateneo.
MacGillivray, J.A.
1987 Pottery workshops and the Old Palaces in Crete. In R. Hägg and N. Marinatos (eds.), *The Function of the Minoan Palace*: 273–79. Göteborg: Paul Åströms Forlag.
Manning, S.W.
1995 *The Absolute Chronology of the Aegean Early Bronze Age*. Sheffield: Sheffield Academic Press.
1999 *A Test of Time*. Oxford: Oxbow Books.
Metaxa-Muhly, P.
1984 Minoan hearths. *AJA* 88: 107–22.
Moody, J.
1987 The Minoan palace as a prestige artifact. In R. Hägg and N. Marinatos (eds.), *The Function of the Minoan Palace*: 235–41. Göteborg: Paul Åströms Forlag.
Mountjoy, P.A.
1983 The Ephyraean goblet reconsidered. *BSA* 78: 265–71.
1986 *Mycenaean Decorated Pottery: a Guide to Identification*. Göteborg: Paul Åströms Forlag.
1999 *Regional Mycenaean Decorated Pottery*. Rahden/Westfalen: Verlag Marie Leidorf GmbH.
Müller, W.
1997 *Kretische Tongefässe mit Meeresdekor: Entwicklung und Stellung innerhalb der Feinen*

Keramik von Spätminoisch IB auf Kreta (Deutsches Archäologisches Institut, Archäologische Forschungen 19). Berlin: Gebr. Mann Verlag.

Novaro, D.

1999 I modellini fittili dalla tomba di Kamilari: il problema cronologico. In V. La Rosa, D. Palermo and L. Vagnetti (eds.), *Epi ponton plazomenoi: Simposio italiano di Studi Egei dedicato a Luigi Bernabò Brea e Giovanni Pugliese Carratelli*: 151–60. Rome: Scuola Archeologica di Atene.

Reese, D.S., M.J. Rose and S. Payne

1995 The Minoan fauna. In J.W. and M.C. Shaw (eds.), *Kommos 1,1: the Kommos Region, Ecology, and Minoan Industries*: 163–291. Princeton: Princeton University Press.

Reese, D.S., M.J. Rose and D. Ruscillo

2000 The Iron Age fauna. In J.W. and M.C. Shaw (eds.), *Kommos 4,1–2: the Greek Sanctuary*: 415–646. Princeton: Princeton University Press.

Rehak, P. and J.G. Younger

2001 Review of Aegean prehistory 7: Neopalatial, Final Palatial, and Postpalatial Crete. In T. Cullen (ed.), *Aegean Prehistory: a Review* (AJA Supplement 1): 383–473. Boston: Archaeological Institute of America.

Rethemiotakis, G.

1999 The hearths of the Minoan palace at Galatas. In P.P. Betancourt, V. Karageorghis, R. Laffineur and W.-D. Niemeier (eds.), *MELETEMATA: Studies in Aegean Archaeology Presented to Malcolm H. Wiener as He Enters His 65th Year* (Aegaeum 20): 721–28. Liège: Université de Liège.

Rupp, D.W. and M. Tsipopoulou

1999 Conical cup concentrations at Neopalatial Petras: a case for a ritualized reception ceremony with token hospitality In P.P. Betancourt, V. Karageorghis, R. Laffineur and W.-D. Niemeier (eds.), *MELETEMATA: Studies in Aegean Archaeology Presented to Malcolm H. Wiener as He Enters His 65th Year* (Aegaeum 20): 729–39. Liège: Université de Liège.

Ruscillo, D.

n.d. The fauna. In J.W. and M.C. Shaw (eds.), *Kommos 5: the Monumental Minoan Buildings of the Southern Area*. Princeton: Princeton University Press.

Rutter, J.B.

1999 Cretan external relations during Late Minoan IIIA2 – B (ca. 1370 – 1200 B.C.): a view from the Mesara. In W. Phelps, Y. Lolos and Y. Vichos (eds.), *The Point Iria Wreck: Interconnections in the Mediterranean ca. 1200 B.C.*: 139–86. Athens: Hellenic Institute of Marine Archaeology.

n.d. Neopalatial and Later Minoan pottery. In J.W. and M.C. Shaw (eds.), *Kommos 5: the Monumental Minoan Buildings of the Southern Area*. Princeton: Princeton University Press.

Shaw, J.W.

1995 The exploration and excavation of the Kommos site. In J.W. and M.C. Shaw (eds.), *Kommos 1,1: the Kommos Region, Ecology, and Minoan Industries*: 8–29. Princeton: Princeton University Press.

1996 Introduction to the Kommos site. In J.W. and M.C. Shaw (eds.), *Kommos 1,2: the Minoan Hilltop and Hillside Houses*: 1–14. Princeton: Princeton University Press.

2000a The architecture of the temples and other buildings. In J.W. and M.C. Shaw (eds.), *Kommos 4,1–2: the Greek Sanctuary*: 1–100. Princeton: Princeton University Press.

2000b Ritual and development in the Greek sanctuary. In J.W. and M.C. Shaw (eds.), *Kommos 4,1–2: the Greek Sanctuary*: 669–731. Princeton: Princeton University Press.

2001 The excavation and the structure of the kiln. In J.W. Shaw, A. Van de Moortel, P.M. Day, and V. Kilikoglou, *A LM IA Ceramic Kiln in South-Central Crete: Function and Pottery Production* (Hesperia Supplement 30): 5–24. Princeton: American School of Classical Studies at Athens.

Shaw, J.W. and M.C. Shaw

1993 Excavations at Kommos (Crete) during 1986–1992. *Hesperia* 62: 129–90.

n.d. *Kommos 5: the Monumental Minoan Buildings of the Southern Area*. Princeton: Princeton University Press.

Shaw, J.W., A. Van de Moortel, P.M. Day, and V. Kilikoglou

2001 *A LM IA Ceramic Kiln in South-Central Crete: Function and Pottery Production* (Hesperia Supplement 30). Princeton: American School of Classical Studies at Athens.

Shaw, M.C.

1990 Late Minoan hearths and ovens at Kommos, Crete. In P. Darcque and R. Treuil (eds.), *L'habitat égéen préhistorique* (BCH Supplement 19): 231–54. Athens: École française d'Athènes.

1996 Town arrangement and domestic architecture. In J.W. and M.C. Shaw (eds.), *Kommos 1,2: the Minoan Hilltop and Hillside Houses*: 345–77. Princeton: Princeton University Press.

Shaw, M.C. and L.F. Nixon

1996 The hilltop settlement at Kommos. In J.W. and M.C. Shaw (eds.), *Kommos 1,2: the Minoan Hilltop and Hillside Houses*: 15–138. Princeton: Princeton University Press.

Shay, C.T. and J.M. Shay

1995 The modern flora and plant remains from Bronze Age deposits at Kommos. In J.W. and M.C. Shaw (eds.), *Kommos 1,1: the Kommos Region, Ecology, and Minoan Industries*: 91–162. Princeton: Princeton University Press.

Tzedakis, Y. and H. Martlew (eds.)

1999 *Minoans and Mycenaeans: Flavours of their Time*. Athens: Greek Ministry of Culture, National Archaeological Museum.

Van de Moortel, A.M.P.A.

1997 *The Transition from the Protopalatial to the Neopalatial Society in South-Central Crete: a Ceramic Perspective*. PhD dissertation, Bryn Mawr College.

2001 The area around the kiln, and the pottery from the kiln and the kiln dump. In J.W. Shaw, A. Van de Moortel, P.M. Day and V. Kilikoglou, *A LM IA Ceramic Kiln in South-Central Crete: Function and Pottery Production* (Hesperia Supplement 30): 25–110. Princeton: American School of Classical Studies at Athens.

Watrous, L.V.

1992 *Kommos 3: the Late Bronze Age Pottery*. Princeton: Princeton University Press.

Wright, J.C.

1995 Empty cups and empty jugs: the social role of wine in Minoan and Mycenaean societies. In P.E. McGovern, S.J. Fleming and S.H. Katz (eds.), *The Origins and Ancient History of Wine*: 287–309. Philadelphia: Gordon and Breach Publishers.

Wright, J.C. and J. McEnroe

1996 The central hillside at Kommos. In J.W. and M.C. Shaw (eds.), *Kommos 1,2: the Minoan Hilltop and Hillside Houses*: 139–242. Princeton: Princeton University Press.

5

Mycenaean Drinking Services and Standards of Etiquette

James C. Wright

In this paper I examine the archaeological manifestations of etiquette or manners. Etiquette is a behavioural mechanism for the expression and signification of group identity. Its construction reflects the process of formalizing ranked status among elites competing for leadership. Its standardization is effected by functionaries of the leaders as they administer the emerging institutions of the society. Also etiquette serves as a social mechanism for integrating the entire populace into the ideology and political economy of the society. I will use evidence of drinking in ritualized settings to illustrate different ways in which this behaviour is manifest in the archaeological record.

Notions of etiquette are naturally heterogeneous. Etiquette prescribes the performance of ritualized activities which signify socio-political and socio-economic relations within a bounded social group. Tied as it is to fundamental human activities, from bodily functions to forms of address, the performance of etiquette is constrained by the limits of those activities, yet infinite in the potential for variation of signification. As a consequence standards of etiquette are open to manipulation *qua* etiquette and potentially independent of controlling authority. Thus, inherent in the establishment of prescribed ways of acting is the potential to use manners as a form of promotion, regulation, enfranchisement, and resistance.

Because of its social nature, etiquette is fluid. There is a natural tension in its performance that is derived from individual concern about access to authoritative information about acceptable behaviour and the reliability of that information. This uncertainty leads to a desire to prescribe this behaviour, to regulate its performance, to prohibit variation, and to impose it as a means of reinforcing authority. In like manner, the performance of manners is a public act, scrutinized by its practitioners for any sign of variation, of omission or addition; for such signs may be a cause for delegitimizing authority or, at the very least, inferring change in the balance of power.

The performance of etiquette, according to Elias (1978), evolves in relation to social complexity. Originally etiquette is an unselfconscious standard of identity behaviour within a bounded group of elites, usually a warrior class (Elias 1978: 60–61). Its modes of behaviour set members of the group apart from everyone else, but there is no reason for etiquette to be written down, as it is communicated through its performance and through oral tradition. In such a setting, etiquette is as fluid and dynamic as the evolving social interrelations and regulations within the group (cf. Clarke and Blake 1994). Etiquette becomes prescribed when lesser elites seek to establish themselves in an authentic relation to the leading elites. Notably this group serves the elites and is dependent upon them. As the entire elite group becomes more highly stratified and differentiated, for example as the administrative and priestly classes emerge, fixing etiquette according to published and mandated forms of behaviour becomes a way both to signify the close relationship between the ruling group and its functionaries and a way to assert control over the general populace. For this reason etiquette and orthodox religious behaviour are bound together, and proper behaviour is said to have its origins in the manners of divinities or through their commands and, therefore, is to be imitated by humans (Elias 1978: 100–14). At this point etiquette as a means of differentiating the ruling elite from everyone else becomes devalued, and two things happen. The standards change according to the changing social situation of the group that is recording and standardizing modes of proper behaviour. Thus by documenting behaviour a functionary group also begins to control and manipulate it, causing the ruling elite to seek new ways of differentiation. This process of standardizing and publishing modes of proper behaviour causes a reflux. As Elias puts it, the nobility are 'bourgeoisified' as the functionaries' power to define behaviour increases and puts pressure on the upper elites to conform. This is particularly true in speech, where a 'linguistic polemic' is carried out by whichever group asserts control over language (Elias 1978: 108–13).

Thus mannered behaviour and its material expression are a dynamic expression of vertically ranked statuses carried out across a heterogeneous and changing social landscape. Within this fluid situation etiquette is performed and reformed at such base levels as intra-community factions (Brumfiel 1994), where rivalry for leadership is a primary activity; in inter-community relations, where community and factional identities are displayed and contested; and at broader regional levels of socio-cultural integration, where larger political entities strive to consolidate control over heterogeneous social, political-economic assemblages and territorial landscapes.

For archaeologists, then, any attempt to recover mannered behaviour presents the usual challenges of constructing methods for correlating the temporal and spatial distribution of artifacts with past human action and of fitting that evidence to the appropriate level or form of human behaviour. What follows is a case study, which I hope will show that the process by which a standard service of Mycenaean drinking vessels was developed reflects the emergence of a functionary group, who used its power to define etiquette. In so doing these

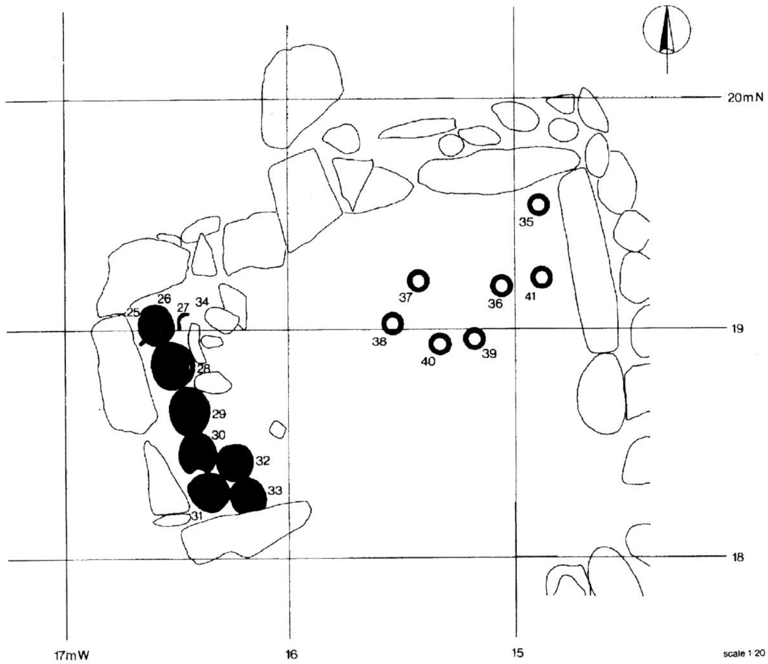

Figure 5.1. Plan of burial 1971-3 at Asine. From Dietz 1980: fig. 32. Reproduced courtesy of the author.

functionaries consolidated their position in the social order and effected an integration of ruling ideologies throughout the overall structure of society.

In southern mainland Greece, vessels that can be associated with drinking begin to appear with some consistency and increasing abundance in burials of the end of the late Middle and beginning of the Late Helladic periods. Table 5.1 lists pottery groups from selected cemeteries of this period. In general they show the pairing of drinking with pouring vessels (Figure 5.1). Thus in the North Cemetery at Corinth (Blegen *et al.* 1964) various forms of rounded cups, and sometimes a kantharos, are consistently found with a jug with cut-away spout. At Prosymna (Blegen 1937) rounded cups, straight-sided cups, kantharoi, and once a goblet occur with the one-handled jar or the jug with cut-away spout. In three the goblet appears, either solo or with semi-globular cups and/or the jug with cut-away spout. At Argos one-handled and straight-sided cups are popular with the spouted jug. Goblets appear, as do semi-globular cups with everted rims (Dietz 1991: 132–40). At Asine a rich grave of LHI date in the east cemetery (Figure 5.1) displays a different character (Dietz 1980: 34–55 [grave 1971–3]). In it six goblets appear; they were prominently displayed arranged along one end of the large cist burial of an important male, who was buried with a dagger. Also in this burial were a straight-sided cup and a conical cup, both in Mainland panelled style (# 126 and 36, Dietz 1980; Davis 1978), and two kantharoi. A matt-painted

Table 5.1. Pottery Groups from Selected Cemeteries in the Corinthia and Argolid

Site & Burial	**Cup Form**							**Kantharos Form**			**Jar Form**						**Jug Form**			
●=1 ●=2 ●=3 ●=4 ●=5 ●=6 ●=7 ●=8 ●=9	GM Stemmed, carinated	One-handled	Basket-handled mug	Straight-sided	Conical/Panelled	Semi-globular, everted rim	Goblet	Shallow without foot	Carinated with foot	Carinated with pedestal	Hemispherical	Hole-mouth	Spherical bridge-spouted	One-handled	Hydria & Stamnos	Amphoriskos	One-handled	Spouted jar/jug	Cut-away spout	Askos
Asine																				
B12								2												
B15		1					1			1										
B30			1		2														1	
B32	1							1		1								1		
LT-18		1																3		
1971-3		1		1	1		5		2				1	1					3	
Argos																				
Gamma 82		1						1											1	
Delta 161		1						1										1	1	
Delta 1, 132		4	1	2														3		
Delta 1,137		1					1											2		
Gamma 22	1	1	1															2		
Gamma 61			3	1														8		
Gamma 2				1						1									1	
Gamma 27			1			1												1		
Gamma 29				2		2														
Prosymna																				
I			2											1		1		1		
III						1	1													
IV			2				1												1	
XII																		1		
XII														1						
XIII	1		1																	
XV								1									1			
XVI				1										1						
XVII		1												1						
XVIII			1											4						
XIX			1	2										5						
XX		1	4	1										5						
XXI			1																1	
XXIV														1			1			
XXV																				1
XXVI		2															1		1	
XXVIII								1												
XXXI			1					1											1	
Corinth																				
1		1																		2
2			1			1														1
3																			1	
5		1						1											1	1
6																				1
7		1																		
8			1						1											1
9								1						1						
10					1															
11			1																	1
13			1																	1

Figure 5.2. Floor Deposit of LH I house at Tsoungiza. Photograph by Taylor Dabney.

bridge-spouted jar and three cut-away spouted jugs also appear. This burial illustrates the emergence of a distinct Mycenaean set of drinking vessels, which also appear in domestic deposits at Asine (Nordquist 1987: 85–86). A contemporary floor deposit from a house at Tsoungiza in the Nemea Valley illustrates this set (Figure 5.2; Wright 1982; Rutter 1989). It contains two coarse-ware cooking pots, two kantharoi, a goblet, two jugs with cut-away spouts, and a ladle.

The high-status burial at Asine is also contemporary with the high status group that was being interred in Circle B at Mycenae (Table 5.2, following Graziadio 1988). In the Circle B burials the shift in preference of vessels is marked. Goblets are ubiquitous. The semi-globular cup is present (eight) but no longer dominant: there are more kantharoi (ten), and the Vapheio shape appears in pottery (five) and metal (five). Also occurring are the Mainland Panelled cup (seven), loop-handled cups (four), teacups (two), and bronze phialai (two). One-handled matt-painted jars and their successor LHI squat jars appear (seven), as do cut-away spouted jugs (six), a spherical bridge-spouted jar, and a bronze spouted jug. Also present are many hydriai and stamnoi. Ten of these burials are of males, eight of which were accompanied by bronze weapons. Two are of females, one of which was exceedingly wealthy.

This diversity resulted from the desire of elites to display their elevated status and from their efforts to consolidate their power. A major aspect of the change in grave goods is the adoption of foreign pottery and vessels of silver and faience, as well as the acquisition of cups of bronze, silver and gold. This process continues even more forcefully in the burials of Circle A (Table 5.3), in which

Table 5.2. Pottery Groups from Mycenae, Grave Circle B (Graziadio 1988)

Site & Burial: ●=1 ●=2 ●=3 ●=4 ●=5 ●=6 ●=7 ●=8 ●=9

Site & Burial	Cup Form: GM Stemmed, carinated	One-handled	Basket-handled	Straight-sided	Conical/Panelled	Semi-globular, everted rim	Goblet	Kantharos Form: Shallow without foot	Carinated with foot	Carinated with pedestal	Jar Form: Hemispherical	Hole-mouth	Spherical bridge-spouted	One-handled	Piriform	Hydria & Stamnos	Amphoriskos	Jug Form: One-handled	Spouted jar/jug	Cut-away spout	Askos
Z male weapons				●			●	●											●	●	
H male weapons						●	●	●	●					●						●	
I early				●				●												●	
I late male weapons							●							●		●					
Lamda 2 male			●																	●	
Xi early							●		●				●	●							
Rho		●					●	●													
B male weapons							●														
E fill					●		●														
Lamda fill				●			●														
Lamda male weapons					●	●	●									●			●		
N roof							●														
Y female							●									●	●				
MYC 58 female				●	●	●	●		●					●						●	
Delta fill							●							●							
A male weapons							●		●						●					●	
E inside later																					
N later male																					
Pi							●											●	●	●	
K-112								●								●				●	
Lamda1								●													
M early			●			●	●					●		●							
N							●									●					●
Pi							●												●		
Gamma male weapons		●		●	●	●	●	●	●					●		●	●			●	●
Delta																					
O						●	●	●					●			●	●				●

Table 5.3. Pottery Groups from Mycenae, Grave Circle A

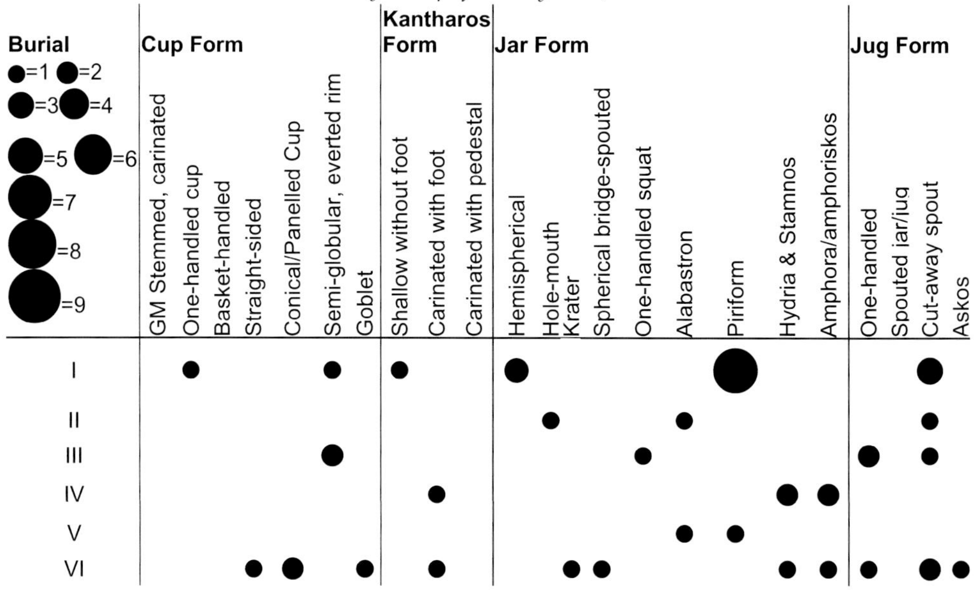

there are many fewer pottery vessels (and they are largely imports); instead vessels of precious metal predominate (Table 5.4). A Mycenaean drinking service was being created at this time and it merged indigenous pottery forms with exogenous ones. In an earlier study, I emphasized that this shift reflects

> 'an amplification of traditions which were already a part of indigenous behaviour; thus, foreign objects are introduced alongside prestigious items of local origin. Accompanying these objects must be a change of behaviour that explains their presence. . . . The prestige enhancement that accompanies the introduction of foreign but not altogether new ceremonies of drinking, and the social distance expressed by the luxurious vessels used in the ceremonies are fundamental aspects of the emergence of chiefly groups at developing Mycenaean centers. Hybrid vessels incorporate all these elements and document the syncretistic nature of early Mycenaean social and political ideology. ' (Wright 1995: 295)

Dietler (1990: 375–80, 382–90) and Arnold (1999) have studied a similar adoption of Greek and Etruscan drinking customs by the Celts. This phenomenon has also been explored by Clark and Blake (1994) in a study of how foreign ceramics are adopted by aggrandizing elites in Lowland Mesoamerica during the Early Formative period (see also the study by Junker [2001] of the use of high-status ceramics in feasting in the prehispanic Philippines). Clark and Blake emphasize what I have shown above, that in order for the symbolic meaning of the foreign items to be transferred to their community, it is necessary for the meaning to be

Table 5.4. Gold and Silver Vessels from the Shaft Graves at Mycenae (after Davis 1977)

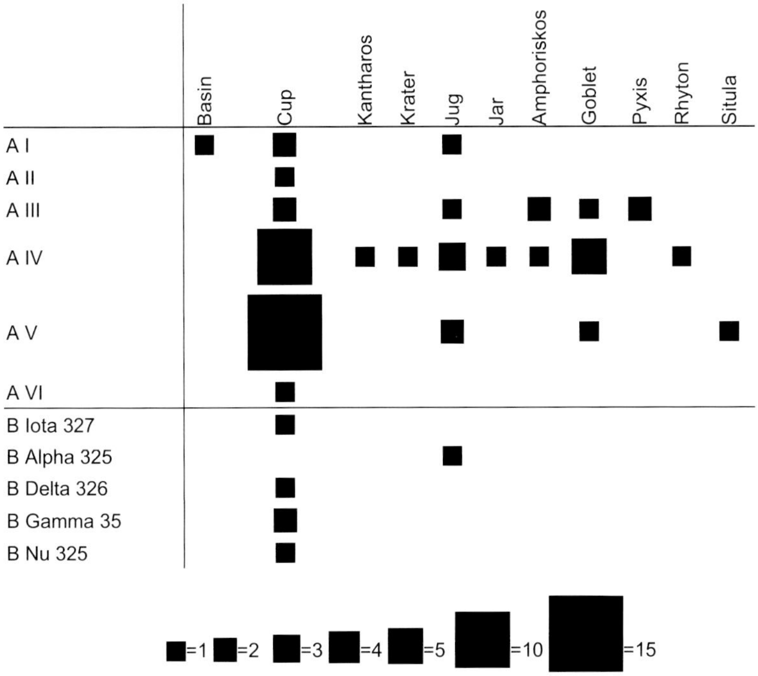

expressed in the familiar material and social code of their community. In the case they study, the foreign technology of ceramic production is introduced by imitating the shape of gourd vessels current in the community. Notably the vessels selected for this transfer were those used for serving and drinking liquids.

What is happening in these rich burials is the product of the competitive atmosphere for power among the factional leaders within and among the emerging communities of the early Mycenaean world. The variation in the display of items of wealth and of vessel forms is a function of the lack of a single recognized authority. Clark and Blake describe (1994: 29) these early leaders as 'aggrandizers' whose actions and displays are not governed by the rules and trappings of any institutions of authority, and therefore are characterized by variation, innovation, and excess. Thus the archaeological manifestations of these leaders are recognizable by the degree to which they stand out as items of prestigious display among other such displays. Two examples from Grave IV in Circle A at Mycenae best illustrate this process at work. Each is a unique object both familiar and foreign in appearance. First is the so-called 'golden cup of Nestor', which combines the Vapheio cup, the chalice stem, and the handles of a kantharos (Figure 5.3). Next is the silver goblet with *niello* inlay that combines the Minoan iconographic element of a floral display (Shaw 1993) with the Mycenaean

Figure 5.3. Golden Nestor Cup from Mycenae. From Karo 1930/1933. Reproduced courtesy of Hirmer Verlag, Munich.

Figure 5.4. Silver goblet with niello *inlay from Mycenae. From Karo 1930/1933. Reproduced courtesy of Hirmer Verlag, Munich.*

preferences for a stemmed base and a carinated shape (Figure 5.4). These eclectic preferences can also be seen in the succeeding LHII and IIIA periods – for example in the pair of gold cups from Vapheio (Davis 1974) and in the repoussée octopus bowl from Dendra (Hurwit 1979), each of which incorporates Minoan elements into a product of Mycenaean craftsmanship.

After the Shaft Graves at Mycenae there are only a few tombs dated within LHII, and the Vapheio tholos is the most important. Although it was largely robbed, the pit in the floor disclosed four Vapheio cups (two of gold and two of silver), a spouted silver jug, a shallow silver-plated copper teacup with broad, ornate gold rim and ring-handle, a bronze ladle, and a bronze brazier (Davis 1977: #103–108; Matthäus 1980: #447, #468). At this time the fluid situation recognized in LHI still obtains, although the shallow teacup with ornate, broad rim and ring handle occurs with regularity (Shaft Grave I, Kazarma tholos tomb, Peristeria Tholos III: Davis 1977: #97, 137, 101), and this cup form along with the one-handled goblet and Ephyraean goblet are increasingly popular in elaborate decorated pottery form in chamber tombs of this date (e. g. Mycenae, Kalkani C. T. 516, 517, 518; Wace 1932: 63–87). As we turn to LHIIIA1, however, a very different picture emerges.

LHIIIA1 is when the citadels were first consolidated as fortified centres with monumental palaces erected within them (Kilian 1987; Dabney and Wright 1990). At this time authority is established in the palaces and their surrounding territory and, through interpalatial exchange, unified cultural expressions are achieved. It is apparent in all areas of endeavour, from architecture to pottery. Dickinson describes pottery at this time as 'extremely homogeneous throughout the

Figure 5.5. Silver vessels from Dendra. From Persson 1942: fig. 103. Reproduced courtesy of Swedish Institute at Athens.

Figure 5.6. Tinned vessels from Dendra. From Persson 1942: fig. 109. Reproduced courtesy of Swedish Institute at Athens.

Mycenaean region', which extends across the Mainland, the islands and on Crete (Dickinson 1994: 118–19). Social expression, as recorded in burial assemblages, achieves a standard formal expression exemplified by the set of silver drinking vessels found in Tomb 10, shaft II of the cemetery at Dendra (Figure 5.5; Persson 1942: 87–88). In this service there are two single-handled goblets, a deep stemmed repoussée-decorated cup with high-swung handle, a silver two-handled krater, a silver teacup with broad gold rim and ring handle, and a small repoussée-decorated silver spoon. These shapes in precious metal appear in a number of other tombs of this period: the tholoi at Dendra, Kazarma, Kokla, Marathon, Peristeria, and Pylos (Table 5.4). That they were recognized as a set is demonstrated by their emulation in similar pottery sets that were tinned to look like silver. One appears in Shaft II of Tomb 10 at Dendra (Figure 5.6), and others are known at Asine, Prosymna, Mycenae, Berbati, in the Athenian Agora and elsewhere (Persson 1942: 98; Immerwahr 1971: 127–28, 171–76; Gillis 1991).

This standardization of a drinking service is not merely the result of the growth of craft industries, which were able to turn out items of standardized shape and size, but much more an indication of the emergence of standards of taste and a burgeoning demand for commodities which represented status and that could be used in displays of status. These consumers must be the newly enfranchised functionaries of the palace-centred system, and, as Brian Burns has demonstrated, they participated in and stimulated a burgeoning market in international goods (Burns 1999: 182–87). This group accounts for the proliferation of chamber tombs at this time, and they were a diverse group, who served the many needs of the society: exercising and regulating religious practices, policing the state, handling commercial exchanges, overseeing estates, and so forth (Chadwick 1976). Certainly the so-called warrior graves are products of this group (Matthäus 1980: 68–75; 1983; Kilian-Dirlmeier 1985), and the diversity of functions they carried out has been explored by Kilian-Dirlmeier in her study of the objects from the Vapheio tholos tomb (Kilian-Dirlmeier 1987).

These consumers were not merely interested in standardizing the drinking service; they also began to rewrite customs by introducing new forms for which there are not good precedents. Excellent examples are found among bronze assemblages deposited in tombs, notably the lekane and the wishbone type handle, both of which are introduced in metal and flourish during LHIIIA; they may owe their origin to the wider world in which these functionaries were involved (Matthäus 1980: 74), especially that of Cyprus and the Eastern Mediterranean. On this subject Brian Burns has shown in his brilliant dissertation how this broader system of consumption of foreign-made items evolved in the Argolid during the LHIIIA and B periods (Burns 1999).

After LHIIIA the deposition of vessels in bronze and in precious metals in burials virtually ceases. Matthäus has argued that this can only be accounted for by a change in mortuary practice on the Mainland and on Crete, since there is no evidence of a fall-off in the supply of copper and the production of bronze (1980: 74–75). Indeed, since his study, the discovery of the Ulu Burun wreck, continuing discoveries of the vitality of the Cypriot metal industries, and Burns, examination of the distribution of foreign-made items in the Argolid (Burns 1999: 86–101) underscore his argument. Why, then, did sumptuary displays in mortuary practice cease to be so important?As a consequence of the change in the nature of the political economy that accompanied the establishment of the palace-centred society, the nature of social relations also changed. Although personal relations continued to count in establishing and maintaining status, the emergence of a bureaucracy of office-holders stabilized status positions, and the activities of these functionaries became more cosmopolitan, as Burns' examination of the trade in foreign-made items and the production of ivories and glass convincingly demonstrates (Burns 1999: 124–346, 158–75). These officials must have been primarily concerned with the management of the palace-state: the mobilization and organization of labour, the administration of territory, the command of military forces, and conduct of religious ceremony; and these concerns contributed to the shift away from personal sumptuary display toward state-sponsored activities. These are seen at Mycenae in the public monumental displays of the Atreus tholos, the Lion Gate, and the refurbishing of Grave Circle A – all of which are part of a 'royal' building program to advertise the power and centrality of rule at Mycenae (Wright 1987). They are evident in state forms of management of craft production (Shelmerdine 1985; Tournavitou 1995), and the founding of centres of cult within the palaces and throughout the territories they controlled (Wright 1994; Kilian 1992).

Concomitantly the values and customs of the palace and its court would have served as another way to enlarge the sense of community. This is the time when the palace began to sponsor feasts on a wide scale (Killen 1994; 1998), and Dabney (Dabney *et al.* 2004) suggests in her study of the feasting deposit at Tsoungiza that the palace was also involved in the sponsoring of feasting in the territories. With this there developed a social etiquette that was broadly shared by the populace, ritualized in oral traditions, and practised on festival days. Etiquette continued to be controlled by the functionary agents of the palaces, but it was also increasingly subject to regional variation and local custom. On the one hand this would account for the emergence of the kylix as a universal drinking form at this time, yet on the other it explains the persistence of local traditional forms, as explored by Borgna at Phaistos (this volume and 1999), and the appearance of a distinct service in Cyprus, as studied by Steel (1998; 1999). The increasing regionalism at this time is manifested in pottery production and seems to be a reflection of the difficulty central authority has maintaining its control over production and innovation (Rathje 1975; Sherratt 1980; Wright 1984: 29; Mountjoy 1990). It is in this situation of increasing flux and heterogeneity at the end of LHIIIB and throughout LHIIIC that we witness the break-up of the court society of the Mycenaean palaces. I imagine that officials in the palaces must often have muttered to themselves, 'Nobody shows any respect anymore!Nobody seems to know his manners!', but unfortunately they never thought to record these thoughts on the Linear B tablets.

Acknowledgements

I wish to thank John Barrett and Paul Halstead for inviting me to participate in this colloquium and the participants for their useful comments on my paper.

Bibliography

Arnold, B.
1999 'Drinking the feast': alcohol and the legitimation of power in Celtic Europe. *Cambridge Archaeological Journal* 9: 71–93.

Blegen, C.
1937 *Prosymna*. Cambridge: Cambridge University Press.

Blegen, C. , H. Palmer and R. Young
1964 *Corinth, 13. The North Cemetery*. Princeton: American School of Classical Studies.

Borgna, E.

1999 Circolazione della ceramica nello scambio cerimoniale tra mondo miceneo palaziale e Creta tardominoica: la prospettiva di Festòs nel TM III. In V. La Rosa, D. Palermo and L. Vagnetti (eds.), *Epi ponton plazomenoi. Simposio italiano di Studi Egei dedicato a L. Bernabò Brea e G. Pugliese Carratelli*: 199–205. Rome: Scuola archeologica italiana di Atene.

Brumfiel, E.

1994 Introduction. In E. Brumfiel and J. Fox (eds.), *Factional Competition and Political Development in the New World*: 3–13. Cambridge: Cambridge University Press.

Burns, B.

1999 *Import Consumption in the Bronze Age Argolid: Effects of Mediterranean Trade on Mycenaean Society*. PhD dissertation, University of Michigan, Ann Arbor.

Chadwick, J.

1976 *The Mycenaean World*. Cambridge: Cambridge University Press.

Clark, J. and M. Blake

1994 The power of prestige: competitive generosity and the emergence of rank societies in lowland Mesoamerica. In E. Brumfiel and J. Fox (eds.), *Factional Competition and Political Development in the New World*: 17–30. Cambridge: Cambridge University Press.

Dabney, M. , P. Halstead and P. Thomas

2004 Late Mycenaean feasting on Tsoungiza at ancient Nemea. In J. Wright (ed.), The Mycenaean Feast. *Hesperia* 73, 2.

Dabney, M. and J. Wright

1990 Mortuary customs, palatial society and state formation in the Aegean area: a comparative study. In R. Hägg and G. C. Nordquist (eds.), *Celebrations of Death and Divinity in the Bronze Age Argolid*: 45–53. Stockholm: Swedish Institute at Athens.

Davis, E.

1974 The Vapheio cups: one Minoan and one Mycenaean? *Art Bulletin* 56: 472–87.

1977 *The Vapheio Cups and Aegean Gold and Silver Ware*. New York: Garland.

Davis, J.

1978 The Mainland panelled cup and panelled style. *AJA* 82: 216–22.

Dickinson, O.

1994 *The Aegean Bronze Age*. Cambridge: Cambridge University Press.

Dietler, M.

1990 Driven by drink: the role of drinking in the political economy and the case for Early Iron Age France. *Journal of Anthropological Archaeology* 9: 358–72.

Dietz, S.

1980 *Asine II. Results of the Excavations East of the Acropolis, 1970–1974, 2. The Middle Helladic Cemetery, the Middle Helladic and Early Mycenaean Deposits*. Stockholm: Paul Åströms Forlag.

1991 *The Argolid at the Transition to the Mycenaean Age*. Copenhagen: National Museum of Denmark, Aarhus University Press.

Elias, N.

1978 *The History of Manners*. New York: Urizen Books.

Gillis, C.

1991 Tin in the Aegean Bronze Age. *Hydra* 8: 1–30.

Graziadio, G.

1988 The chronology of the graves of Circle B at Mycenae: a new hypothesis. *AJA* 92: 343–72.

Hurwit, J.
1979 The Dendra octopus cup and the problem of style in the fifteenth century Aegean. *AJA* 83: 413–26.
Immerwahr, S.
1971 *Excavations in the Athenian Agora, 13: the Neolithic and Bronze Ages.* Princeton: American School of Classical Studies.
Junker, L.
2001 Ritual feasting systems in prehispanic Philippine chiefdoms. In M. Dietler and B. Hayden (eds.), *Feasts: Archaeological and Ethnographic Perspectives on Food, Politics, and Power*: 267–310. Washington, DC: Smithsonian Institution Press.
Karo, G.
1930/1933 *Die Schachtgräber von Mykenai.* Munich: R. Habelt.
Kilian, K.
1987 L'architecture des résidences mycéniennes: origin et extension d'une structure. In E. Lévy (ed.), *Le système palatial en Orient, en Grèce et à Rome*: 203–17. Strasbourg: Université des sciences humaines de Strasbourg.
Kilian, K.
1992 Mykenische Heiligtümer der Peloponnes. In H. Froning, T. Hölscher and H. Mielsch (eds.), *Kotinos, Festschrift für Erika Simon*: 10–25. Mainz: Philipp von Zabern.
Kilian-Dirlmeier, I.
1985 Nochmal zu den 'Kriegergräber' von Knossos. *Jahrbuch des Römisch-Germanischen Zentralmuseums Mainz* 32: 196–213.
1987 Das Kuppelgrab von Vapheio (Lakonien): die Beigabenausstattung in der Steinkiste: Untersuchungen zur Sozialstruktur in späthelladischer Zeit. *Jahrbuch des Römisch-Germanischen Zentralmuseums Mainz* 34: 197–212.
Killen, J.
1994 Thebes sealings, Knossos tablets, and Mycenaean state banquets. *BICS* 39: 67–81.
1998 The Pylos Ta tablets revisited. *BCH* 122: 421–22.
Matthäus, H.
1980 *Die Bronzegefässe der Kretisch-Mykenischen Kultur* (Prähistorische Bronzefunde 2,1). Munich: Beck.
1983 Minoische Kriegergräber. In O. Kryzyszkowska and L. Nixon (eds.), *Minoan Society:* 203–15. Bristol: Bristol Classical Press.
Mountjoy, P. A.
1990 Regional Mycenaean pottery. *BSA* 85: 245–70.
Nordquist, G.
1987 *A Middle Helladic Village. Asine in the Argolid* (Boreas 16). Uppsala: Academia Upsaliensis.
Persson, A.
1942 *New Tombs at Dendra near Midea.* London: Humfry Milford.
Rathje, W.
1975 The last tango in Mayapan: a tentative trajectory of production distribution systems. In J. Sabloff and C. Lamberg-Karlovsky (eds.), *Ancient Civilizations and Trade*: 409–48. Albuquerque: School of American Research.
Rutter, J.
1989 A ceramic definition of Late Helladic I from Tsoungiza. *Hydra* 6: 1–9.
Shaw, M.
1993 The Aegean Garden. *AJA* 97: 661–85.

Shelmerdine, C.
1985 *The Perfume Industry of Mycenaean Pylos*. Göteborg: Paul Åström's Forlag.

Sherratt, S.
1980 Regional variation in the pottery of Late Helladic IIIB. *BSA* 75: 175–202.

Steel, L.
1998 The social impact of Mycenaean imported pottery in Cyprus. *BSA* 93: 285–96.
1999 Wine kraters and chariots: the Mycenaean pictorial style reconsidered. In P. Betancourt, V. Karageorghis, R. Laffineur and W. -D. Niemeier (eds.), *Meletemata: Studies in Aegean Archaeology Presented to Malcolm H. Wiener as He Enters His 65th Year* (Aegaeum 16): 803–10. Liège: University of Liège.

Tournavitou, I.
1995 *The 'Ivory Houses' at Mycenae* (BSA Supplement 24). London: British School at Athens.

Wace, A.
1932 Chamber tombs at Mycenae. *Archaeologia* 82.

Wright, J.
1982 Excavations at Tsoungiza (Archaia Nemea) 1981. *Hesperia* 51: 375–92.
1984 Changes in form and function of the palace at Pylos. In T. G. Palaima and C. W. Shelmerdine (eds.), *Pylos Comes Alive*: 19–29. New York: Lincoln Center, Fordham University.
1987 Death and power at Mycenae: changing symbols in mortuary practice. In R. Laffineur (ed.), *Thanatos. Les coutumes funéraires en Egée à l'Age du Bronze* (Aegaeum 1): 171–84. Liège: University of Liège.
1994 The spatial configuration of belief: the archaeology of Mycenaean religion. In S. Alcock and R. Osborne (eds.), *Placing the Gods, Sanctuaries and Sacred Space in Ancient Greece*: 37–78. Oxford: Clarendon Press.
1995 Empty cups and empty jugs: the social role of wine in Minoan and Mycenaean societies. In P. McGovern, S. Fleming and S. Katz (eds.), *The Origins and Ancient History of Wine*: 287–309. Amsterdam: Gordon and Breach.

6

Fit for a King? Hierarchy, Exclusion, Aspiration and Desire in the Social Structure of Mycenaean Banqueting

L. M. Bendall

It has long been known that feasting was a prominent feature of Mycenaean life. In recent years, however, new evidence for the specific nature and practices associated with Mycenaean ceremonial banqueting has emerged, provoking new interest. Both Linear B and archaeological data are available for Mycenaean banqueting, and banqueting studies thus provide an opportunity to combine different types of evidence to an unusually high degree (Bennet 1984; 1988). The present paper draws upon Linear B and archaeological data in an attempt to elucidate one aspect of Mycenaean social practice displayed in banqueting: the use of communal feasts to display and negotiate social status in Mycenaean palace society.

The Benefits of Giving: Gifts of Banqueting Foodstuffs

Three types of Linear B documents relate to state-organized banqueting: lists of foodstuffs and sacrificial animals for feasts (e.g. Killen 1964: 1; 1992; 1994; 1996; Chadwick 1976: 95–96, 132; Palaima 1989: 108–10; Piteros *et al.* 1990; Godart 1999); lists of rations for support staff and participants at religious festivals (Killen 2000; 2001b); and records of furnishings and other paraphernalia (Killen 1998; Speciale 1999). Our focus here will be on one particular feature of interest in the lists of foodstuffs: the phenomenon of provision of banqueting supplies by persons other than the palaces, and by the palaces to towns outside the centres.

There are numerous examples of such practices. For instance, Linear B text Cn 418 from Pylos records a contribution of animals for sacrifice (carefully selected for colour and other physical attributes) by a man named **we-u-da-ne-u*:

Cn 418 .1 pa-ro , **we-u-da-ne-we**
.2 re-u-ko , a-ko-ro-we-e BOS+*SI* 2
.3 re[-u-]ko , ma-ra-pi , pe-ko , a-ko-ro-we BOS+*SI* 1
.4 OVIS^{m}?]3 CAP^{m} 3 *WE* 3 CAP+*E* 3

.5	]2 [	]3	[	note: possibly]BOS^{x} 3
.6	] *vestigia* [	] *vestigia* [		

.7 re-u-ko[ ]ma-ra-[pi]pe-ko , a-ko-ro-we[BOS+*SI*
.8 OVIS^{m} 1 CAP^{m} 3 *WE*[ ]CAP+*E* [ ] SUS^{x}[
.9 *vacat*
mutila

**we-u-da-ne-u* is known from a variety of other Pylian texts. He contributes rowers for the palace fleet (An 610), is a major land holder (Es series, Na 856, Na 1041, Un 1193) and is one of the four so-called 'collectors' at Pylos (Cn 40+). The nature of the 'collectors' is still a matter of debate (e.g. Ventris and Chadwick 1973: 201–02, 413, 434, 437; Palmer 1963; Killen 1976; 1979b: esp. 176–79; 1983a; 1985; 1992–1993; 1995: esp. 214, 222; 2001a; Bennet 1985: 204; 1992; Carlier 1992; Driessen 1992; Godart 1992; Rougemont 2001; Olivier 2001). I take John Killen's view that they are most plausibly explained as 'members of the ruling elite (members of the royal family, high palace officials and the like) who have been assigned part of the productive capacity of the kingdoms for their own benefit' (Killen 1995: 213; also 1979b: 177). It has further been suggested (Lindgren 1973: 134–36) that **we-u-da-ne-u* may be the *ra-wa-ke-ta*, the *lāwāgetās* (literally 'leader of the host'; see Aura Jorro 1993: 230–31), thought of as the 'second in command' after the *wanax*. However that may be, he is clearly one of the more important personages in the polity.

Another individual who contributes banqueting provisions is *du-ni-jo* in Un 138:

Un 138 .1 pu-ro , qe-te-a$_{2}$, pa-ro , du-ni-jo
.2 HORD 18 T 5 po-qa OLIV 4 T 3 V 5
.3 VIN 13 OVIS^{m} 15 *WE* 8 OVIS^{f} 1 CAP^{m} 1 SUS 12
.4 SUS+*SI* 1 BOS^{f} 1 BOS^{m} 2
.5 me-za-wo-ni HORD 4 T 8 V 1 ka-pa OLIV 7

The list includes foodstuffs such as barley and olives, animals for sacrifice, and wine. Like **we-u-da-ne-u*, *du-ni-jo* may well have been an important figure. At least two different men of this name appear in the tablets, in the contexts of land tenure (Ea 59+, Ep 705+), festival rations records (Fn 79) and lists of officials (An 192, On 300). Though it is not certain which, if any, of these persons is the *du-ni-jo* of Un 138, all are important officials (where we can tell), so there must be a good chance that the same holds good for the *du-ni-jo* here, particularly in view of the large quantities of food with which he is associated on the tablet.

Further contributions are seen in Pylos Un 718.

Un 718 .1 sa-ra-pe-da , po-se-da-o-ni , do-so-mo
.2 o-wi-de-ta-i , do-so-mo , to-so , e-ke-ra$_{2}$-wo
.3 do-se , GRA 4 VIN 3 BOS^{m} 1
.4 tu-ro$_{2}$, *TURO*$_{2}$ 10 ko-wo , **153* 1
.5 me-ri-to , V 3
.6 *vacat*
.7 o-da-a$_{2}$, da-mo , GRA 2 VIN 2

.8 OVIS^{m} 2 *TURO*$_2$ 5 a-re-ro , *AREPA* V 2 **153* 1
.9 to-so-de , ra-wa-ke-ta , do-se ,
.10 OVIS^{m} 2 me-re-u-ro , FAR T 6
.11 a -ma
VIN S 2 o-da-a$_2$, wo-ro-ki-jo-ne-jo , ka-
.12 GRA T 6 VIN S 1 *TURO*$_2$ 5 me-ri[
.13 *vacat* [me-]ri-to V 1

The tablet records wine, animals for sacrifice, and foodstuffs such as cheese and wheat contributed in the context of land tenure obligations connected with Poseidon. The contributors are a man *e-ke-ra*$_2$*-wo* (line 2), the *dāmos* (line 7), the *lāwāgetās* (line 9) and a man *wroikiōn*, who has a special type of land-holding known as a *ka-ma*. *e-ke-ra*$_2$*-wo* is again an important person. He is involved in land tenure (Er 880), contributes rowers to the palace fleet (An 610) and so forth. He may be the *wanax* himself (Lindgren 1973: 153) although this is not universally agreed (Chadwick 1975; Killen 1999: 352–53). For our purposes here it is enough to note his high status. The *lāwāgetās*, mentioned above, is also a person of high status.

Contributions of banqueting provisions by persons of high status are also witnessed at Knossos and Thebes. Some examples from the group of Thebes sealings found in 1982 are below:

Wu 60	.α	SUS^{m}	**Wu 65**	.α	OVIS^{f}
	.β	pa-ro , sa-me-we		.β	te-qa-de /*Theq*^{w}*ans-de*/ 'to Thebes'
	.γ	*vacat*		.γ	qe-te-a$_2$
Wu 50	.α	CAP^{f}	**Wu 52**	.α	SUS+*SI*
	.β	qe-te-o		.β	a-ko-ra-jo
	.γ	a-ko-ra		.γ	*vacat*

As elucidated by Piteros *et al.* (1990: 171–84, esp. 172, 181), the sealings record provisions for a feast. They have formulaic similarities to tablets such as Cn 418 and Un 138 from Pylos, seen above. Further, like **we-u-da-ne-u* of Cn 418, some of the contributors at Thebes are likely to have been 'collectors', as indicated by the appearance of the words *a-ko-ra*/*a-ko-ra-jo*, indicating a connection with 'collector' flocks (Killen 1976; 1994: 76–77; Piteros *et al.* 1990: 147–50).

'Collectors' also appear in records of banqueting contributions at Knossos. Some examples are as follows:

C(2) 913
.1 pa-ro , e-te-wa-no , *a*$_3$ CAP^{m} 1[
.2 pa-ro ko-ma-we-te CAP^{m} 1 pa[

C(2) 941 + 1016 + *fr.*
.A OVIS^{m} 8[
.B pa-ro / a-pi-qo-ta , sa-pa-ka-te-ri-ja OVIS^{f} 10 [

v. .A [[ ]][
.B [[wi-ja[ ]][

C(2) 915

.A	] OVIS^f 10 [
.B	] pa-ro , a-pi-qo-ta / pa-ro , do-e-ro CAP^f 10 [
	.B CAP^f perhaps over [[ ]].

Killen notes that two of the men appearing in C(2) banqueting records, *ko-ma-we* (913.2) and *a-pi-qo-ta* (915.B; 941.B) are Knossian 'collectors' (Killen 1994: 76). It is also possible that the oxen on C 902 and the animals on the C(3) tablets represent contributions by officials (J.T. Killen pers. comm.).

This evidence, coming as it does from numerous tablets at several different sites, suggests that the making of contributions of banqueting foodstuffs by individual high-status members of society was a standard feature of Mycenaean banqueting practices. Interestingly, there are also records of contributions by persons of lower status. In C(2) 915 above, for instance, we have a contribution by *a-pi-qo-ta* and another contribution by his slave (*doelos*, corresponding to Attic δοῦλος). Now it is likely that this 'slave' was himself a person of somewhat high status, rather than an ordinary chattel slave. *Doelos* appears to have indicated more a position of dependency with regard to another person rather than a state of abject servitude (Aura Jorro 1985: 186; also Lejeune 1971: 63–82; Killen 1979a; it is relevant that the 'women of Pylos', many of whom very likely had the status of chattel slaves, are never actually called *doelai*; Chadwick 1988: 89–93, esp. 90, 92). We may compare some Pylian land tenure records, where a high official *a-pi-me-de* has a holding of land (Ep 539.14) alongside smaller holdings by three of his 'slaves' (Ep 539.10–12). There is evidence that land tenure denoted an elevated status, though not necessarily the highest. For instance, the Pylian records show holdings by important religious officials and personal craftsmen of the *wanax*. The 'slaves' of *a-pi-me-de* and *a-pi-qo-ta* may have been highly-placed retainers, whatever their precise legal status in terms of 'freedom' (for examples of the potential fluidity of ancient concepts of slavery, see Finley 1981).

The contribution by a 'slave' in C(2) 915 can be compared with a similar contribution from a Pylos tablet, Cn 1287:

	MN's	**occupations**	**female goats**	
Cn 1287				
.1	a-*64-jo ,	a-ke-ro	CAP^f 1	/*angelos*/? 'herald'?
.2	te-re-do	ka-na-pe-u	CAP^f 1	/*knapheus*/ 'fuller'
.3	na-ma-ru-ko		CAP^f 1	
.4	qe-ta-ko	ke-ra-me-u	CAP^f 1	/*kerameus*/ 'potter'
.5	da-u-da-ro ,	pe-re-ke-u	CAP^f 1	/*plekeus*/? 'weaver'?
.6	mu-ti-ri-ko ,	di-u-ja , do-e-ro	CAP^f 1	slave of a goddess, *di-u-ja* (see Tn 316)
.7	a_2-ra-ka-wo	ke-re-ta-o do-e-ro	CAP^f 1	slave of a man, **ke-re-ta*
.8	a-sa-ma-o		CAP^f 1	
.9	mo-ri-wo		CAP^f 2	
.10	ma-ni-ko		CAP^f 1	
.11	*vacat*			

Verso Drawing of a labyrinth

Line 7 records a contribution of a female goat – the same type of animal as in C(2) 915 – by a man who is described as a 'slave' of another man, **ke-re-ta*. In line 6 a 'slave' of the female deity *di-u-ja* makes a similar contribution. Other contributors are a fuller, a potter and (probably) a weaver. While the status of these people would not have been on the level of the 'collectors' and other important officials seen in the first group of documents examined, there is no reason to suppose that they were at the bottom ranks of society. There is evidence for craftsmen holding different positions in society, even those serving within the same industry. For instance, a differential status apparently obtained between those who held plots of land and those who received rations. As Killen suggests, the perfumer Eumedes, mentioned in a land tenure record at Pylos, may have been in charge of the industry (Killen 2001a: 180; see also Shelmerdine 1985: 24), while a perfumer who may have been subordinate received rations (albeit a large one).

So what is it that we are witnessing in these records? Why are high officials and (perhaps prominent) craftsmen contributing supplies for banqueting, and why are these contributions recorded in the palatial archives? To answer this, we need also to examine evidence for regional banqueting. Gifts for banqueting on the parts of the officials and craftsmen are mirrored in records of gifts from the palaces to regional centres. The main example is Vn 20 from Pylos, to which Cn 608 might possibly be added. The texts of these tablets are as follows:

Vn 20			**Cn 608**		
	.1	o-a_2 , e-pi-de-da-to		.1 jo-a-se-so-si , si-a_2-ro	
	.2	pa-ra-we-wo , wo-no		.2 o-pi-da-mi-jo	
	.3	pi-**82*-de 50		.3 pi-**82*	SUS+*SI* 3
	.4	me-ta-pa-de 50		.4 me-ta-pa	SUS+*SI* 3
	.5	pe-to-no-de 100		.5 pe-to-no	SUS+*SI* 6
	.6	pa-ki-ja-na-de 35		.6 pa-ki-ja-si	SUS+*SI* 2
	.7	a-pu_2-de 35		.7 a-pu_2-we	SUS+*SI* 2
	.8	a-ke-re-wa-de 30		.8 a-ke-re-wa	SUS+*SI* 2
	.9	e-ra-to-de 50		.9 e-ra-te-i	SUS+*SI* 3
	.10	ka-ra-do-ro-de 40		.10 ka-ra-do-ro	SUS+*SI* 2
	.11	ri-jo-de 20		.11 ri-jo	SUS+*SI* 2
	.12	*vacat*			

Vn 20 shows wine being distributed to the nine major towns of the Hither Province (note that each town has the directional suffix *-de*), while Cn 608 records pigs being fattened at those places (the toponyms are in dative-locative). These two circumstances are plausibly connected: the pigs may have been intended to accompany the wine in regional feasts. We cannot be certain of this since the heading of Cn 608 merely states that the */opi-dāmioi/* (apparently 'those in charge of the *dāmos*') are fattening pigs, and it could be that the pigs are intended as contributions from the regional centres to the palace (Palaima 1989: 117–18). Another possibility is that the palace was monitoring activities of officials under its jurisdiction, who were operating under its orders but had themselves to supply the pigs; in terms of the present argument, this would still constitute 'regional banqueting' and might still be perceived as palatial beneficence. Whatever the case for Cn 608, it is at least clear that Vn 20 concerns banqueting supplies intended for regional centres (note that wine was not an item of standard rations; Palmer 1994: 119).

R. Palmer makes some relevant comments regarding these tablets in the context of her discussion of wine in the Mycenaean palatial economy:

> The palaces could not have held a royal monopoly on wine, because vine growing and winemaking formed an integral part of traditional agriculture. However, all the Mycenaeans did not have equal access to wine. Only those farmers with enough land and labor to grow vines in addition to the staple crops would have been able to make wine. For those with little or no land to devote to vines, and not enough resources to barter for it, access would have been severely limited. (Palmer 1994: 187)

> Wine was not a staple of the Mycenaean economy as figs and grain were, but ranked with meat, milk products and honey as high status foods, items available to the poorer inhabitants on a limited basis, and hence equated with wealth and luxury. The palaces advertised their role as guardians and controllers of agricultural wealth by displaying this wealth on ceremonial occasions, and in particular by offering it to the gods. (Palmer 1994: 195)

> The palace provided these commodities to honour the gods and to emphasize the dependence of the gods and the people upon the generosity of the palace centre. The palace effectively demonstrated its position as the most powerful and the richest entity in the kingdom by making these 'luxury' foods available to people who otherwise could rarely afford meat and wine. (Palmer 1994: 191)

But, as we have seen, it was not only the palace which could demonstrate wealth and enhance prestige in this way. Officials, craftsmen and others made use of this social strategy. Personal prestige may have been enhanced by individuals through provision of goods for ceremonial banqueting in the same way as by the palaces. To be able to contribute would emphasize individual wealth as well as commitment to the social structure. In this sense the contributions of important persons such as *du-ni-jo* and **we-u-da-ne-u* would perhaps have been seen not as taxation-type obligations (though they may have been *social* obligations for some), but as marks of privilege. Similarly, with the 'slaves' and craftsmen of KN C(2) 915 and PY Cn 1287, it is difficult to take the contributions by these persons at a lower level of the hierarchy as 'tax' in the ordinary sense (note that no deficits [*o-pe-ro*] appear on these records, though deficits are common on ordinary tax records), but the ability to contribute goods might have been a means of securing or enhancing social prestige, displaying personal wealth, and invoking reciprocal obligations. While the donations on Cn 1287 are not as lavish as those seen in Un 138 and Cn 418, this could be in keeping with the lower status (and presumably inferior wealth) of the contributors. Yet it might have been considered worthwhile (and prestigious) to make lesser contributions - even if it be, in the case of Cn 1287, only a single goat. Not everyone in the society would have been in a position to give even this much; our craftsmen may have been among the wealthy and prominent of their professions.

A number of standard models can be called upon to explain the banqueting contributions, above all 'conspicuous consumption' and 'reciprocity', but neither of these precisely fits the Mycenaean evidence. Regarding 'consumption', it is probable that the officials, craftsmen and the like would have themselves participated in the feasts, but that is hardly the issue. Consumption *is* relevant to the present situation in terms of display, but what we have here is not so much (or rather, not merely) 'conspicuous consumption' as 'conspicuous giving' or 'conspicuous generosity' (cf. Hamilakis 1996), a concept more connected with reciprocity (Mauss 1954). Linear B administrators were, as a rule, highly selective in terms of what was recorded and what was not. The fact that the *names* of contributors of foodstuffs are carefully documented indicates the considerable importance placed on this type of information by the palaces.

But what ethic is attached to this conspicuous generosity? The Mycenaean banquets do not look like a potlatch. Contributions of banqueting supplies may have functioned to evoke reciprocal obligations, but there is a difficulty with imposing the classic model in the present instance. Reciprocity normally functions where the social status of participants is roughly equivalent (or, at least, where the society is small enough for reciprocity to be evoked on an individual basis - note that potlatch does not exist where there is central government; Dalton 1977: 207). That is not the case here. The villages, for instance, in the case of regional banqueting, could not have been expected to make reciprocal returns to the palace. To be sure, they paid taxes, but to speak of this in terms of 'reciprocal obligation' is grossly to distort the true relationship – not in terms of wealth or 'who gave more' (in absolute terms, the villages would have given more to the palaces than *vice versa*), but in terms of social power. The fact that the palaces extracted taxes from the population – including an extremely onerous sort of tax, corvée labour (An 1, An 610, Ac series – Killen 1983b; Bendall 2003: 206) – indicates a starkly non-egalitarian relationship. Similarly, with the contributions of the craftsmen to the palaces, the contrast between the wealth and status of contributors and recipients is too great to speak in terms of mutuality. The explanation lies more along Palmer's lines of expressing dependence and generosity, but this does not entirely work either, since we see the mechanism functioning in both directions. The palaces were not 'dependent' on the craftsmen (except in the sense in which a factory owner may be 'dependent' on his workers for their labour – but the power dynamics in such cases are unfortunately not normally weighted in favour of the workers), and the gift of a few goats would be unlikely to have convinced anyone to the contrary. So what precisely is going on with all this 'conspicuous giving'? It is possible that the answer is related to archaeological evidence for banqueting hierarchies in Messenia, to which we now turn.

You are Where you Eat: Banqueting Locations as Expressions of Social Status

Our focus here will be on the palace of Pylos and on Malthi, a small settlement in northern Messenia. We begin with the palace.

The Palace of Pylos

It has long been suggested that Court 63 and the Southwest Building were locations of banqueting activities (Säflund 1980; Shelmerdine 1998: 84, 87–88; 1999; Davis and Bennet 1999: 110; Whitelaw 2001: 58). Banqueting (or at least drinking or the pouring of libations) is thought also to have taken place in Room 6 (Blegen and Rawson 1966: 88; Säflund 1980; McCallum 1987a; 1987b; Hägg 1995: 389–90, with further bibliography; Palaima 1995: 132–33; Shelmerdine 1999: 21; Davis and Bennet 1999: 115–16; see also Hägg 1985: 211, 215–16). The present study supports the identification of these areas for banqueting, proposes a third area and above all investigates the social status of participants in activities in the various areas.

The question of social status can be approached through an examination of the distribution of kylikes throughout the palace. Kylikes are the classic Mycenaean drinking vessel and, while they may have been used in ordinary domestic contexts, there is various evidence that they were particularly associated with banqueting. For example, the Campstool Fresco at Knossos shows groups of men drinking from kylikes in what may be a ceremonial feast (Cameron 1964; Immerwahr 1990: 95; Shelmerdine 1997: 563, 579; Wright 1996: 292).

Table 6.1 shows the numbers of kylikes found in different rooms of the palace, based on the data presented by Blegen and Rawson (1966); some refinements of the picture may emerge from new work being done on Pylos (e.g., Davis 1998; Nelson and Cooper 1998). The numbers include both whole vessels and stems. Kylix stems, unlike other types of sherds, are relevant to how many vessels were originally extant, since each item must relate to *one* vessel. Their distribution is thus significant in a way that distributions of ordinary body sherds are not. There are, however, some complicating factors. First, kylix stems are highly durable and will not necessarily give a synchronic picture since a single deposit could include a long accumulation of debris (for instance, in the OSWB many stems were identified as LHIIIA). Second, such objects were sometimes included in mudbrick, so their distribution might show little beyond variations in mudbrick composition. It happens that we do see both of these factors operating at Pylos, but – crucially – it is possible to identify them. That is, it is possible to tell when we are seeing distortions due to depositional factors and when we are seeing distributions reflecting activities which took place within a reasonably short span of time before the destruction of the palace.

A first point to note about Table 6.1 is that the difference in counts from room

Table 6.1. Numbers of kylikes in rooms at Pylos

lowest

Room	count
36	1
50	2
53	[2]
72	3
48	3
62	4
35	5
13	5
28	6
71	6+
34	8
23	ca. 9
38	9
39	9
70	10
21	12
68	12
41	14

low

Room	count
8	many
77	many
78	as 77
69	good many
5	great many
76	abundant
44	18
4	20+
25	20
55	22
43	23
12	25+
2	26
46	31
32	32
40	32
93	32
31	38+
33	39
16	ca. 40??
10	43

low-medium

Room	count
100	53
chasm	60
58	76 [329]
94	79
1	80
88	80
95	87
102	90
3	92

medium-high

Room	count
104	118
96	145
98	197
26-27	199

high

Room	count
101	243
47	255
63	275
92	275
20	279
60	267
97	300
18+18/20	309
42	348
99	352

highest

Room	count
65	442
91	445
9	500-600
105	761
19	2854
OSWB	3142

Notes

Both stems and whole vessels are counted. Diminutive kylikes are not included. Figures in brackets were found in drains.

No kylix sherds are reported from the following rooms: 11, 14-15, 17, 22, 29, 52, 59, 66, 67, 74 (no floor), 75, 79, 87, 103. No inventories are given for: 51, 56, 57, 80, 81, 83-86. Kylix sherds, but no stems or bases are reported from some rooms/areas: 6, 7, 23, 24, 30, 37, 45, 49, 54, 61, 64, 73, 82, 89-90, aqueduct. These appear to be random scatter, e.g. for the aqueduct they are described as 'small nondescript pieces' (Blegen and Rawson 1966: 366).

Chasm = The channel created by post-destruction ashlar quarrying in the area of Rooms 7, 8, 9, 10, 12 (Blegen and Rawson 1966: 92, 95-96).

OSWB = 'Outside Southwest Building'. This is spill down the slope of the citadel. The inventory is divided in sections giving: 650 + 516 + 1,147 + 385 = 2698. There were also 208 labelled 'earlier' and 236 considered

possibly LHIIIA, for a total of 444 + 2698 = 3142.
Rooms where 'many' or 'abundant' kylikes are recorded, but not counted, are assigned to 'low'.
Room 9: Some 500-600 'drinking cups or kylikes of the tall-stemmed type' recorded (Blegen and Rawson 1966: 102). The wording is ambiguous about whether drinking cups and kylikes is meant or whether kylix is a specification of drinking cup. Whitelaw (2001: 54) states that all the vessels were kylikes.
Room 12: 'some 25 or more' (Blegen and Rawson 1966: 110).
Room 16: '120 miscellaneous potsherds, mainly fragments of kylikes and flat-bottomed bowls and cups' (Blegen and Rawson 1966: 117); most of this is presumably spill out from the main pantry.
Room 18: Count includes vessels found in the doorway 18/20 (see Blegen and Rawson 1966: 121 n. 46). Many are whole vessels.
Room 19: Most are whole vessels.
Rooms 26-27: Material for both rooms was combined at the time of the excavation (Blegen and Rawson 1966: 146).
Room 31: 'at least 38 stems' (Blegen and Rawson 1966: 56).
Room 32: A large decorated kylix (unnumbered) was put together from scattered sherds found near floor level; 31 stems were found in debris above floor (Blegen and Rawson 1966: 160).
Room 42: Only stems 'from below black stratum' (mixed context including Geometric) are included. 183 more were found above (Blegen and Rawson 1966: 185) [348 + 183 = 567].
Room 43: 19 whole kylikes, 4 stems.
Room 53: Two restored from sherds in drain (Blegen and Rawson 1966: 220).
Court 58: 76 kylix stems in court (Blegen and Rawson 1966: 230), and another 329 in the drain extending from Room 7 to the SW wall of Room 60 (Blegen and Rawson 1966: 235) [329 + 76 = 405].
Room 60: Most are whole vessels.
Room 65: Finds from 'debris accumulated over the eroded slope under Room 65' (Blegen and Rawson 1966: 258, 259) shown in room.
Room 72: four stems, one of a votive (Blegen and Rawson 1966: 269).
Room 98: 6 whole, 4 semi-whole, 187 stems [= 197].
Rooms 104-105: 173 stems came from a layer of ploughed earth overlying both rooms (Blegen and Rawson 1966: 348). 118 came from below the ploughed layer in Room 104 (Blegen and Rawson 1966: 344); 2 whole vessels and 759 'bases' came from the 'burned debris filling Room 105' (Blegen and Rawson 1966: 349).

to room is very large. Some rooms have a very few items, while others have hundreds or even thousands. This is a first indication that the pattern of distribution among the various rooms is significant. Table 6.1 groups together rooms with comparable counts: 1–14 ('lowest'), 18–43 ('low'), 53–92 ('low-medium'), 118–199 ('medium-high'), 243–352 ('high'), and 442+ ('highest'). The disparity cannot be explained merely by a factor such as erosion from the mudbrick, since this should produce a more uniform distribution (being relevant wherever there are walls). Nor is this merely random background scatter. In fact, we do have what is very probably 'background noise' in the rooms with the 'lowest' counts and some of the smaller counts from the 'low' category may also be 'noise'. Figure 6.1 plots the remaining four groups on a plan of the palace. The highest numbers of vessels are concentrated in six places: three – Room 19, Room 65 and the spill from off the slope (OSWB) – are related to the Southwestern Building; the other three are Room 9, Ramp 91 and Room 105. Our primary interest here is in the concentration of kylikes in the Southwest Building, but we should first briefly discuss the others.

Room 9 was a pantry containing some 500–600 drinking vessels, which were found lying on the floor in a broken fused mass. The excavators suggested that

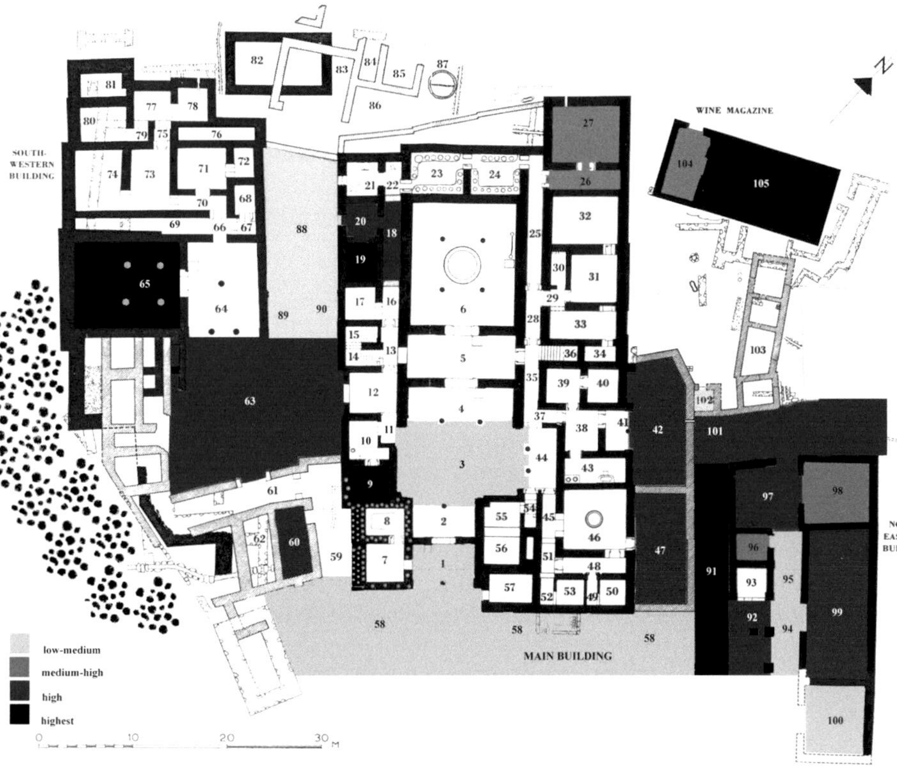

Figure 6.1. The distribution of kylikes at the Palace of Nestor, Pylos

the pantry served guests or other visitors who were offered refreshment on entering the palace: 'This was surely a serving room from which guests in the adjoining apartment could be offered refreshment while they waited' (Blegen and Rawson 1966: 102). The location of the room would well suit such a function, as would the existence in Room 10 of a built-in stand for jars or pithoi, perhaps for wine (Blegen and Rawson 1966: 104–05; Whitelaw 2001: 57). The positioning of the associated doorways and partition walls suggests that the pantry served the area of Court 3, and the scatters of vessels in this courtyard and the connected areas (2, 4 and 44) could reflect use in the vicinity. Scatters in Rooms 8, 10 and 12 are probably accidental. The Room 10 deposit probably reflects spill out from Room 9, perhaps combined with the fall-out from the 'chasm', a result of post-destruction ashlar quarrying, affecting Rooms 7, 8, 9, 10 and 12. The back-fill in the trench was a jumble of mixed deposits, and the hundred or so kylix stems and cup/bowl bases found in it may have to do with an original presence in Room 9, rather than being specifically related to any of the other rooms.

The high counts of kylikes in the fill in Ramp 91 and surrounding areas – the Northeastern Building, and Courts 42 and 47 – are more difficult to explain and may relate to a number of factors. Other peaks in Figure 6.1 are either themselves pantries or (as we shall see for the SWB) are associated with pantries. That is not the case here. Room 98 of the Northeastern Building was a *minor* pantry – a few pots were stored there along with a good many other things, but the number of pots is insufficient to account for the high concentrations in the area. A mere 36 whole vessels were found in Room 98 (only five of them kylikes), with another 20 or so from the rest of the building, yet nearly 3000 stems and bases were found in 91–101. The small number of whole vessels found in the Northeastern Building does not encourage belief that vessels stored in the building were the source of the scatter. Further, Courts 42 and 47, which also had high numbers of stems (some 603 together), were accessed from the *interior* of the palace, not from the Northeastern Building or Ramp 91.

It is likely that several different factors are operating here. First, *some* of the vessels can be accounted for by minor drinking activities in the area. The Northeastern Building was a place to which goods arriving on the palace citadel were brought (for new interpretations of the building, see Flouda 2000; Hofstra 2000; Bendall 2003). It might be that some of the carriers and officials associated with such movements would have needed to be served with something, and this could account for small amounts of vessels for casual and occasional use being kept in Room 98; Hofstra (2000) brilliantly observes that vessels in Room 98 comprise banqueting 'sets', but agrees that these are probably intended for reception rather than feasting. Courts 42 and 47, on the other hand, may have been gardens (Hollister 1998: 416; Cooper 1999: 49–50) rather than perfume workshops (Shelmerdine 1985: 59–62). There could be ample reason for taking refreshments in such places, even though they are not obviously associated with a pantry. (They could have been served from Room 9, though it is not the most conveniently placed for such a purpose.) Also, many of the vessels in these courts were associated with mixed contexts containing Geometric pottery plus some stray Linear B tablets from the Northeastern Building. There was evidently considerable disturbance of deposits in this area.

Another factor that could be operating in the case of Ramp 91 is the very fact that it is a ramp. Kylix stems roll, and debris in this area might have become concentrated in the ramp through such action. A final factor which may have been in play is erosion from the mudbrick. The outer walls of Courts 42 and 47, and the whole of the Northeastern Building were, along with the Wine Magazine, the very latest structures built at the palace (Wright 1984: esp. 22, 26, 20 n. 2 for a summary of Blegen and Rawson's views; Shelmerdine 1985: 59–60; 1997: 560–64; 1998: 88). It is possible that the mudbrick used to construct them had higher densities of inclusions than the brick used for the original construction. (Perhaps because higher concentrations of waste had accumulated in the area of the palace by the time of their construction?) If so, this cluster would not primarily reflect vessel usage in the final stage before the destruction of the palace. The same explanation may possibly apply to the peak of kylikes in Room 105. (It is worth bearing in mind that Room 105 may have served Courts 88 and 63. It is on the same orientation with other new buildings behind the blocking wall of Court 88 and it is possible that this wall did have a gate in it [Whitelaw 2001].)

Let us finally turn to the Southwest Building. Rooms 64 and 65 were identified by the excavators as a 'megaron complex', with Room 65 being 'the principal hall of the Southwestern Building' (Blegen and Rawson 1966: 247–59, esp. 258). (It is uncertain whether Room 65 was a classic Mycenaean 'megaron' in the sense of a square room with central hearth and symmetrically placed columns – six columns might be reconstructed rather than four and it is unclear whether there was a hearth [Blegen et al. 1973: 36–37]; on difficulties with the term 'megaron' see Darcque 1990.) The large numbers of pots found in Rooms 18–22 were considered to be primarily everyday domestic service for persons living and working in the palace (Blegen and Rawson 1966: 352), although kylikes are recognized as connected to drinking activities (Blegen and Rawson 1966: 124; the idea that the vessels were intended for sale is rightly rejected [Blegen and Rawson 1966: 350–51, also 240; Whitelaw 2001: 54]). More recently, numerous scholars have identified the Southwestern Building as a site for banqueting rather than domestic service (see references above), but the extent to which the pantries serving the area functioned as an integrated whole has not been hitherto described in detail (but see Davis and Bennet 1999: esp. 110; Whitelaw 2001: 55–60).

It is important first to note that Rooms 18–20, though they lie in the main palace block, cannot be accessed from within the palace. As discussed by J. Wright (1984: esp. 20, 23), Room 18 was originally a hallway, which was blocked off at either end sometime late in LHIIIB, creating a new area for pottery storage. Access to these pottery stores was from the Southwest Area through a door in the wall of Room 20 – they thus served the Southwest Area, not the main palace. Also serving the Southwest Area were Rooms 21–22. These too were pottery pantries, but they contained a different range of vessels. As can be seen from Table 6.2, the major concentrations of pottery types were complementary in their distribution (note in particular the figures in bold). Kylikes were primarily stored in Room 19, cups and bowls in Room 21, and dippers in Room 22. The organization is for the most part systematic, and this is true also for the arrangement of pots *within* rooms. A great many vessels were found actually stacked within one another, with different vessel types kept together (Blegen and Rawson 1966: 351). While Rooms 19, 21 and 22 have large numbers of a few vessel shapes, Rooms 18 and 20 are remarkable for their variety of wares. Diminutive vessels appear primarily to have been stored in Room 18 (with diminutive kylikes in the doorway – possibly hung from string?). Room 20, opening immediately onto the feasting area and thus the most accessible pantry, appears to contain a *selection* of vessels held in the other rooms – perhaps to keep an assortment 'on hand'.

It is attractive to associate the dippers of Room 22 with Rooms 23 and 24, which lead on from Room 22. These rooms contained over 30 large pithoi set permanently into clay benches. Numerous Linear B tablets from Room 23 suggest

Table 6.2. Pottery from Rooms 18-22

vessel (shape nos.)	**19**	**18**	**18/20**	**20**	**21**	**22**
kylix, two-handled (29-31)	**2854**	308	1	105		
kylix, one-handled (27)				174	12	
kylix, diminutive (26)			43	19		
krater, pedestaled (62)				24		
cup, one-handled, 'teacup' (12)				72	**1024**	55
cup, with clay moulding (13)		4				
cup, two-handled (18, 19)		9				
tankard (33)			2	1		
basin (1)		14	1	1		
bowl, basin-like (4)		2	2	75	**1099**	147
bowl, basin-like (5)				1		
bowl, spouted (9)		3				
cup/bowl, diminutive (3)		7				
dipper/scoop (21, 23, 24, 25)		48	1	16	7	**399**
dipper, diminutive (20)		16	1	7		
jug, medium (36)		3		5		
jug, small (34, 35)		27	10	6		
jug, stemmed (42)		1				
amphora, small (46)		1	1	2		
amphora, diminutive (47)		23		6		
jar, small (51)				3		
lid (77)					1	

Notes
18/20 = Doorway between Rooms 18 and 20, catalogued separately in Blegen and Rawson (1966).
Chance sherds noted at the end of each inventory list are not included here.
Kylikes: all from Room 19 were Shape 29b-c; most from Room 20 were Shape 27, some were Shape 29; Room 18 and the doorway contained Shapes 29-31.
The vast majority of bowls were Shape 4; the one example of Shape 5 is very similar; basins (Shape 1) are the same shape, but larger.

that at least some of these pithoi held perfumed oil, but there is no need to believe that all of them did. Wine and foodstuffs such as grains and olives may have been stored in the pithoi as well. The idea of food being served from these rooms works well with the distribution of pottery in our pantries. It should be noted that the so-called 'teacups' (Shape 12; Blegen and Rawson 1966: 359–60) of Room 21 may have been for eating rather than drinking, as the bowls (Shape 4; Blegen and Rawson 1966: 356) found there certainly were. We thus have food

Table 6.3. Pottery from Rooms 67-68

vessel type (shape nos.)	67	68
krater (59)		30
domestic jar (48a-b)	11	41
jar, small, wide mouth (52)	1	
lid, small-medium (74)	2	
pan (78)		3
tripod 'cup' (69, 70)	52	
brazier (67)	51	

Notes

Pots from other rooms past the doorway of 64/66 are as follows. Rooms 70-71 contained a jar (Shape 49); Room 71 had a larnax and several pithoi (one plus a fragment; six in Shapes 56-57). Only chance sherds were found in Rooms 69 and 72-78. Shapes represented are for the most part those noted from the other rooms; pithoi fragments were frequent. Items of particular note include a diminutive kylix stem from Room 72 and fragment of a spit-holder from Room 76.

service ware in Room 21, foodstuffs (possibly) in Rooms 23–24 and dippers – the appropriate service ware for conveying foods from pithoi to tableware – in the room between, Room 22. Room 19 completes the group by supplying drinking vessels, so that what we essentially have in these rooms are basic elements of a 'banqueting set', systematically stored in separate areas of a unified pantry complex.

A final type of vessel we should expect in connection with banqueting is cooking pots, and in fact a large supply of these was kept nearby, in the Southwestern Building itself, primarily in Rooms 67 and 68, the first two rooms to the right of the entrance past Hall 64 (Table 6.3). Shape 59, called a 'krater', is actually a cooking pot ('very similar' to cooking pots at Zygouries [Blegen and Rawson 1966: 396]), as is the coarseware 'domestic jar' (Shapes 48a and 48b, with one and two handles, respectively – Blegen and Rawson 1966: 383–84; cf. 'cooking jars' in Tzedakis and Martlew 1999: e.g. 102, 121, 122, 126, 127, 131, 135, 170, 185, 186, 188, 198). Such vessels may have been put on clay stands, or used directly over fires. The coarseware 'tripod cups', Shapes 69 and 70, are also cooking vessels, with their own tripod 'stands'; Shape 69 has one handle and a small pinched-out spout; 70 has two handles and is somewhat larger (Blegen and Rawson 1966: 413–14; cf. cooking vessels in Tzedakis and Martlew 1999: 120, 170, 183, 196, 248). The braziers (Shape 67) were probably for carrying coals, a function which may have been related to food preparation (Blegen and Rawson 1966: 412, see also 352).

Altogether, some 139 cooking vessels were stored in Rooms 67 and 68 (not counting the braziers). The cooking wares in these pantries neatly complement the tableware of Rooms 19–22. Given the unity of these 'sets' of vessels, it is no surprise to find high densities of kylix debris in the areas where the actual feasting would probably have taken place: Hall 65, Court 63 and possibly Court 88. It is not clear whether the Court 88 material reflects an actual use area, or spill from Court 63 and the pantries, but the point is unimportant for present purposes.

What is clear is that the *main* 'use areas' were Hall 65 and Court 63. Also, the high number of kylikes in the OSWB is probably related to this group. The thousands of kylikes found here were evidently rubbish pushed over the slope following feasts in Court 63. The attribution of many of them to LHIIIA suggests that banqueting had been going on in the area of this court for a very long time.

We now turn to another large pantry in the area of the Southwest Building, Room 60, located on the ramp (59) which led up to the entrance to Court 63. The purpose of this pantry has never been fully elucidated (but see Säflund 1980: 239; Davis and Bennet 1999: 110; Whitelaw 2001: 57–60). The excavators commented that:

> Although the tall-stemmed drinking cup [i.e. the kylix] is the commonest shape here as well as in Pantries 19 and 20, and some of the other pots too are similar to types found in the five storerooms of the Main Building, the wares themselves differ conspicuously and each group contains pots of a good many shapes that are not represented in the other. It seems logical therefore to conclude that the selections of the types of vessels themselves and the wares were intended for different purposes and users. (Blegen and Rawson 1966: 240)

By 'five storerooms of the Main Building', the excavators meant Rooms 18, 19, 20, 21 and 22. Some scholars have continued to see a difference in the vessel assemblage between Room 60 and the others, with the implication of a different function, but in actuality the make-up of the pottery assemblage in Room 60 does resemble that seen in the other pantries, *when Rooms 67–68 are included in the latter group*. Table 6.4 compares the assemblages. Both groups comprise a range of drinking and eating vessels, service ware and cooking pots and are dominated by the same types in similar proportions: kylikes, basins, cups and dippers, with the other pantries containing about eleven to thirteen times as many vessels of each type as Room 60. The main difference is that far greater numbers of vessels were found in the other pantries and they display a somewhat greater variety of shapes, in particular of diminutive shapes (Room 60 only has diminutive kylikes). But essentially, we are looking at the same type of 'set', and if the purpose of the pantries grouped around Court 63 was to serve feasting activities, this is likely to have been the purpose of Room 60 too (as recognized by Davis and Bennet 1999: 110; see also Whitelaw 2001: 58).

But if so, where were these activities taking place? It has been suggested that Room 60 served the Southwest Area, as the other pantries did, but there is a difficulty. Between Room 60 and Court 63 are two major gateways, one at the top of Ramp 59 and another at the entrance to Court 63. Access to the area was quite strictly controlled – this was not a place that one might casually wander in and out of. Room 60 is very poorly placed to serve the Southwestern Area. An alternative is that it was serving the area in front of the main gate of the palace, Court 58, and I should like to suggest that banqueting may have taken place in this courtyard; indeed, bones found in Room 7, identified as remains of sacrificed animals (Halstead and Isaakidou, this volume; Isaakidou *et al.* 2002), may be

Table 6.4. Pottery assemblage of Room 60 compared with 'others' (Rooms 18-22 and 67-68)

	60	shapes	others	shapes
drinking vessels				
kylix	267	(27-28, 30c, 32)	3454	(27, 29-31)
krater, pedestaled (may be service vessel)			24	(62)
tankard			3	(33)
eating vessels				
basin or basin-like bowl	126	(2, 4)	1342	(1, 4, 5)
drinking/eating vessels				
cup, two-handled	3	(19)	9	(18, 19)
cup, one-handled	84	(12, 15)	1155	(12, 13)
cup, upright rod handle	2	(16)		
cup, one-handle, low foot	4	(17)		
Total	93		1164	
cooking vessels				
krater, semi-coarse	31	(59)	30	(59)
tripod cup			52	(69, 70)
domestic jar			52	(48a-b)
pan			3	(78)
Total	31		137	
dipper/scoop	39	(66)	471	(21, 23-25)
pouring vessels				
bowl, spouted, decorated			3	(9)
bowl, spouted	56	(6-8)		
bowl, spouted, large, deep	33	(10)		
jug			52	(34-36, 42)
jug, 'teapot', heavy plain ware	20	(41)		
diminutive vessels				
kylix, diminutive	82	(26)	62	(26)
cup/bowl, diminutive (3)			7	(3)
dipper, diminutive			24	(20)
amphora, diminutive			29	(47)
other vessels				
amphora, small, wide mouth			4	(46)
brazier			51	(67)
jar, pithoid, small	1	(52)	4	(51, 52)
tripod 'incense-burner'	5	(71)		
lids for 'incense-burner'	6	(72)		
lids, various			3	(74, 77)
squat jar/alabastron, decorated	1	(64)		
stirrup jar	1	(65b3)		

Notes

Basins: Shapes 1 and 2 are functionally similar.

Cups: Shapes 12-13 and 15 are functionally similar; 15 is more roughly made, with the handle simply looped inside rather than smoothed onto the outside of the vessels.

Cups: Shape 19 is a low kylix-type vessel; 17 is a carinated cup.

Dippers: Room 60 dippers are Shape 66, while the other rooms have Shapes 21 and 23-25. The main differences are that the latter have higher handles and are fineware; those from Room 60 are coarseware. The sizes are similar and the functions could be the same.

related to activities in Court 58. A reception function for the area should also be considered. Much of the courtyard is badly eroded, but it is probable that entrance onto the citadel would have been from this direction (Cooper 1998: 56, fig. 79; Nelson and Cooper 1998: 399–400; Davis and Bennet 1999: 110). Thus, a person approaching the palace would come first to Court 58. It may be that such persons would have been received with refreshments before progressing (or not) to the interior of the palace, similar to what was suggested by Blegen for Room 9. The possibilities are not exclusive: the area may have been used for both banqueting *and* receptions.

If this is correct, it may be significant that Room 60 is serving an area where people *have not got into the palace yet*. They are on the citadel, but have not passed through the Propylon into Court 3 or through the double-gateway leading to Court 63. One wonders whether this might relate to the fabric of the Room 60 pottery, which differs from that found in the other pantries. Specifically, it seems to be inferior in quality. The excavators comment:

> Pantry 60 offers a strong contrast in comparison with the foregoing group: here, with few exceptions, the vases are dark and smoky-looking. This difference cannot be attributed solely to local effects of the fire that wrecked the palace; **it is manifest at the outset that the clay itself is not of the same fine kind as that used for the pots stored in Pantries 18 to 22. It is coarser in texture** possibly because of admixture of different tempering matter…The utensils and the pots kept in Room 60 **must surely have been made for other purposes and for other people than the types that were supplied from the five pantries in the Main Building.** (Blegen and Rawson 1966: 352; my emphases)

While doubting that the 'purpose' of the assemblage was different (for reasons above), the idea that the 'people' it was serving were different may well be right (as recognized by Whitelaw 2001: 58). Is it possible that we are seeing here a hierarchy in banqueting (or reception) service with a distinction made between people who were served outside the main palace gates and those who were admitted to the carefully-controlled area of Court 63? (Or, in terms of reception, those who were served with superior quality vessels in Court 3?)

One reason for thinking along these lines concerns an interesting lacuna in our kylix distribution: Room 6, the main megaron, is almost entirely empty. Only a few random stems were found here, plus some diminutive kylikes, associated with an offering table. Yet there is various evidence suggesting that Mycenaean megara were locations of drinking activities. In Room 6, for instance, a curiously-shaped trough cut into the floor next to the throne was probably for making libations, and the frescoes in the room and the Propylon (Room 5) depict a procession and feast (Lang 1969: 193–95, pls. 119, 125; McCallum 1987a: 78, 96, 108–41; 1987b).[1] If we are not actually wrong in associating megara with banqueting, where are the vessels?

An answer may emerge through plotting fragments of metal vessels found in the palace (Figure 6.2).[2] They seem to be concentrated in the megaron, although

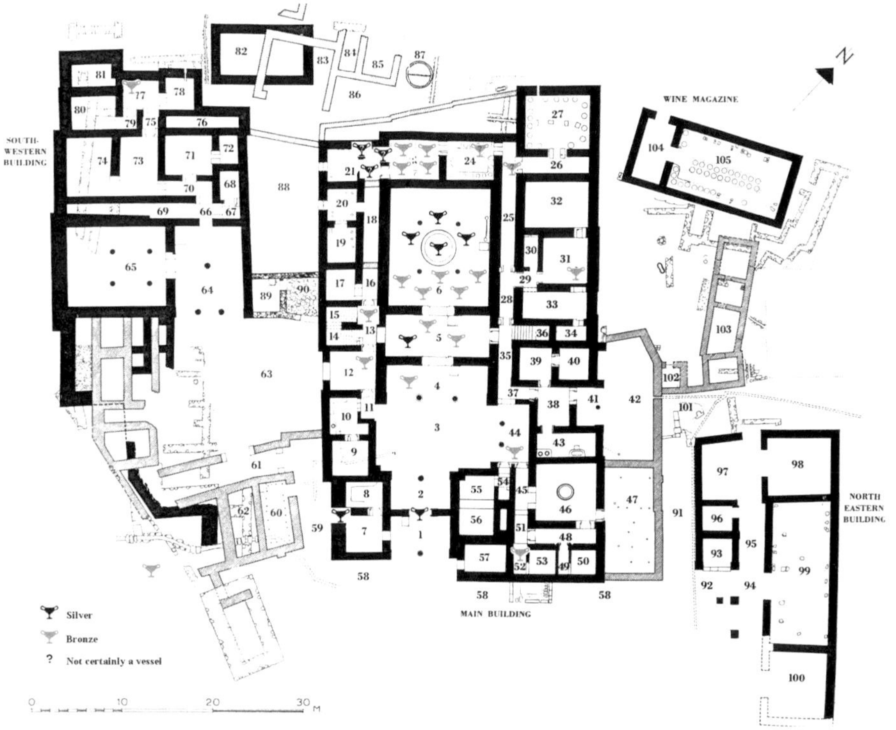

Figure 6.2. The distribution of metal vessels at the Palace of Nestor, Pylos

some may have fallen from an upper floor (e.g. fragments of a silver cup reported as coming 'from layer of fallen debris' [Blegen and Rawson 1966: 90]; see also Hofstra 2000: 108). Silver and bronze vessels are present, and in the vestibule are more of bronze. Pieces of a silver cup with inlaid gold and niello heads found principally in the Propylon may be related (Blegen and Rawson 1966: 57–58). A few other vessels are scattered about the palace (those in Rooms 12 and 21 may be related to banqueting in the Southwest Building), but the megaron does seem to stand out. It may be suggested that there *was* drinking in the megaron, but participants drank from metal vessels, not clay ones.

Let us return now to the question of whether different qualities of vessels might be linked with the social status of the persons using them. In the case of the megaron, the answer must be 'yes', which may encourage us to draw similar conclusions elsewhere. We would thus have three tiers of quality: metal vessels, fineware, and inferior ware. These tiers are neatly linked to varying degrees of access to the interior of the palace. The inferior ware comes from a pantry serving people who have not proceeded to the interior of the palace, an area *outside* both the main gate and the gate leading into Court 63. Next, in Court 63 and the Southwest Building, we have fineware being used, in an area where access was carefully controlled by two separate gateways. A higher degree of exclusion of access is witnessed here than in the case of the area served by Room 60. Finally, in the heart of the palace, the megaron, we would have the highest quality, metal vessels, being used. It is not necessary to insist that access to the megaron would have been very closely controlled indeed. This room must have been amongst the most exclusive at the palace, with the high status of the participants stressed and articulated by their use of superior vessels.

One feature of interest in this 'banqueting hierarchy' is a sense of simultaneous exclusion and inclusion. People served in Court 58 have not got into the palace yet, but they are still on the citadel. People served in Court 63 are not in the megaron itself, but they are still within the palace. Banqueting can be a means of emphasizing social ties, but can also emphasize differences from those outside the group (e.g., Mars 1987 and other articles in Douglas 1987). There can be various sorts of differences – gender, ethnicity, wealth, class and so forth – but it is likely that the distinction we are seeing here is one of social rank. Access to banqueting in different areas – the ability to participate – may have marked a privilege, which would not have necessarily been extended to all members of society. This raises the question of which members of society *were* admitted. Was banqueting a generalized feature of Mycenaean society (wherever the feasts were held)? Or were such activities restricted to the socio-political elite? That is, was exclusion not merely in terms of access to different areas, but in terms of being able to take part in such activities at all?

We have already anticipated some answers to these questions with our Linear B evidence for regional banqueting: there was banqueting in regional centres. This is corroborated by archaeological evidence for banqueting at settlements in Messenia outside Pylos. For instance, Nichoria, a Late Bronze Age village lying atop a ridge overlooking the major road from Pylos to the Pamisos River Valley, had a small building which was identified as a megaron (McDonald and Wilkie 1992: 407, fig. 7–36), as did the hill-top settlement of Malthi, in northern Messenia.

Malthi

We will focus here on the megaron at Malthi (Figure 6.3). The stratigraphy of the site is highly problematic,[3] but we may hazard some comments. The town is divided into two areas: an upper terrace in the middle of the site, and groups of houses lying along the walls. On the upper terrace was a building which was evidently the chief house of the town and probably the residence of whatever person(s) held dominant authority. One hall of the structure, A1, is a likely location for banqueting. A hearth against the back wall was associated with ash and animal bones, and a large number of kylikes was found. Interestingly, some of these were of local red clay, slipped with yellow. One wonders whether this was to make them look like the more classic fineware, examples of which were also found.

Another room, almost certainly used for banqueting, was the small megaron,

Figure 6.3. Banqueting areas at Malthi

B85 (Valmin 1938: 173). This room has the classic features of a central hearth surrounded by four columns. It lacks the usual propylon, but does seem to be correctly interpreted as a megaron. The pottery is not described in sufficient detail to allow comment on its nature (whether kylikes were present is not mentioned), but the hearth is reported as 'covered with ashes, charred wood and fragments of burnt bones of small animals (birds?)' (Valmin 1938: 174). More hearths stood in rooms nearby which may have formed a single complex with B85. B74 contained a hearth and a couple of pithoi (Valmin 1938: 176). Tripod cooking pots, blackened on the outside, were found near the hearth (Valmin 1938: 177). Another hearth was located in B82, which also contained a pithos with a stone cover (Valmin 1938: 177). In the so-called 'Sanctuary of the Double Axe' (B69) was found a great quantity of 'vases'. None of these are described in the text, but five were given museum numbers (nos. 11, 31, 32, 33, 54) and can be identified among those illustrated (Valmin 1938: plate 20). They turn out to be: a plainware jar (11), two decorated jars with multiple handles (32, 22), a jug (31), and a one-handled bowl (54). Valmin argued that the vases must be offerings, but this need not be, and given the evidence for cooking in the area it may have been that B69 was in reality a small pantry serving the megaron complex (Vermeule 1964: 348, n. 4, rightly dismisses Valmin's identification of the room as a shrine, noting it was 'only a closet').

While it is unfortunate that the data are insufficient to investigate the pottery and layout of the banqueting areas in detail, the mere fact that banqueting activities took place at Malthi (and Nichoria, although the megaron belongs to an earlier period) at all is of considerable importance. Banqueting was not confined to the palaces, as anticipated by the evidence for regional banqueting seen in Linear B tablets such as Vn 20 and possibly Cn 608. We noted in our discussion of those tablets that the provision of banqueting foodstuffs by the palaces may have functioned to enhance prestige and political control through demonstrations of generosity and piety. Such demonstrations may also have worked to foster and underpin social cohesion. This may tie into our discussion about social exclusion within the Palace of Nestor. An interesting feature of banqueting at Malthi is the way in which it *imitated* banqueting at Pylos, though on a reduced scale. The megaron has the main appropriate features, but it is very small and lacks a propylon. It expresses itself in the standard vocabulary, but it is a poorer expression. It may be relevant that it apparently was built in the LHIIIB period (though Valmin's stratigraphy is questionable, this does seem to be one of the later buildings on the site). Why was it built? There was already a large hall (A1) suitable for banqueting in the 'palace', whose foundations go back to the Middle Helladic. But Hall A1 is not a proper megaron, and it would have been difficult architecturally to make it one. For instance, it had one central column, not four, and the hearth was located at the back wall, not in the centre of the room. To make the hearth central, one would have had to displace the column – with implications for the integrity of the roof. In LHIIIB the older banqueting location was apparently no longer felt sufficient (or appropriate?) by the elites at Malthi. Could their incorporation into the hierarchical society focused on the palace have been responsible (for the expansion of Pylian political power, see Bennet 1995)? Did they aspire to become *bona fide* members of the system, for which participation in banqueting, with a 'proper' megaron, was apparently a criterion? The yellow-slipped kylikes might be relevant here. Again, we see attempts at imitation. Local red clay did not yield vessels of the 'right' colour to suit the Mycenaean standard. And the standard was evidently important. Were the vessels slipped to make them look more like 'proper' ware of the type associated with the palace elite (cf. Davis and Bennet 1999: 114–15)?

Banqueting and Hierarchy in Late Bronze Age Messenia

We may now suggest four levels of banqueting 'quality', three attested at Pylos and one at regional settlements such as Malthi and Nichoria. (It would be interesting to know whether there was a range *within* these smaller sites, but the data are not adequate to allow investigation.) The highest level is displayed in the heart of the palace itself, in the main megaron. A secondary level is seen in the more accessible, but still highly protected, Court 63 and the Southwestern Building. A third level is associated with the courtyard before the main block of the palace. And finally, we have a fourth level, at smaller towns in Messenia.

Each level represents a step in the hierarchy of a highly stratified society. Banqueting *is* seen at the lower levels; it simply is not as lavish. One is reminded of Wallace-Hadrill's analysis of houses at Pompeii. At Pompeii the up-and-coming members of the society chose to emulate the rich rather than to form or select an alternative means of expression. This might seem an obvious thing to do in one sense, but such social strategies are not imperative; alternatives do exist. Roman society was rigidly stratified, and all the indications are that Mycenaean society was also, although it had its own forms and methods of articulating this and of course the social institutions were radically different. Wallace-Hadrill speaks of Roman lower-class imitation of the houses of the rich in the following terms:

> This phenomenon is not simply one of mimicry ('aping one's betters'); the sheer insecurity of the freedman or the *novus homo* in the social structure drove him to affirm and legitimate his social standing by drawing on the cultural language of the dominant class. Since this language is designed to express the axes of differentiation which are central to the upper class, it is ineffective to express any other type of differentiation. There is not one language for the rich and one for the poor: but a common language in which the rich are eloquent and the poor dumb. (Wallace-Hadrill 1988: 58)

The same may have been true for the Late Bronze Age Messenians. It may be that all this exclusion, inclusion, hierarchy and imitation is linked to the gift-giving that we saw in the tablets. Regional banqueting was evidently not a threat to the socio-political elite: they positively encouraged it. But the matter is not a simple case of reciprocity, since the participants differed so entirely in wealth and social status. Nor is it simply a matter of generosity, piety and prestige as legitimizations of power (though that is doubtless part of the picture). The instances of contributions by lesser personages to palatial feasting are relevant here. Functionally, they appear similar: means of enhancing prestige and securing obligations. But the fact that these ends can be achieved through precisely the same mechanisms as used by the elite (though on a reduced scale) is of interest. It is not so in all societies. One can have situations where the very activity in itself is an elite marker. In the Mycenaean world, participation in banqueting was apparently generalized, but not everyone feasted with equal degrees of lavishness. It was not participation itself that served as a social mark (an elite badge), but rather differentiation was shown through degrees of finery and access to (thus social inclusion in) politically significant areas.

This may relate to the difficulty in explaining why 'town shrines' (e.g. Asine) look rather like 'palace shrines', with regard to the 'official cult' question (Hägg 1981). The palaces did not mark themselves through a different *sort* of religious practice: they followed the old and traditional, but with superior luxury (cf. Wright 1996: 294–95, 300). The ware, the location and presumably one's companions marked one's place in the hierarchy. We may suspect that the Mycenaean elites had not invented banqueting, but it may be that this was a type of religious or semi-religious activity which proved particularly amenable to their appropriation. This might help explain why palace shrines often seem to be surprisingly small and located in somewhat marginal areas (as for instance at Mycenae and Tiryns). Perhaps 'official' and 'popular' cult were not differentiated, but some aspects of 'popular' cult had gone out of vogue with the palaces, perhaps because they were less amenable to socio-political control and less relevant to a warrior elite (cf. Murray 1991, on the importance of commensal feasting to the formation of a warrior elite; Davis and Bennet 1999: esp. 107, on Mycenaean warfare). Therefore banqueting was adopted as the Mycenaean elite religious expression *par excellence*.

It is an effective mechanism of social power to convince everyone that the way in which you do things is the right way to do them and then to demonstrate that they cannot do them as well as yourself. The palatial gifts of wine and perhaps pigs for regional banqueting were not so much an expression of generosity as an expression of patronizing: 'You can't do as well as we, so we'll help you.' Wonderfully effective: it does two things at once – it both encourages perpetuation of the paradigm and imposes a sense of superiority and domination (on the part of the palace), with a concomitant sense of helplessness and inferiority on the part of the recipients. The fact that such gifts were accepted suggests that the Mycenaean populace had bought into the *status quo*.

To participate in banqueting was to accept the hierarchical inequality of the Mycenaean social world, to affirm and maintain it. If other forms of expression were available, they were not adopted. All members of society used the same forms of expression, and were thus drawn together through equal participation in Mycenaean religious life but, within this common expression, status and rank were articulated through excluding the majority from the more important venues and access to prestige artefacts. To participate in banqueting was thus to acquiesce in the inequalities inherent in the fabric of the Mycenaean social structure and to accept one's own place in it.

This was not apparently a society of rebels. The Mycenaean *koine*, which persisted with remarkably little change for some 130 years, is an extreme example of cultural homogeneity, and though many scholars have recently – rightly – stressed local differences, the similarities still call for explanation. People made choices, to be similar, rather than different, and those choices lay along the lines of an essential strand of Mycenaean society. Banqueting was an important arena through which those choices, that strand of the social fabric, were expressed. A Mycenaean feast was truly 'the bread of servitude' – a rather grim conclusion.

Acknowledgements

The text here is essentially that submitted as chapter six of my doctoral dissertation (Cambridge 2001). I am very grateful to my supervisors, John Killen and John Bennet, for their help and comments, and to my examiners, S. Voutsaki and C. Shelmerdine, for comments which I have tried to take into account in this published version. I am also grateful to R. Anderson for comments and general assistance, to T. Stevens for help with the illustrations, and to Valasia Isaakidou for her work on the printed versions of the illustrations. I am grateful to P. Halstead and J. Barrett for inviting me to attend the conference. I am grateful to Lisa French for first raising with me years ago the issue of pottery inclusions (e.g., kylix stems) eroding from mudbrick. Travel to the conference was funded by the University of Sheffield; the research was made possible by support from the British Academy (now AHRB), the Classics Faculty, Jesus and Fitzwilliam Colleges, Cambridge, and my family. The final draft was prepared at the British School at Athens, to which I am grateful for use of its outstanding facilities. All remaining faults in this work are my own.

Endnotes

1 In fact, the feast is depicted as taking place outside (McCallum 1987a: 132) and it is indeed likely that many Mycenaean feasts did take place out of doors (e.g. recently, Hägg 2001: 176). This is not at odds with our argument here because there is no reason that banqueting should not have taken place in different locations on different (and perhaps different types of) occasions. McCallum (1987a: 119–20), with justification, criticises some of Säflund's arguments for placing banquets in the megaron. However, while agreeing that some of his remarks would not meet with current approval, it is not necessary that we actually envisage a bull being led through the door of Room 6 (as McCallum objects) to contemplate banqueting taking place in the room. The festival programme which McCallum convincingly reconstructs need not have depicted a specific occasion, but an ideal connecting banqueting and the room itself with an ideology of power (McCallum 1987a: 140–42, 148–49).

2 The fragments all come from different vessels; in the cases where a single vessel was broken into fragments, these were counted as one, so we are not simply seeing many bits of the same vessel. The Blegen and Rawson (1966) data have been supplemented by Hofstra (2000: esp. 101–04; and a personal communication to the effect that there were more silver vessels represented in the megaron than reported by Blegen and Rawson). I am very grateful to S. Hofstra for permission to mention this here. I show four by way of a conservative representation, but the precise number is uncertain pending completion of Hofstra's study. It should also be noted that, although I use a kylix shape to illustrate the distribution, a few of the vessels were jugs. It would be useful in the future to produce an account which better distinguishes vessel types, but there are too many uncertainties to do this at present. Blegen and Rawson (1966: 350) also suggest that the king would have used metal vessels.

3 McDonald and Rapp (1972: 130–31, also 132–37) note 'it is now impossible to check typologically most of the material he [Valmin] recovered'. Hope Simpson and Dickinson (1979: 174) comment that Valmin's 'Adriatic ware' was probably MH-LH plain and coarse ware, while the many tiles were Byzantine. This calls into serious question the whole of Valmin's stratigraphic sequencing. See also McDonald and Hope Simpson 1969: 141; McDonald 1975: 111; Hope Simpson 1981: 138. Dickinson (1994: 60) cites P. Darcque's unpublished doctoral dissertation (*L'architecture domestique mycénien*, Paris, 1980: 32–33) for Malthi stratigraphy (*non vidi*).

Bibliography

Aura Jorro, F.
1985 *Diccionario Micénico, 1: Diccionario Griego-Español, Anejo 1*. Madrid: Consejo Superior de Investigaciones Científicas.
1993 *Diccionario Micénico, 2: Diccionario Griego-Español, Anejo 2*. Madrid: Consejo Superior de Investigaciones Científicas.

Bendall, L.
2003 A reconsideration of the Northeastern Building at Pylos: evidence for a Mycenaean redistributive center. *AJA* 107: 181–231.

Bennet, J.
1984 Text and context: levels of approach to the integration of archaeological and textual data in the Late Bronze Age Aegean. *Archaeological Review from Cambridge* 3, 2: 63–75.
1985 The structure of the Linear B administration at Knossos. *AJA* 89: 231–49.
1988 Approaches to the problem of combining Linear B textual data and archaeological data in the Late Bronze Age Aegean. In E.B. French and K.A. Wardle (eds.), *Problems in Greek Prehistory*: 509–18. Bristol: Bristol Classical Press.
1992 'Collectors' or 'owners'? An examination of their possible functions within the palatial economy of LM III Crete. In J.-P. Olivier (ed.), *Mykenaïka: Actes du IXe Colloque international sur les textes mycéniens et égéens* (BCH Supplement 25): 65–102. Athens, Paris: École française d' Athènes.
1995 Space through time: diachronic perspectives on the spatial organisation of the Pylian state. In R. Laffineur and W.-D. Niemeier (eds.), *Politeia: Society and State in the Aegean Bronze Age* (Aegaeum 12): 587–602. Liège: University of Liège.

Blegen, C.W. and M. Rawson
1966 *The Palace of Nestor at Pylos in Western Messenia. Volume I. Part 1: Text. Part 2: Illustrations.* Princeton: Princeton University Press.

Blegen, C.W., M. Rawson, W. Taylour and W.P. Donovan
1973 *The Palace of Nestor at Pylos in Western Messenia. Volume III.* Princeton: Princeton University Press.

Cameron, M.
1964 An addition to 'la parisienne'. *Kr Chr* 18: 38–53.

Carlier, P.
1992 Les collecteurs sont ils des fermiers? In J.-P. Olivier (ed.), *Mykenaïka: Actes du IXe Colloque international sur les textes mycéniens et égéens* (BCH Supplement 25): 159–66. Athens, Paris: École française d' Athènes.

Chadwick, J.
1975 Who was *e-ke-ra$_2$-wo*? In J. Bingen, G. Cambier and G. Nachtergael (eds.), *Le monde Grec: Pensée, littérature, histoire, documents: Hommages à Claire Préaux*: 450–53. Brussels: Éditions de l'Université de Bruxelles.
1976 *The Mycenaean World.* Cambridge: Cambridge University Press.
1988 The women of Pylos. In J.-P Olivier and T.G. Palaima (eds.), *Texts, Tablets and Scribes: Studies in Mycenaean Epigraphy Offered to Emmett L. Bennett, Jr.* (Minos Supplement 10): 43–96. Salamanca: University of Salamanca.

Cooper, F.A.
1998 Minnesota Pylos Project. In D.J. Blackman, Archaeology in Greece 1997–98. *AR* 44: 55–56.
1999 Minnesota Pylos Project. In D.J. Blackman, Archaeology in Greece 1998–99. *AR* 45: 47–51.

Dalton, G.
1977 Aboriginal economies in stateless societies. In T.K. Earle and J.E. Ericson (eds.), *Exchange Systems in Prehistory*: 191–212. New York: Academic Press.
Darcque, P.
1990 Pour l'abandon du terme 'mégaron'. In P. Darcque and R. Treuil (eds.), *L'habitat égéen préhistorique* (BCH Supplement 19): 21–32. Paris: École française d' Athènes.
Davis, J. (ed.)
1998 *Sandy Pylos. An Archaeological History from Nestor to Navarino*. Austin: University of Texas Press.
Davis, J. and J. Bennet
1999 Making Mycenaeans: warfare, territorial expansion, and representations of the other in the Pylian kingdom. In R. Laffineur (ed.), *Polemos: le contexte guerrier en égeé à l'âge du bronze* (Aegaeum 19): 105–20. Liège: University of Liège.
Dickinson, O.P.T.K.
1994 *The Aegean Bronze Age*. Cambridge: Cambridge University Press.
Douglas, M. (ed.)
1987 *Constructive Drinking. Perspectives on Drink from Anthropology*. Cambridge, Paris: Cambridge University Press, Editions de la Maison des Science de l'Homme.
Driessen, J.
1992 'Collector's Items'. Observations sur l'élite mycénienne de Cnossos. In J.-P. Olivier (ed.), *Mykenaïka: Actes du IXe Colloque international sur les textes mycéniens et égéens* (BCH Supplement 25): 197–214. Athens, Paris: École française d' Athènes.
Finley, M.I.
1981 Between slavery and freedom. In B.D. Shaw and R.P. Saller (eds.), *Economy and Society in Ancient Greece. Collected Essays of M.I. Finley*: 116–32. New York: Viking Press.
Flouda, G.
2000 Inscribed Pylian nodules: their use in the administration of the storerooms of the Pylian palace. *SMEA* 42(2): 213–45.
Godart, L.
1992 Les collecteurs dans le monde égéen. In J.-P. Olivier (ed.), *Mykenaïka: Actes du IXe Colloque international sur les textes mycéniens et égéens* (BCH Supplement 25): 257–84. Athens, Paris: École française d' Athènes.
1999 Les sacrifices d'animaux dans les textes mycéniens. In S. Deger-Jalkotzy, S. Hiller and O. Panagl (eds.), *Floreant Studia Mycenaea. Akten des X. Internationalen Mykenologischen Colloquiums in Saltzburg*: 249–56. Vienna: Verlag der Österreichischen Akademie der Wissenschaften.
Hägg, R.
1981 Official and popular cults in Mycenaean Greece. In R. Hägg and N. Marinatos (eds.), *Sanctuaries and Cults in the Aegean Bronze Age*: 35–40. Stockholm: Paul Åströms Förlag.
1985 Pictorial programmes in the Minoan palaces and villas? In P. Darcque and J.-C. Poursat (eds.), *L'Iconographie minoenne* (BCH Supplement 11): 209–17. Paris: École française d' Athènes.
1995 State and religion in Mycenaean Greece. In R. Laffineur and W.-D. Niemeier (eds.), *Politeia: Society and State in the Aegean Bronze Age* (Aegaeum 12): 387–91. Liège: University of Liège.
2001 Ritual action in Mycenaean religion. *BICS* 45: 175–76.
Hamilakis, Y.
1996 Wine, oil and the dialectics of power in Bronze Age Crete: a review of the evidence. *OJA* 15: 1–32.

Hofstra, S.U.
2000 *Small Things Considered: The Finds from LH IIIB Pylos in Context*. PhD dissertation, University of Texas at Austin.

Hollister, A.B.
1998 A garden at Pylos. *AJA* 102: 416.

Hope Simpson, R.
1981 *Mycenaean Greece*. New Jersey: Noyes Press.

Hope Simpson, R. and O.P.T.K. Dickinson
1979 *A Gazetteer of Aegean Civilisation in the Bronze Age, 1: the Mainland and Islands*. (SIMA 52). Göteborg: Paul Åströms Förlag.

Isaakidou, V., P. Halstead, J. Davis and S. Stocker
2002 Burnt animal sacrifice at the Mycenaean 'Palace of Nestor', Pylos. *Antiquity* 76: 86–92.

Immerwahr, S.A.
1990 *Aegean Painting in the Bronze Age*. University Park, London: Pennsylvania State University Press.

Killen, J.T.
1964 The wool industry of Crete in the Late Bronze Age. *BSA* 59: 1–15.
1976 Linear B *a-ko-ra-ja/-jo*. In A. Morpurgo Davies and W. Meid (eds.), *Papers in Greek, Italic, and Indo-European Linguistics Offered to L. R. Palmer*. Innsbruck: 117–25.
1979a The Linear B tablets and economic history: some problems. *BICS* 26: 133–34.
1979b The Knossos Ld (1) tablets. In E. Risch and H. Mühlestein (eds.), *Colloquium Mycenaeum: Actes du sixième colloque international sur les textes mycéniens et égéens:* 151–81. Neuchâtel: Université de Neuchâtel.
1983a Mycenaean possessive adjectives in *-e-jo*. *Transactions of the Philological Society* 1983: 66–99.
1983b PY An 1. *Minos* 18: 71–79.
1985 The Linear B tablets and the Mycenaean economy. In A. Morpurgo Davies and Y. Duhoux (eds.), *Linear B: a 1984 Survey*: 241–98. Louvain-le-Neuve: Louvain University Press.
1992 Observations on the Thebes sealings. In J.-P. Olivier (ed.), *Mykenaïka: Actes du IXe Colloque international sur les textes mycéniens et égéens* (BCH Supplement 25): 365–80. Athens, Paris: École française d' Athènes.
1993 *ke-u-po-da e-sa-re-u* and the exemptions of the Pylos Na tablets. *Minos* 27–28: 109–22.
1994 Thebes sealings, Knossos tablets, and Mycenaean state banquets. *BICS* 39: 67–84.
1995 Some further thoughts on 'collectors'. In R. Laffineur and W.-D. Niemeier (eds.), *Politeia: Society and State in the Aegean Bronze Age* (Aegaeum 12): 213–26. Liège: University of Liège.
1996 Thebes sealings and Knossos tablets. In F. De Miro, L. Godart and A. Sacconi (eds.), *Atti e Memorie del Secondo Congresso Internazionale di Micenologia*: 71–82. Rome: Gruppo Editoriale Internazionale.
1998 The Pylos Ta tablets revisited. *BCH* 122: 421–22.
1999 New readings and interpretations in the Pylos tablets. In S. Deger-Jalkotzy, S. Hiller and O. Panagl (eds.), *Floreant Studia Mycenaea. Akten des X. Internationalen Mykenologischen Colloquiums in Saltzburg*: 343–54. Vienna: Verlag der Österreichischen Akademie der Wissenschaften.
2000 Religion at Pylos: the evidence of the Fn tablets (abstract). *Journal of Prehistoric Religion* 14: 31–32.
2001a Some thoughts on *ta-ra-si-ja*. In S. Voutsaki and J.T. Killen (eds.), *Economy and Politics*

in the Mycenaean Palace States (Cambridge Philological Society, Supplementary Volume 27): 161–80. Cambridge: Cambridge Philological Society.

2001b Religion at Pylos: the evidence of the Fn tablets. In R. Laffineur and R. Hägg (eds.), *Potnia. Deities and Religion in the Aegean Bronze Age (Aegaeum* 22): 435–43. Liège: University of Liège.

Lang, M.

1969 *The Palace of Nestor at Pylos in Western Messenia. Volume II.* Princeton: Princeton University Press for University of Cincinnati.

Lejeune, M.

1971 Textes mycéniens relatif aux esclaves (1958). In *Mémoires de Philologie Mycénienne. Deuxième Série (1958–1963):* 63–83. Rome: Edizioni dell'Ateneo.

Lindgren, M.

1973 *The People of Pylos: Prosopographical and Methodological Studies in the Pylos Archives* (Boreas 3). Uppsala: Uppsala University.

Mars, G.

1987 Longshore drinking, economic security and union politics. In M. Douglas (ed.), *Constructive Drinking. Perspectives on Drink from Anthropology*: 91–101. Cambridge, Paris: Cambridge University Press, Editions de la Maison des Science de l'Homme.

Mauss, M.

1954 *The Gift. Forms and Functions of Exchange in Archaic Societies.* London: Cohen and West.

McCallum, L.R.

1987a *Decorative Program in the Mycenaean Palace of Pylos: The Megaron Frescoes.* PhD dissertation, University of Pennsylvania.

1987b Frescoes from the Throne Room at Pylos. *AJA* 91: 296.

McDonald, W.A.

1975 Excavations at Nichoria in Messenia: 1972–1973. *Hesperia* 44: 69–141.

McDonald, W.A. and R. Hope Simpson

1969 Further explorations in southwestern Peloponnese. *AJA* 73: 123–77.

McDonald, W.A. and G.R. Rapp (eds.)

1972 *The Minnesota Messenia Expedition: Reconstructing a Bronze Age Regional Environment.* Minneapolis: University of Minnesota Press.

McDonald, W.A. and Wilkie, N.C. (eds.)

1992 *Excavations at Nichoria in Southwest Greece, 2: the Bronze Age Occupation.* Minneapolis: University of Minnesota Press.

Murray, O.

1991 War and the symposium. In W.J. Slater (ed.), *Dining in a Classical Context:* 83–103. Ann Arbor: University of Michigan Press.

Nelson, M.C. and F.H. Cooper

1998 Minnesota archaeological researches at Pylos, 1996–1997 seasons. *AJA* 102: 399–400.

Olivier, J.-P.

2001 Les 'Collecteurs': leur distribution spatiale et temporelle. In S. Voutsaki and J.T. Killen (eds.), *Economy and Politics in the Mycenaean Palace States* (Cambridge Philological Society Supplementary Volume 27): 139–59. Cambridge: Cambridge Philological Society.

Palaima, T.G.

1989 Perspectives on the Pylos oxen tablets. In T.G. Palaima, C.W. Shelmerdine and P.Hr. Ilievski (eds.), *Studia Mycenaea (1988):* 85–124. Skopje: Macedonian Academy of Sciences and Arts.

1995 The nature of the Mycenaean wanax: non-Indo-European origins and priestly functions. In P. Rehak (ed.), *The Role of the Ruler in the Prehistoric Aegean* (Aegaeum 11): 119–41. Liège: Université de Liège.

Palmer, L.R.

1963 *The Interpretation of Mycenaean Greek Texts.* Oxford: Oxford University Press.

Palmer, R.

1994 *Wine in the Mycenaean Palace Economy* (Aegaeum 10). Liège: Université de Liège.

Piteros, C., J.-P. Olivier and J.L. Melena

1990 Les inscriptions en linéaire B des nodules de Thèbes (1982): la fouille, les documents, les possibilités d'interprétation. *BCH* 144: 103–84.

Rougemont, F

2001 Some thoughts on the identification of the 'collectors' in the Linear B tablets. In S. Voutsaki and J.T. Killen (eds.), *Economy and Politics in the Mycenaean Palace States* (Cambridge Philological Society Supplementary Volume 27): 129–38. Cambridge: Cambridge Philological Society.

Säflund, G.

1980 Sacrificial banquets in the 'Palace of Nestor'. *Opuscula Atheniensia* 13: 237–46.

Shelmerdine, C.W.

1985 *The Perfume Industry of Pylos* (SIMA Pocket-book 34). Göteborg: Paul Åströms Förlag.

1997 Review of Aegean prehistory 6: the palatial Bronze Age of the southern and central mainland. *AJA* 101: 537–85.

1998 The palace and its operations. In J. Davis (ed.), *Sandy Pylos. An Archaeological History from Nestor to Navarino:* 81–96. Austin: University of Texas Press.

1999 Administration in the Mycenaean palaces. Where's the chief? In M. Galaty and W. Parkinson (eds.), *Rethinking Mycenaean Palaces: New Interpretations of an Old Idea*: 19–24. Los Angeles: University of California at Los Angeles, Institute of Archaeology Press.

Speciale, M.-S.

1999 La tavoletta PY Ta 716 e i sacrifici di animali. In V. La Rosa, D. Palermo and L. Vagnetti (eds.), *Epi ponton plazomenoi: Simposio italiano di Studi Egei:* 291–97. Rome: Scuola Archeologica Italiana di Atene.

Tzedakis, Y. and H. Martlew (eds.)

1999 *Minoans and Mycenaeans: Flavours of their Times.* Athens: Greek Ministry of Culture, General Directorate of Antiquities.

Valmin, M.N.

1938 *The Swedish Messenia Expedition.* Lund: C.W.K. Gleerup.

Ventris, M.G.F. and J. Chadwick

1973 *Documents in Mycenaean Greek.* Second Edition. Cambridge: Cambridge University Press.

Vermeule, E.

1964 *Greece in the Bronze Age.* Chicago and London: University of Chicago Press.

Wallace-Hadrill, A.

1988 The social structure of the Roman house. *Papers of the British School at Rome* 56: 43–97.

Whitelaw, T.M.

2001 Reading between the tablets: assessing Mycenaean palatial involvement in ceramic produce and consumption. In S. Voutsaki and J.T. Killen (eds.), *Economy and Politics in the Mycenaean Palace States* (Cambridge Philological Society Supplementary Volume 27): 51–79. Cambridge: Cambridge Philological Society.

Wright, J.C.

1984 Changes in form and function of the palace at Pylos. In C.W. Shelmerdine and T.G. Palaima (eds.), *Pylos Comes Alive: Industry and Administration in a Mycenaean Palace*: 19–29. New York: Lincoln Center, Fordham University.

1996 Empty cups and empty jugs: the social role of wine in Minoan and Mycenaean societies. In P.E. McGovern, S.J. Fleming and S.H. Katz (eds.), *The Origins and History of Wine*: 287–309. Philadelphia: Gordon and Breach.

7

Faunal Evidence for Feasting: Burnt Offerings from the Palace of Nestor at Pylos

Paul Halstead and Valasia Isaakidou

Introduction

Bioarchaeological studies of consumption have tended to emphasize the biological or nutritional significance of food, while neglecting its cultural meaning (Dennell 1979; Hamilakis 1999). A salient characteristic of the human consumption of food (and drink) is that it is highly differentiated in time, space and social/cultural context. What one consumes (ingredients and methods of preparation), how one consumes it (associated material culture and etiquette) and who one consumes it with (kin, colleagues, strangers) are shaped by and help to define time (e.g., breakfast/dinner; Lent/Easter), place (e.g., home/work/eating out), personal identity (e.g., age, gender, ethnicity) and membership of social groups (e.g., family, club, class).

The differentiated nature of consumption is thus of great intrinsic interest, because of its pervasive role in defining the social world (e.g., Goody 1982; Crabtree 1990; Wright 1996). It is also, indirectly, of fundamental importance to the analysis of bioarchaeological evidence of consumption, whether this analysis is targeted at nutritional or cultural questions or both. If the consumption of food and drink is indeed highly variable in content, quantity, timing, location and social/cultural context, the discard of consumption debris will inevitably be discontinuous and uneven and also, in consequence, subject to very variable likelihood of survival and retrieval (e.g., Maltby 1985: 49–57; Hill 1994).

Bioarchaeologists have of course long recognized this discontinuity in patterns of deposition. Zooarchaeologists have often responded by excluding 'special deposits' (e.g., whole or part-skeletons) from any overall quantitative assessment of consumption (e.g., Grant 1991) – a practice which has been criticized for its implicit failure to recognize that all acts of consumption, and not just the most dramatic and infrequent rituals, are shaped by cultural rules (Hill 1994). On the other hand, insistence that all acts of consumption are laden with symbolism risks, in turn, losing sight of the fact that, in many human societies, qualitatively or quantitatively unusual acts of consumption serve to mark special occasions or places or gatherings or relationships (e.g., Goody 1982). The approach adopted here is pragmatic: temporal, spatial and contextual variation in the material remains of consumption should be explored for its intrinsic importance and as a necessary prelude to (and not as a demonstration of the futility of) any nutritional or 'economic' analysis.

Although much of the preceding discussion will be familiar to bioarchaeologists, especially zooarchaeologists, working in other geographical regions, the cultural dimension of consumption has largely been neglected in Aegean bioarchaeology (Hamilakis 1996; 1999). The methodological implications of the approach advocated here should thus be clarified before illustrating their application with an example drawn from Mycenaean Greece. Although the general thrust of what follows is arguably relevant to any bioarchaeological study of consumption, the remainder of this paper focuses on the zooarchaeological investigation of meat consumption.

Methodology

To explore cultural and social variability in consumption, a basic prerequisite is contextual or sub-contextual analysis of bioarchaeological remains in order to isolate, where possible, individual episodes of deposition and particular types of predepositional activity. This practice is relatively well established in archaeobotany (Jones 1991), perhaps because the preservation and retrieval of charred plant remains are so obviously discontinuous. Conversely, animal bones are perhaps more ubiquitous than charred plants in archaeological deposits and are usually far more easily visible during excavation, while individual stratigraphic units (e.g., a pit or hearth) are less likely to contain enough specimens for reliable interpretation. As a result, despite cogent arguments to the contrary by some practitioners (e.g., Maltby 1985: 57; O' Connor 1984), faunal remains are particularly likely to be grouped into site-period assemblages in order to achieve samples large enough for quantitative analysis (cf. Gamble 1978). On the other hand, in many cultures, meat (or meat of certain types) is not eaten on a daily basis but rather plays a prominent role in marking rare consumption events or those of wide social significance. Arguably, therefore, in the case of faunal remains, contextual analysis is both especially desirable and especially likely to be revealing of the differentiated nature of consumption.

The starting point for such contextual analysis is a group of bags or 'bone lots', each containing the osteological material from an individual stratigraphic unit or from an arbitrary excavation unit (e.g., a 'spit' within a deep pit fill or a grid-square within an extensive layer). The zooarchaeologist must explore three broadly sequential, if overlapping, stages in the formation of this material:

(1) the degree of depositional and post-depositional mixing and distortion to which each bone lot has been subjected;
(2) the range and nature of any pre-depositional human activities involved in the creation of each bone lot;
(3) the nature and context of any consumption episodes implied, directly or indirectly, by (2).

Approaches to investigating each of these stages are now discussed with particular emphasis on the potential role of faunal evidence, followed by some observations on the importance of collaboration between zooarchaeologist and excavator.

Exploring Depositional and Post-depositional Mixing and Distortion

After deposition in the ground, groups of discarded and buried animal bone may be contaminated or redeposited by subsequent human activity (including archaeological excavation) or non-human agencies (such as burrowing animals). Where deposits of very different composition or age become mixed, this may be apparent in the heterogeneous colour and texture of the osteological material, but the faunal analyst is often dependent for such insights on stratigraphic observations by the excavator or information from colleagues studying intrinsically more datable materials, such as pottery. Contaminating faunal material can occasionally be isolated with confidence (e.g., where a recent burrow has cut into an ancient deposit – von den Driesch and Boessneck 1990: 88), but bone lots subjected to post-depositional mixing are usually of little value for a detailed analysis of human consumption patterns.

Animal bone may also become mixed during deposition, if waste material from different activities is discarded in the same place, or is discarded separately but disturbed before burial by agencies such as scavengers or flowing water. Faunal material mixed during deposition may be recognizable as such, on the basis of heterogeneous taphonomic history (e.g., a combination of burnt and unburnt, canid-gnawed and rodent-gnawed, or weathered and unweathered specimens). Moreover, evidence of post-discard disturbance (e.g., traces of gnawing) or delayed burial (e.g., weathering of bone surfaces) increases the likelihood that bone from different places or times, and hence perhaps from different activities, has been mixed. Material of mixed depositional origin often makes up a large proportion of a faunal assemblage and may be of archaeological interest, not least because it must be considered in order to evaluate whether unmixed deposits are representative or atypical, in terms of taxonomic and anatomical composition and of human modification, of the assemblage as a whole. Unmixed and rapidly buried material, however, has greater potential for fine-grained investigation of pre-depositional human activity, because of the greater likelihood that it is the recognizable product of a restricted range of activities or limited number of episodes. For this reason, indications of a restricted range of predepositional activities (e.g., selective representation of body parts) or of a limited number of depositional episodes (e.g., a small 'minimum number of individuals' represented by many body parts) are also likely indirect indications that a bone lot is relatively unmixed. The occurrence of articulating or paired bones (e.g., Pappa *et al.* this volume [LN Makriyalos]; Jordan 1975: 33–34, 87–88 [FN Pevkakia]; Isaakidou 2004 [Neolithic and Bronze Age Knossos]) is a more direct indication that a particular bone lot has not undergone severe post-depositional disturbance.

As well as mixing deposits of different origins, depositional and post-depositional processes may also transform the composition of bone samples in other ways (e.g., Brain 1981; Payne 1972; 1985; Lyman 1994; Munson and Garniewicz 2003). For example, gnawing by dogs or partial retrieval by archaeologists may selectively destroy or lose certain body parts or bones from particular species and age categories. Equally, degradation of bone surfaces by weathering or root-etching may obscure traces of butchery. Because these variables play a central role in the ensuing analysis of consumption patterns, prior consideration of the distorting forces involved in the formation of archaeological bone samples is essential.

Exploring Pre-depositional Human Activities

If a bone group appears to represent rapid burial of material with a homogeneous discard history, the prospects are relatively good for identifying the pre-depositional activity or activities that gave rise to this material. Archaeological context may be illuminating: for example, bone splinters in human faeces are direct evidence of consumption. More commonly, however, the analysis of body part composition and butchery marks, in terms of 'utility' and anatomical position respectively, serves to determine which stages of carcass processing between slaughter and consumption may be represented osteologically (Binford 1978; 1981; O' Connor 1993). Dumps of horncores or foot bones, such as are often found on historical urban sites, are likely to be associated with horn working, hide preparation or glue making (e.g., MacGregor 1989; Serjeantson 1989); groups of mixed head and foot bones may be waste discarded at the site of slaughter and primary butchery; and bones from the trunk and upper limbs are more likely to represent waste products of food preparation or consumption. If bone surfaces are well enough preserved, cut marks from skinning, dismembering or filleting may support such inferences about carcass processing tentatively drawn from body part representation.

Industrial use of carcass parts, in hide or horn working, may be far removed in time and space from food consumption and may even involve animals (e.g., old work-horses) not eaten by humans. Unmixed deposits of bone discarded during the preparation or clearing up of meals clearly offer the most direct information on the nature and context of consumption. Bone discarded in the initial stages of butchery (skinning and dressing of the carcass), however, although likely to be further removed in time and space from food consumption, may still be informative. The segregation of primary butchery waste and food preparation/consumption debris is intrinsically interesting, whether it reflects a cultural perception that one type of carcass by-product is more polluting than another (e.g., Hodder 1982; Moore 1982) or a more practical distinction between the large-scale butchery of animals, for example in a meat market or temple precinct, and subsequent small-scale consumption of joints of meat in a domestic context. For example, at late LB Nemea Tsoungiza in southern Greece, a dump of tableware, associated with a terracotta figurine of a type found at other sites in shrines, appears to represent refuse from a religious ceremony involving drinking and perhaps eating (Wright 1994). Animal bones from the same deposit were dominated by primary butchery waste (heads and feet) of cattle, implying that the ceremony also involved slaughter and butchery but that the meaty parts of the carcasses were consumed, or at least discarded, elsewhere (Dabney *et al.* 2004).

Discrete dumps of primary butchery waste are also of interest because of their implications for the scale of carcass processing. In archaeozoological assemblages, the spatial segregation of different skeletal parts is often far more marked for large than for small animals. This tendency arguably reflects basic practical considerations of food preparation and consumption familiar in our own society: whereas a dressed hare or chicken may be placed in a cooking pot more or less whole, a sheep is likely to be butchered into 'joints' of single or contiguous bones, and beef is relatively likely to be filleted from the bone for cooking. The more intensively an animal is butchered for cooking and consumption, the more likely it is that different skeletal parts will be discarded at different times or in different places and so give rise to anatomically selective bone groups. For similar reasons of scale, the greater the number of animals butchered and the larger the quantity of meat available for consumption, the greater the likelihood that the discard of different body parts will be segregated. Thus modern Nunamiut hunters are more likely to discard high- and low-utility carcass parts at different locations after mass kills than single kills (Binford 1978: 61–62). Likewise, specialist butchers are thought to have been responsible for dumps of primary butchery waste, common on Roman and Medieval urban sites in NW Europe: initial carcass processing was on a large scale and so, on the one hand, generated enough refuse to require rapid disposal (Maltby 1985: 55) and, on the other hand, was divorced in time and/or space from consumption and its associated bone waste. Conversely, deposits containing mixed waste from all or most parts of the skeleton may be suggestive of small-scale, perhaps 'domestic', carcass processing in which primary butchery and consumption were relatively close in time and/or space. For example, at Nemea Tsoungiza, a bias towards butchery waste in the late LB settlement (including the 'shrine' dump discussed above) contrasts with a more balanced mixture of carcass parts in the assemblage from the preceding late MB-early LB settlement (Halstead in prep.). Thus, while unmixed bone debris from meals may be most *directly* related to the consumption of meat, both unmixed primary butchery waste and mixed debris from a range of carcass processing stages may be suggestive as to the scale of consumption. Because the segregation of different categories of bone refuse is also shaped by cultural perceptions of pollution, however, the evidence of anatomical composition should play only a heuristic role in exploring scale of consumption and should be integrated with estimates of the minimum numbers of animals and minimum quantities of meat involved (Charles and Halstead 2001).

Also of importance for any consideration of the scale of consumption is the timespan over which a deposit has formed. Stratigraphic detail may reveal that a layer has built up incrementally, while joining bone fragments and articulating or paired parts of the same skeleton may, like joins between potsherds, suggest that different excavation units were deposited in a single episode. In exceptional cases, associated bioarchaeological materials may even afford some indication of the number of seasons (e.g., Wright *et al.* 1989) or years (Schibler et al. 1997) over which deposition took place. Stratigraphic arguments for rapid deposition are central to the interpretation of a bone-rich pit at LN Makriyalos in N Greece in terms of feasting debris (Pappa *et al.*, this volume).

Exploring the Nature and Context of Consumption Episodes

Having established that the composition of a group of bones is likely to have been structured by a stage of carcass processing related more or less directly to food consumption, the nature and context of consumption may be clarified by further examination of any evidence for selective use of particular species, age/sex categories, body parts or methods of preparation. For example, in medieval England, deer are almost exclusively found in elite contexts (Grant 1988), while, at Archaic Miletus in Asia Minor, there are higher proportions of young cattle in the sanctuary site of Zeytin Tepe and of older cattle in the associated settlement site of Kalabak Tepe (Peters and von den Driesch 1992; Peters 1993). At Zeytin Tepe, the bones of sheep and goat are dominated by burnt specimens of femur and sacrum – a combination not readily accounted for in terms of either similar utility or anatomical proximity. At the sanctuary of Apollo at Kourion on Cyprus, where burnt specimens from the upper hind limb of sheep or goat again predominate, a preference for the right side of the body represents an even clearer example of a cultural choice which cannot be reduced to practical reasoning (Davis 1996: 182); similarly unambiguous examples of cultural choice include the selective deposition of right femurs from immature cattle in EIA graves at Kastri, Thasos (Halstead and Jones 1992), and of the same body part from young pigs in a LB house at Pevkakia, Thessaly (Jordan 1975: 88). In these examples, the context of consumption is defined very clearly by other lines of evidence and faunal remains serve to show how various animal-based categories were used to differentiate particular contexts.

In the faunal assemblage from the 'Workmen's Village' at LB Amarna in Egypt (Luff 1994), demographic and anatomical evidence suggests that pigs and goats were reared and seasonally slaughtered in this area, together with a few cattle, and that prime hind-limb joints of pigs and goats were exported from the site, while articulated limbs of cattle were introduced, perhaps from the 'Main City'. Careful analysis of butchery evidence indicates different methods of carcass processing for these three species. Most cattle were clumsily chopped up with cleavers, suggesting mass-processing under time stress – perhaps by temple butchers, while pigs, goats and a few cattle were carefully butchered with knives – arguably on a domestic scale by local residents. Moreover, while goats were often butchered when freshly killed, because joints were flexed to facilitate dismembering, many pigs and cattle seem to have been butchered after the joints had stiffened, suggesting the cutting up of cured meat. In this case, while architectural remains define the social context of consumption (the 'Workmen's Village'), faunal evidence sheds light on both the social context of food preparation and the temporal pattern of consumption. Contextual variation in consumption is thus well documented for later prehistory and early history, when sacrifice and feasting often took place in architecturally segregated areas devoted to ritual activity or elite-residence, but variation is also identifiable on earlier or less blatantly segregated sites by detailed contextual analysis of faunal remains.

The Importance of Information on Archaeological Context

The fundamental importance of information on archaeological context will have been self-evident in the discussion of the nature and context of consumption, but is no less true at the earlier stages of analysis. The exploration of depositional and post-depositional mixing demands fine stratigraphic distinctions of the excavator, together with detailed information on the presence of residual or intrusive artefactual material. Conversely, even with excellent conditions of preservation and retrieval, individual excavation units often contain too few bone fragments for pre-depositional activities to be recognizable in clear patterns of anatomical representation. Successful exploration of pre-depositional activities is thus greatly facilitated by guidance on which excavation units are arbitrary subdivisions of a single deposit and may potentially be combined at this stage of analysis. Moreover, because individual bone fragments tend to be less distinctive than decorated potsherds, the faunal analyst searching for 'joins' or 'matches' between bones, as a means of establishing the homogeneity of a deposit, is even more dependent than the ceramic specialist on prior guidance as to which excavation units should be 'strewed' at the same time. In sum, no matter how rigorous and imaginative the faunal analyst, the quality of zooarchaeological insights into consumption will rarely be better than the quality of information on archaeological context made available to the specialist – usually by the excavator.

Animal Remains from the 'Palace of Nestor' at Pylos

Excavations by Blegen at the Bronze Age site of Pylos (Blegen and Rawson 1966) yielded a large faunal assemblage. A brief report on part of this assemblage has been published by Nobis (1993). Subsequently, during reorganization of the Blegen stores, Stocker and Davis located a much larger body of material and, through careful study of Blegen's excavation notebooks, have clarified the date and provenance of individual bone lots (Stocker and Davis 2004). The entire assemblage is now under study by the authors of this chapter.

During a preliminary evaluation, prior to detailed study, Davis and Halstead noted that the assemblage comprised a mixture of species, body parts and taphonomic conditions, typical of settlement material derived from a variety of habitation contexts. Six groups of bone stood out from the rest of the assemblage because they consisted entirely, or almost entirely, of burnt bones representing selected parts of the skeleton of cattle and deer (probably red deer [*Cervus elaphus*], but fallow deer [*Dama dama*] cannot be ruled out because burning and fragmentation hinder precise identification). All six groups were dated to the final destruction of the 'Palace of Nestor, ca 1200 BC, or slightly earlier (Stocker and Davis 2004). These distinctive groups of material, which have obvious potential for contextual analysis, are subjected to the three stages of analysis outlined above.

Depositional and Post-depositional Mixing and Distortion

Each group of burnt bones represented the contents of a particular excavation context or was identified during excavation as a discrete concentration (i.e., the heap on the floor of archive Room 7 – Blegen and Rawson 1966: 93). The few unburnt bones in some groups included different body parts and different species from the burnt material (Table 7.1) and so seemed likely to represent slight contamination from neighbouring deposits, probably during excavation.

These groups of burnt bone were evidently recognized by the excavators as unusual, because they were stored separately from other osteological material, in some cases leading to loss of precise contextual information. The discovery of physical joins, however, with small fragments of burnt bone left in the more precisely labeled pottery lots, has now restored accurate information on provenance. This exercise showed that parts of the burnt bone deposit in area PNW were removed with contiguous stratigraphic units, strongly supporting the proposition that unburnt bone in this group represents contamination during excavation. Similar 'detective work' demonstrated joins between burnt bone from Room 7 and that from the neighbouring 'West Chasm', a later cut from the robbing of the west wall of Room 7 (see also Stocker and Davis 2004). On this basis, the bone from the West Chasm has been combined in Table 7.1 with that from Room 7; significantly, the unburnt bone from this combined group is all derived from the West Chasm and so probably results from mixing during wall robbing. The resulting five groups of burnt bone each exhibited a more or less distinctive degree and type of burning, suggesting derivation from single combustion episodes rather than the collection for disposal of bones burnt independently.

As well as making these deposits so distinctive, burning inevitably had an adverse effect on their preservation. Some bones were heavily calcined and

Table 7.1. Composition of burnt bone deposits from the Palace of Nestor, Pylos, in Minimum Number of Elements (MNE) and Minimum Number of Individuals (MNI)

	Cow		**(Red) Deer****		**Pig**		**Sheep(/goat)**	
	MNE	**MNI**	**MNE**	**MNI**	**MNE**	**MNI**	**MNE**	**MNI**
*Room 7 + West Chasm**								
Mandible	**24**	13			1	1	3	2
Humerus	1 + **24**	14	**1**	1	1	1	2	1
Radius					1	1	1	1
Ulna					1	1		
Metacarpal					1	1	1	1
Pelvis	**1**	1			2	1		
Femur	1 + **35**	19	**1**	1	1	1	1	1
Tibia					1	1		
Metatarsal					1	1	1	1
PNW								
Mandible	**6**	4			1	1		
Humerus	**10**	6	1	1				
Radius							2	1
Femur	**17**	10						
EBW								
Mandible	**6**	3						
Humerus	4 + **9**	7						
Femur	2 + **12**	10						
WK4								
Humerus	**7**	5						
Femur	**7**	5						
WK6								
Mandible	**2**	2						
Humerus	**1**	1						
Radius	**1**	1						
Ulna	**2**	1						
Femur	**1**	1						

Key: unburnt bones in plain text, **burnt bones highlighted in bold**

* all bones of pig and sheep(/goat) and all (possibly) unburnt bones of cow are from the West Chasm rather than Room 7

** the identification of the cervid humerus and femur in Room 7 + W Chasm to red deer rather than fallow deer is uncertain because of distortion by burning; the fragmentary humerus in PNW is also assigned to red(/fallow) deer with uncertainty distorted and most were very brittle and had been heavily fragmented. The degree of fragmentation made identification and quantification difficult, particularly of the less diagnostic shaft fragments, and rendered standard metrical analysis virtually impossible. On the other hand, unlike much of the assemblage from the 'Palace of Nestor', the burnt bones had not suffered damage from gnawing, nor had butchery marks on their surfaces been obscured by root-etching.

Pre-depositional Human Activities

The body parts represented in the four largest groups of burnt bone were mandible, humerus and femur (Table 7.1, Figure 7.1), and included both left- and right-sided specimens. Humerus and femur are both prime meat-bearing bones, but the mandible is often discarded at an early stage of butchery and so the presence of this body part suggests that slaughter is likely to have taken place in or near the palace. This combination of body parts is not easily explicable in terms of either the practicalities of carcass processing (e.g., Binford 1978; O' Connor 1993) or biases of preservation (Lyman 1994) and is perhaps most plausibly interpreted as a deliberate cultural statement, albeit of unclear meaning.

The pre-depositional treatment of these bone groups is otherwise fairly clear. Butchery marks (Isaakidou *et al.* 2002: 89 fig. 1) suggest that the carcass was

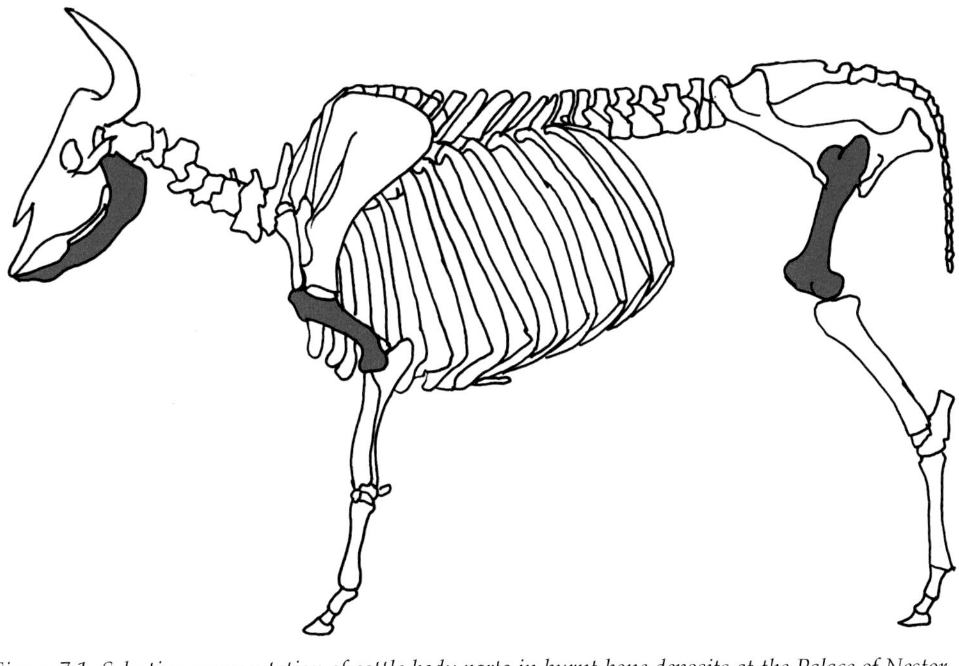

Figure 7.1. Selective representation of cattle body parts in burnt bone deposits at the Palace of Nestor, Pylos

dismembered and the bones filleted (i.e., stripped of meat). In contrast with much of the unburnt assemblage from the palace, however, there is no evidence that these bones were broken open to extract marrow: although the material was highly fragmented, many of these breaks were fresh and most or all of the old breaks appeared, from the nature of the fractures, to have occurred after burning. Thus it seems that whole, bare bones were burnt. Moreover, while the bones found on the floor of the archive Room 7 may have been burnt fortuitously in the final destruction of the palace, other groups predate the destruction and so are presumed to have been burnt deliberately. The extreme rarity of gnawing, which again contrasts sharply with the unburnt assemblage from the Palace, implies that these bones were either burnt soon after butchery or were stored until burning in a place inaccessible to dogs (perhaps the floor of Room 7). Finally, the burnt bone was buried with sufficient care that minimal mixing took place with other bone refuse (Isaakidou *et al.* 2002).

The treatment of this material is thus highly unusual and the apparently deliberate destruction of selected parts of the carcass with unexploited nutritional value (marrow) is consistent with burnt sacrifice of bones, similar to that described in the *Odyssey*. The bones in Room 7 were closely associated with a group of miniature *kylikes* or cups, suggesting that some form of libation or toasting ceremony accompanied the ritual of burnt sacrifice. The meat filletted from the burnt bones, and that from the remainder of the carcasses from which these bones were removed, would also have been available for human consumption (Isaakidou *et al.* 2002; Stocker and Davis 2004).

The Nature and Context of Consumption Episodes

The episodes of meat consumption implied by the burnt bone deposits seem likely to have been of very great cultural and social significance. First, the animals selected for burnt sacrifice were cattle and (red?) deer, both of which are far less common than pigs and sheep in the remaining unburnt assemblage. The consumption of these animals would thus have been a fairly unusual event. Moreover, although the burnt material is highly fragmented, the best preserved groups seem to be dominated by cattle bones from the upper end of the size range encountered at Pylos, suggesting that many of these animals were adult bulls or steers. Conversely, ongoing analysis of the unburnt assemblage suggests a higher proportion of small, perhaps adult female, cattle.

Secondly, each of the burnt bone groups includes parts of several animals (Table 7.1): WK6 – two cattle; WK4 – five cattle; EBW – ten cattle; PNW – ten cattle and perhaps one deer (though unburnt, the bone is a humerus – consistent with sacrificial deposition); and Room 7/West Chasm – nineteen cattle and one deer. Moreover, given the fragmentary state of the material, these numbers are very likely to be underestimates and, for methodological reasons, the probability of underestimation is greatest in the largest groups. It is possible that each animal was killed on a separate occasion and that the selected bones were then accumulated for burnt sacrifice at a later date, but this would have entailed the stock-piling of malodorous bones, perhaps within the palace, and would have divorced sacrifice from both slaughter and feasting. It seems both more plausible and more parsimonious to conclude that the burnt bone deposits resulted from single episodes of slaughter as well as of sacrifice. If several of the cattle were indeed adult males, then each slaughtering episode may have yielded between a few hundred kilograms and as much as two or more tons of meat – enough, by the rules of thumb of modern British receptions, to feed between several hundred and several thousand guests. Taken together, the quantity and type of meat represented by the burnt bone deposits suggests large-scale feasting on a special occasion, rather than everyday catering for palace residents.

Evidence that feasting played an important part in the life of the palaces comes from several different sources. Linear B texts describe the mobilization of animals (including fattened cattle and pigs) and other high-value (or, at any rate, scarce) foodstuffs, probably for banquets (Palaima 1989; Piteros *et al.* 1990; Killen 1994; 1999; Palmer 1994; Bendall this volume; Killen this volume), and also stock-taking of furniture, which may well have been used on such occasions (Killen 1998). Most of these texts do not specify venue and so arguably refer to feasts taking place at or in the vicinity of the palaces, but several specify the subordinate communities or persons responsible for supplying animals (Killen 1994). The texts are concerned with monitoring the *provisioning* of animals and so, perhaps not surprisingly, make no reference to burnt sacrifices. Individual texts usually record the mobilization of several species of animal, however, and list fewer cattle than are attested in the larger burnt bone deposits. For example, the Pylos text Un 2, which seems to deal with a feast to mark the initiation of the king, lists 32 sheep, four goats and seven pigs, but only one head of cattle, of unspecified age and sex (Killen 1994). The Pylos text Ua 25 impressively lists eight male and two female cattle, three fattened pigs and 67 sheep, but the nature of the occasion celebrated is not specified. It might reasonably be argued that the selection of cattle and deer bones for burnt sacrifice does not preclude the slaughter of sheep, goats and pigs on the same occasion. The number of cattle indicated by the burnt bone deposits, however, suggests feasts of a magnitude barely, if at all, represented in the surviving sample of Linear B texts dealing with this subject and, ostensibly, of far greater importance to the Pylos polity than the initiation of the king.

Fragments of wall painting from Pylos make clear the importance of feasting to palatial society, perhaps imply that feasting took place within the palace itself, and concur with the faunal evidence in according pride of place in such ceremonies to the slaughter of cattle (Wright 1996; Bennet and Davis 1999; Shelmerdine 1999). Stores of tableware in pantries around the palace suggest that large-scale drinking ceremonies or receptions took place in the palace (Wright 1996; Whitelaw 2001); vessels obviously intended for the serving or eating of food are far less well represented, but the scarcity of such provision may reflect the niceties of palatial dining etiquette or modern misconceptions of vessel function rather than the absence of feasting (cf. Bendall this volume). Finally, consideration of the architectural organization of the palace, and in particular the accessibility of the pantries, suggests that feasts may have taken place in the inner courtyard 63/88 (Shelmerdine 1999; Bennet and Davies 1999; Whitelaw 2001). If, as Whitelaw has argued, this courtyard was only large enough to accommodate a few hundred guests (Whitelaw 2001: 58), then the suggested quantities of meat represented by the burnt deposits would have been enough for guests to take considerable quantities of meat away with them or, alternatively, enough to feed further large groups of feasters in other parts of the palace (Bendall this volume).

Discussion

In the palatial societies of the Aegean Bronze Age, as in many other ethnographically or historically attested societies, feasting is widely regarded as a means of attracting or securing clients or allies, of promoting social solidarity and of legitimizing the authority of the sponsors (Moody 1987; Hamilakis 1996; Wright 1996; Bennet and Davis 1999; Whitelaw 2001: 58). The large scale of meat consumption inferred from the burnt bone deposits certainly implies mass participation in these events. Accepting Whitelaw's thoughtfully reasoned, ballpark population estimates of 3000 for Pylos town and 50,000 for the Pylos polity (Whitelaw 2001: 63–64), two tons of meat could plausibly have provided generous hospitality for all local residents or for household heads from the polity as a whole. While estimates of human population, available meat and allocation of meat per head are all subject to large margins of error, this exercise underlines the potential importance of such feasts in attracting supporters or promoting social solidarity.

Feasts on this scale will also surely have reinforced the prestige of the palace. The identity of the generous host was arguably made plain not only by the venue for these feasts, and the incorporation of the remains of burnt sacrifice within the palace building, but also by the particular animals consumed. Deer were presumably acquired by hunting, an activity prominent in Mycenaean art (Morris 1990; Bennet and Davis 1999; Hamilakis 2003), and so perhaps symbolized an elite contribution to the feasts (Bennet 2001: 35). Equally, adult male cattle would have been among the largest animals seen in the Pylian landscape and their slaughter would have been an act of very conspicuous consumption not lost on any witnesses. Textual evidence (Palaima 1989; Killen 1994) raises the further possibility, sadly not verifiable osteologically, that these cattle may have been of a colour distinctive enough to reveal the identity of their donor. It might even be argued that the reason why provision for feasts of this nature and scale is more or less unparalleled in the relevant Linear B texts is that these cattle were not mobilized, with written administrative monitoring, from dependent communities or high-ranking individuals elsewhere in the Pylos polity, but were drawn instead, with little or no bureaucratic involvement, from livestock controlled directly by the 'royal household'.

As well as promoting the prestige of the palace and securing the loyalty of followers, such feasts will also have served to naturalize the sharp inequalities within Mycenaean society. Whether the guests at these occasions were numbered in hundreds or thousands, those who participated will have been marked out as different from those who did not. The closed courtyard 63/88 will have underlined the divide between those admitted to this part of the palace and those who either did not participate in the feast or participated in a more public venue (Bendall this volume). Feasting will have offered further opportunities to mark a host of social distinctions: perhaps in the food or drink served (e.g., beef versus venison), in the serving vessels used (e.g., ceramic versus metal – cf. Bendall this volume), in the furniture provided (Killen 1998; the tables and chairs of the Ta texts are surely both too few and too elaborate to be destined for the same social group as the plain ceramic tableware in pantries 18–22), or in the garments worn (Killen 1994). In such contextual details, the structure of palatial society may have been laid bare at feasts.

The mass participation in feasting, implied by the burnt bones and pottery stores, also contrasts sharply with the restricted number of miniature *kylikes* found near the bone group in archive Room 7. The linking of these feasts with burnt sacrifice ensured divine participation and so served to legitimate the social distinctions and relationships encapsulated by such gatherings. If the spatial association of miniature kylikes and cattle bones in Room 7 is significant, then the social implications of such divine legitimation were further underscored by restricting participation in sacrifice to just a few individuals, probably of very high rank, and by eventual deposition of the burnt remains within the palace.

Conclusions

Animal bones from the Palace of Nestor at Pylos confirm existing archaeological and textual evidence for the importance of feasting in Mycenaean palatial society, while offering new insights into the location and scale of palatial feasting and its relationship with burnt sacrifice. Although impressive, the scale of meat consumption at Pylos may be dwarfed by that inferred for Late Neolithic Makriyalos, several millennia earlier (Pappa *et al.* this volume). On the other hand, the Makriyalos case displays evidence neither for the ritualized treatment of parts of the carcass nor for the elaborate ceremonial and material culture revealed at Pylos variously by iconographic, textual and artefactual evidence. At Pylos, this elaboration served to highlight social distinctions within palatial society, which were in turn legitimated by the burnt sacrifice of selected body parts. Conversely, the evidence from Makriyalos is at least consistent with relatively unrestricted participation in feasting. Arguably, the distinctive feature of Mycenaean palatial feasting is thus neither its existence nor its scale, but rather its cultural elaboration and highly inegalitarian social context.

In addition to its specific relevance to palatial feasting and sacrifice in Mycenaean Greece, the animal bone from Pylos has been discussed here as a means of exploring some more general issues in the zooarchaeological investigation of consumption. This discussion has sought to highlight the potential benefits to zooarchaeology of contextual analysis, which seeks to identify coherent depositional episodes and to understand the underlying carcass processing and consumption activities. The case study demonstrates clearly the extent to which such a contextual approach to faunal analysis is dependent at every stage on guidance from the excavator and other specialists. These principles are well established in the archaeology of some other regions, but have not yet become standard practice in the Aegean. The case study also supports the assertion, made at the start of this chapter, that, while consumption and discard may always be ritualized and symbolically laden, some acts of consumption are invested with greater ceremony and may leave more clearly structured remains than others; at Pylos, comparison between a handful of 'special deposits' and the less blatantly structured remainder of the assemblage proved highly illuminating.

Finally, although this chapter has focused on a rather exceptional and ostentatiously structured case of large-scale consumption, situated in an elite architectural context and attended by overt sacrificial ritual, it must be stressed that more mundane episodes of consumption also deserve investigation and would repay contextual analysis. For example, at the small Early Bronze Age village of Nemea Tsoungiza (Pullen in press), the composition of animal bone differed between pits, floors and fills in degree of fragmentation, frequency of canid gnawing and relative proportions of both taxa and age groups. While some of these differences may plausibly be attributed to more rapid burial and hence lower attrition of bone in pits, others suggest that large and small animals were discarded in different depositional contexts and so probably consumed in contrasting social contexts (Halstead in press).

Acknowledgements

We are indebted to Sharon Stocker and Jack Davis, for the opportunity to study the faunal material from Pylos; to INSTAP and the University of Cincinnati, for funding this work; and to the staff of Khora Museum, for facilitating its execution. Sharon Stocker and Jack Davis have also provided vital contextual information for the Pylos bones, based on study of the original excavation records and pottery lots. Our discussion of 'royal' herds was triggered, rather indirectly, by discussion with Michael Lane. Finally, in writing this chapter, we have benefitted from discussions with John Bennet, Lisa Bendall, Jack Davis, Glynis Jones, John Killen,

Astrid Lindenlauf, Sharon Stocker, Pat Thomas and Jim Wright; Astrid's name should also have featured prominently in the acknowledgements to Isaakidou *et al.* (2002) – profuse apologies!

Bibliography

Bennet, J.
2001 Agency and bureaucracy: thoughts on the nature and extent of administration in Bronze Age Pylos. In S. Voutsaki and J. Killen (eds.), *Economy and Politics in the Mycenaean Palace States* (Cambridge Philological Society Supplementary Volume 27): 25–37. Cambridge: Cambridge Philological Society.

Bennet, J. and J. Davis
1999 Making Mycenaeans: warfare, territorial expansion, and representations of the other in the Pylian kingdom. In R. Laffineur (ed.), *Polemos: le contexte guerrier en égeé à l'âge du bronze* (Aegaeum 19): 105–20. Liège: University of Liège.

Binford, L.R.
1978 *Nunamiut Ethnoarchaeology*. New York: Academic Press.
1981 *Bones: Ancient Men and Modern Myths*. New York: Academic Press.

Blegen, C.W. and M. Rawson
1966 *The Palace of Nestor at Pylos in Western Messenia, 1: the Buildings and their Contents*. Princeton: Princeton University Press.

Brain, C.K.
1981 *The Hunters or the Hunted?* Chicago: Chicago University Press.

Charles, M. and P. Halstead
2001 Biological resource exploitation: problems of theory and method. In D.R. Brothwell and A.M. Pollard (eds.), *Handbook of Archaeological Sciences*: 365–78. Chichester: Wiley.

Crabtree, P.
1990 Zooarchaeology and complex societies: some uses of faunal analysis for the study of trade, social status and ethnicity. In M. Schiffer (ed.), *Archaeological Method and Theory* 2: 171–81. Tucson: University of Arizona Press.

Dabney, M., P. Halstead and P. Thomas
2004 Mycenaean feasting on Tsoungiza at ancient Nemea. In J. Wright (ed.), The Mycenaean Feast. *Hesperia* 73, 2.

Davis, S.J.M.
1996 Animal sacrifices. In D. Buitron-Oliver, *The Sanctuary of Apollo Hylates at Kourion: Excavations in the Archaic Precinct* (SIMA 109): 181–2. Göteborg: Paul Åström.

Dennell, R.
1979 Prehistoric diet and nutrition: some food for thought. *World Archaeology* 11: 121–36.

von den Driesch, A. and J. Boessneck
1990 Die Tierreste von der mykenischen Burg Tiryns bei Nafplion/Peloponnes. In H.-J. Weisshaar, I. Weber-Hiden, A. von den Driesch, J. Boessneck, A. Rieger and W. Böser, *Tiryns Forschungen und Berichte* 11: 87–164. Mainz am Rhein: von Zabern.

Gamble, C.
1978 Optimising information from studies of faunal remains. In J. Cherry, C. Gamble and S. Shennan (eds.), *Sampling in Contemporary British Archaeology* (BAR British Series 50): 321–53. Oxford: British Archaeological Reports.

Goody, J.
1982 *Cooking, Cuisine and Class*. Cambridge: Cambridge University Press.
Grant, A.
1988 The animal resources. In G. Astill and A. Grant (eds.), *The Countryside of Medieval England*: 149–87. Oxford: Blackwell.
1991 Economic or symbolic? Animals and ritual behaviour. In P. Garwood, D. Jennings, R. Skeates and J. Toms (eds.), *Sacred and Profane*: 109–14. Oxford: Oxford University Committee for Archaeology.
Halstead, P.
in press Faunal remains from FN-EH Nemea Tsoungiza: husbandry, butchery, consumption and discard of animals. In D. Pullen, *Nemea Valley Archaeological Project I: The Early Bronze Age Village on Tsoungiza Hill*. Princeton: American School of Classical Studies at Athens.
Halstead, P. and G. Jones
1992 Animal bones and burial customs in Early Iron Age Thasos: the faunal remains from the cemeteries of Kastri settlement. In H. Koukouli-Khrisanthaki, *Proistoriki Thasos*: 753–55. Athens: Ministry of Culture.
Hamilakis, Y.
1996 Wine, oil and the dialectics of power in bronze age Crete: a review of the evidence. *OJA* 15: 1–32.
1999 Food technologies/technologies of the body: the social context of wine and oil production and consumption in bronze age Crete. *World Archaeology* 31: 38–54.
2003 The sacred geography of hunting: wild animals, social power and gender in early farming societies. In E. Kotjabopoulou, Y. Hamilakis, P. Halstead, C. Gamble and P. Elefanti (eds.), *Zooarchaeology in Greece: Recent Advances*: 239–47. London: British School at Athens.
Hill, J.D.
1994 Why we should not take the data from Iron Age settlements for granted: recent studies of intra-settlement patterning. In A.P. Fitzpatrick and E.L. Morris (eds.), *The Iron Age in Wessex: Recent Work*: 4–8. Salisbury: Trust for Wessex Archaeology.
Hodder, I.
1982 *The Present Past*. London: Batsford.
Isaakidou, V.
2004 *Bones from the Labyrinth: Faunal Evidence for the Management and Consumption of Animals at Neolithic and Bronze Age Knossos, Crete*. PhD dissertation, University College London.
Isaakidou, V., P. Halstead, J. Davis and S. Stocker
2002 Burnt animal sacrifice at the Mycenaean 'Palace of Nestor', Pylos. *Antiquity* 76: 86–92.
Jones, G.
1991 Numerical analysis in archaeobotany. In W. van Zeist, K. Wasylikowa and K. Behre (eds.), *Progress in Old World Palaeoethnobotany*: 63–80. Rotterdam: Balkema.
Jordan, B.
1975 *Tierknochenfunde aus der Magula Pevkakia in Thessalien*. Dissertation, University of Munich.
Killen, J.T.
1994 Thebes sealings, Knossos tablets and Mycenaean state banquets. *BICS* 1994: 67–84.
1998 The Pylos Ta tablets revisited. *BCH* 122: 421–22.
1999 Mycenaean *o-pa*. In S. Deger-Jalkotzy, S. Hiller, O. Panagl and G. Nightingale (eds.), *Floreant Studia Mycenaea: Akten des 10 Mykenologischen Kolloquiums 1995, Salzburg*: 325–41. Salzburg: Österreichische Akademie der Wissenschaften.

Luff, R.
1994 Butchery at the Workmen's Village (WV), Amarna, Egypt. In R. Luff and P. Rowley-Conwy (eds.), *Whither Environmental Archaeology?*: 158–70. Oxford: Oxbow Books.

Lyman, R.L.
1994 *Vertebrate Taphonomy*. Cambridge: Cambridge University Press.

MacGregor, A.
1989 Bone, antler and horn industries in the urban context. In D. Serjeantson and T. Waldron (eds.), *Diet and Crafts in Towns* (BAR British Series 199): 107–28. Oxford: British Archaeological Reports.

Maltby, M.
1985 Patterns in faunal assemblage variability. In G. Barker and C. Gamble (eds.), *Beyond Domestication in Prehistoric Europe*: 33–74. New York: Academic Press.

Moody, J.
1987 The Minoan palace as a prestige artefact. In R. Hägg and N. Marinatos (eds.), *The Function of the Minoan Palaces*: 235–41. Stockholm: Swedish Institute at Athens.

Moore, H.L.
1982 The interpretation of spatial patterning in settlement residues. In I. Hodder (ed.), *Symbolic and Structural Archaeology*: 74–79. Cambridge: Cambridge University Press.

Morris, C.E.
1990 In pursuit of the white tusked boar: aspects of hunting in Mycenaean society. In R. Hägg and G.C. Nordquist (eds.), *Celebrations of Death and Divinity in the Bronze Age Argolid*: 149–55. Stockholm: Swedish Institute at Athens.

Munson, P.J. and R.C. Garniewicz
2003 Age-mediated survivorship of ungulate mandibles and teeth in canid-ravaged faunal assemblages. *JAS* 30: 405–16.

Nobis, G.
1993 Archäozoologische Untersuchungen von Tierresten aus dem 'Palast des Nestor' bei Pylos in Messenien, SW-Peloponnes. *Zeitschrift für Archäologie* 27: 151–73.

O' Connor, T.
1984 *Selected Groups of Bones from Skeldergate and Walmgate* (The Archaeology of York 15,1). London: Council for British Archaeology.
1993 Process and terminology in mammal carcass reduction. *International Journal of Osteoarchaeology* 3: 63–67.

Palaima T.G.
1989 Perspectives on the Pylos oxen tablets: textual (and archaeological) evidence for the use and management of oxen in late bronze age Messenia (and Crete). In T.G. Palaima, C.W. Shelmerdine and P. Hr. Ilievski (eds.), *Studia Mycenaea 1988* (Ziva Antika Monograph 7): 85–124. Skopje: University of Texas at Austin, University of Skopje.

Palmer, R.
1994 *Wine in the Mycenaean Palace Economy* (Aegaeum 10). Liège: University of Liège.

Payne, S.
1972 Partial recovery and sample bias: the results of some sieving experiments. In E.S. Higgs (ed.), *Papers in Economic Prehistory*: 49–64. London: Cambridge University Press.
1985 Zoo-archaeology in Greece: a reader's guide. In N.C. Wilkie and W.D.E. Coulson (eds.), *Contributions to Aegean Archaeology: Studies in Honor of William A. McDonald*: 211–44. Minneapolis: University of Minnesota Press.

Peters, J.
1993 Archaic Milet: daily life and religious customs from an archaeozoological perspective. In H. Buitenhuis and A.T. Clason (eds.), *Archaeozoology of the Near East: Proceedings of*

the First International Symposium on the Archaeozoology of Southwest Asia and Adjacent Areas: 88–96. Leiden: W. Backhuys.

Peters, J. and A. von den Driesch
1992 Siedlungsabfall versus Opferreste: Essgewohnheiten im archaischen Milet. In V. von Graeve, Milet 1991. *Istanbuler Mitteilungen* 42: 117–25.

Piteros, C., J.-P. Olivier and J.L. Melena
1990 Les inscriptions en Linéaire B des nodules de Thèbes (1982): la fouille, les documents, les possibilités d' interpretation. *BCH* 114: 103–84.

Pullen, D.
in press *Nemea Valley Archaeological Project I: The Early Bronze Age Village on Tsoungiza Hill.* Princeton: American School of Classical Studies at Athens.

Schibler, J., S. Jacomet, H. Hüster-Plogmann and C. Brombacher
1997 Economic crash in the 37th and 36th centuries cal. BC in neolithic lake shore sites in Switzerland. *Anthropozoologica* 25–26: 553–70.

Serjeantson, D.
1989 Animal remains and the tanning trade. In D. Serjeantson and T. Waldron (eds.), *Diet and Crafts in Towns* (BAR British Series 199): 129–46. Oxford: British Archaeological Reports.

Shelmerdine, C.W.
1999 Administration in the Mycenaean palaces: where's the chief? In M.L. Galaty and W.A. Parkinson (eds.), *Rethinking Mycenaean Palaces*: 19–24. Los Angeles: Cotsen Institute of Archaeology, UCLA.

Stocker, S. and J. Davies
2004 Animal sacrifice, archives, and feasting at the Palace of Nestor. In J. Wright (ed.), The Mycenaean Feast. *Hesperia* 73, 2.

Whitelaw, T.
2001 Reading between the tablets: assessing Mycenaean palatial involvement in ceramic production and consumption. In S. Voutsaki and J. Killen (eds.), *Economy and Politics in the Mycenaean Palace States*. (Cambridge Philological Society Supplementary Volume 27): 51–79. Cambridge: Cambridge Philological Society.

Wright, H., R. Redding and S. Pollock
1989 Monitoring interannual variability: an example from the period of early state development in southwestern Iran. In P. Halstead and J. O' Shea (eds.), *Bad Year Economics*: 106–13. Cambridge: Cambridge University Press.

Wright, J.
1994 The spatial configuration of belief: the archaeology of mycenaean religion. In S.E. Alcock and R. Osborne (eds.), *Placing the Gods: Sanctuaries and Sacred Space in Ancient Greece*: 37–78. Oxford: Clarendon Press.
1996 Empty cups and empty jugs: the social role of wine in Minoan and Mycenaean societies. In P.E. McGovern, S.J. Fleming and S.H. Katz (eds.), *The Origins and History of Wine*: 287–309. Philadelphia: Gordon and Breach.

8

Wheat, Barley, Flour, Olives and Figs on Linear B Tablets

John Killen

This paper sets out and discusses the evidence for the distribution of the five foodstuffs wheat, barley, flour *vel sim.*, olives and figs in the Linear B records. Much of the relevant data has already been presented and analysed in Appendix 2 ('The ideograms **120* and **121* at Knossos, Pylos and Mycenae') of Ruth Palmer's excellent paper, 'Wheat and barley in Mycenaean society', published in 1992. Since that paper was written, however, there has been further discussion of the purpose of some of the groups of records on which the five commodities appear, and there have been new discoveries of relevant texts at Thebes, some of which have been published, though the publication of the remainder is still awaited (February 2002). It would not seem untimely therefore to present and discuss the evidence here afresh.

Prolegomena to a contextual analysis

In Tables 8.1–5, I list attestations of the five commodities under two separate headings: site (Knossos, Pylos, etc.) and context. For the purpose of the second analysis I have divided the relevant tablets into six categories:

- ration records,
- records of issues to participants in religious festivals,
- records of religious offerings,
- records of 'menus' for state-sponsored sacrificial banquets,
- 'harvest' records,
- 'benefit' or 'payment' records viz. texts which contain the term *o-no* (or its plural *o-na*), and which appear to refer to commodities given in exchange or compensation (see further Duhoux 1976: 130–34), and
- records of uncertain purpose.

For the suggestion that the Fn records at Pylos and the Av records at Thebes list issues of food to participants in religious festivals, see Killen (1999a: 218–19;

2001); R. Palmer has previously suggested a religious connexion for these texts, categorizing them as 'rations/handouts for middle level religious personnel' (Palmer 1992: 494). For identification of the Wu sealings at Thebes and Un 2, Un 138 at Pylos as records of animals and other commodities intended for consumption at state-sponsored sacrificial banquets, see Piteros *et al.* (1990; and further Killen 1994). For discussion of the records which show the term *a-ma* or the phrase *a-ma e-pi-ke-re*, and the suggestion that these are records of harvested crops now in store at the places named on the documents, see Killen (1994–1995).

Two other preliminary remarks should be made. First, though it seems certain that the ideograms **120* and **121* both denote major cereals, almost certainly wheat and barley, it is still uncertain which represents which. Though **120* is conventionally transcribed as GRA(NUM), wheat, and **121* as HORD(EUM), barley, and although P. Halstead has defended these identifications (Halstead 1995), R. Palmer has argued in favour of **120* being barley and **121* wheat (Palmer 1992). Given this uncertainty, I have referred to these commodities in Tables 8.1–2 simply as **120* and **121*, and will return towards the end of the paper to discuss their identity further. I also discuss below the identification of **129* as flour or the like.

Second, I have not listed in Table 8.1 references to **120* in contexts (like the E records at Pylos) where this is a measure of land capacity rather than a foodstuff. For the reader's convenience, however, I have set out the references to **120* in certain or possible land measurement contexts in an Appendix. I also omit instances of *NI* where this represents 'fig tree' rather than 'fig' (see KN(2) 841.2.3.5; Killen 1987: 174–77), and of OLIV where this indicates 'olive tree' rather than 'olive' (see KN(2) 841.6; Killen 1987: 174–77) or is used as a measure of land capacity (see TH Ft 140; Killen 1999a: 217).

Tabulation of the data reveals certain patterns in the contextual distribution of attestations of the five commodities.

Contextual distribution of **120, *121* (Cereals) (Tables 8.1–2)

**120, *121* appear in five of the six categories of record described above: ration records, records of 'festival issues', records of religious offerings, records of banquet 'menus', 'harvest' records. Within each of these types of record, various distributional patterns can be observed.

Cereals on ration records

All ration records involve **120* (GRA), *except* three records involving rations for *men*: KN Am(2) 819, PY An 7, and PY An 128 (**1̣2̣1̣* on *verso*, but **120* on *recto*).

Recipients of **120* on ration records are all women, *except* on PY An 128 (**120* on *recto*, but **1̣2̣1̣* on *verso*), PY Fg 374 (recipient is unguent-boiler *ko-ka-ro*), and PY Au 658 (also Eu 654, 655?).

Cereals on 'festival issues' records

Cereals on 'festival issues' records are always **121* (HORD), sometimes plus OLIV or *NI* or F̣ẠṚ, *except* on TH Av 100.2.3.

Cereals on records of banquet 'menus'

Cereals on records of banquet 'menus' are usually, perhaps invariably, **121* (HORD). The only possible exception is on PY Ua 434, a two-line tablet listing]* *1̣2̣0̣* 80[(the reading is reasonably secure) and]CYP+*O* 13[. That this has connexions with the banquet 'menu' records like Un 2, Un 47 and Un 138 is suggested by its hand and stylus (S138 H42), which it shares with Un 47, Un 138. Note, however, the regular occurrence of **120* and CYP+*O* in 'harvest' records at Knossos; is this also a 'harvest' record, and did therefore the interests of this scribe extend beyond banquet 'menus' to records of food more generally?

Cereals on records of religious offerings

Cereals on records of religious offerings are always **121* (HORD), *except* on KN E 842 and PY Un 718.

KN E 842 clearly has religious connexions: note *te-o-i* 'to the gods' and *di-wo* 'of Zeus' on l.1, and the references to *me-na*, probably / *Mēnā(i)*/ 'to the moon', and]*pe-ro-*$_2$*-ṇẹ*[, possibly *u*]*pe-ro-*$_2$*-ṇẹ*['to the sun' (on both terms, see Killen in press), in the recipient position in ll.2,3, the first certainly, the second probably followed by **120*. Other entries on the record, however ( ]ỌḶỊṾ 24 T4 on l.2, *ki-da-ro *120* 2̣1[on l.3), involve much larger amounts than are normally listed on 'religious offerings' records, and may have a different purpose.

On PY Un 718, **120* is part of *do-so-mo*, '[assessment(s) for] contributions', to Poseidon. Is it significant that these contributions, though likely to have been used for a sacrifice to the god, have evidently been made in respect of some of the plots of land, measured in **120*, which are recorded on Er 312, 880? (Compare the *do-so-mo* to Poseidon, again of **120*, recorded on the Es tablets other than 650, which have evidently been made in respect of the land measured in **120* on Es 650).

Cereals on 'harvest' records

Cereals on 'harvest' records are always **120* (GRA).

*Table 8.1. Linear B attestations of commodity *120. Notes continued over the page*

Site	Category of record	List of records
Knossos	Rations	*Ai(2)* 750, 751, 752, 5543, Ai(2) 7026, Ai 9503(?), 9504(?), 9505(?), 9514(?); E 777, 847, 7350, 9178[i]
	Religious offerings	E 842
	'Harvests'[ii]	E(2) 668(?), 669(?), 670(?), E 843(??), 848, 850, 1035, 4466(??), 5000(??), 7338(??), 7340(?); F(1) 157(?), F(2) 844(?), 845, 851, 852, 853(?), 854(?), 5001(?),[iii] 7050(?)
	uncertain	All other texts, except for those shown in Appendix as certain or possible records of land measurement
Pylos	Rations	Ab series; An 128 *recto*; Fg 253, 368, 374, 828
	Religious offerings	Es series (except 650)(?);[iv] Un 718[v]
	Banquet 'menus'	Ua 434(??)
	'Harvests'	Ua 434(??)
	'Benefits'	Ua 158; Un 1332
	uncertain	Un 443, 1319, 1321, 1426
Mycenae	Rations	Au 658; Eu 654, 655
	uncertain	Ue 652[vi]
Thebes	Rations/festival issues	Av 100[vii]

Notes

i Palmer (1992: 493) includes E(2) 668, 669, 670 under 'rations and handouts'. While, however, the fact that they are in hand 103 suggests that the **120* and OLIV these tablets record will in due course be issued as rations to women in the textile industry (a great many of the records of which are by this writer), and while they do not contain the term *a-ma*, 'harvest', they have a number of characteristics in common with the 'harvest' records (they contain toponymic references; they list **120*, sometimes with OLIV; OLIV on 669 is subdivided as OLIV+*A*, OLIV+*TI*; and large quantities of both commodities are recorded), and they are hence most plausibly understood either as 'harvest' records proper viz., if I am correct, records of crops now in store and available for distribution or, alternatively, as records of taxation assessments for such crops.

ii These records either show the term *a-ma*, which may be accompanied by *e-pi-ke-re*, or have one or more characteristics in common with the *a-ma* (*e-pi-ke-re*) texts, which (a) contain a place reference, (b) record very large quantities of agricultural produce, regularly **120*, OLIV (often subdivided as *OLIV+A*, *OLIV+TI*) and less regularly CYP/PYC+*O*, CYP+*KU*, cyperus and (c) are often 2-line records. Tablets showing *a-ma* (*e-pi-ke-re*) are classed as certain 'harvest' records; others are shown as less certainly belonging to this category (?, ??). On E(1) 668, 669, 670, see n.i above; on F(2) 854, see Appendix n.18.

iii Besides the apparent 'harvest' record on l.2 ( ]80 OLIV+*A* 3̣0[ ), this tablet contains an entry on l.4, involving much smaller quantities, which may have a different function (is it a note of an issue of some kind??). See further below: *Contextual distribution of *30 (NI): figs and *122* (OLIV): *olives*.

iv It is unclear whether the *do-so-mo*, */dosmoi/*, '[assessments for] contributions', of **120* recorded on these tablets (which are clearly payable in respect of the landholdings, measured in terms of **120*, which are recorded on Es 650) relate to offerings to Poseidon in the same sense as e.g. the offerings to the gods recorded on the Fr series at Pylos or the Fs series at Knossos, or to what are effectively taxes, payable (to priests?) in respect of sacred land.

v Though the commodities listed on this record are again *dosmoi* to Poseidon (payable in respect of land on his estate), their nature, and the order in which they are listed, strongly suggests that they were used in (sacrificial) offerings to the god. See further Burkert (1977: 87). N.B. There is nothing to indicate that the small numbers of animals and amounts of other foodstuffs, etc. listed on this record were consumed at a large, state-sponsored banquet. Contrast the very much larger numbers and amounts of other foodstuffs listed on the certain banquet 'menu' records like Un 2, and the differences between this and the banquet 'menu' records in terms of the types of commodities both record. Neither of the commodities *AREPA*, 'unguent', or *ko-wo*, 'fleece', on Un 718 recurs on any of the banquet 'menu' texts; *AREPA*, however, is found on Un 6, 853, which likewise deal with offerings to Poseidon, again it would seem likely in respect of some of the land at *sa-ra-pe-da* recorded on Er 312, 880 (see Killen 1999b: 350–53); which appear to have lacked references to the large amounts of **121* recorded on Un 2, 47 and 138; and where some of the pigs are designated as *sus+KA*, probably *kaproi*, 'uncastrated males, boars', a variety not found on Un 2, 138, which instead list *sus+SI*, probably *sialoi*, 'fat(tened) pigs'.

vi Possibly a record of crops in store.

vii or the suggestion that the Av tablets in hand 304 at Thebes are concerned, not with religious offerings like e.g. the Fq records there, but with rations given to persons who have an involvement with cult activity, and may therefore be comparable with the Fn 'festival issue' records at Pylos, see Killen (1999a: 218-19; 2001: 441–43). All the recipients on these records appear to be human; Av 100 records **120*, not **121* like the Fq tablets; and the amounts recorded are considerably larger than most on the Fq records. It is also in keeping with this interpretation that Av 100 and Av 101 contain the term *si-to*, */sītos/*, 'grain', which only appears at other sites in rationing contexts (see KN Am(2) 819; MY Au 658); that Av records the issue of **120* to female recipients, and **120* is the cereal invariably issued to dependent women on rationing records; and that Av 104 almost certainly contains *si-to-ko-wo*, a term which recurs in connexion with dependent women and children at Pylos, and is here plausibly interpreted as */sītokhowoi/*, viz. 'pourers, measurers of grain' (cf. the classical term *sītometrēs*, 'measurer of grain' and *Od.* 2.377–380: *grēus… en de hoi alphita kheuen eurrapheessi doroisi*, 'and the old woman poured barley-groats into well-sewn skins for him'). Godart and Sacconi (1998: 900–05) argue that *si-to* on Av 100, 101 is not *sītos* but a divine name *Sītō* (they compare the theonym *si-to-po-ti-ni-ja* at Mycenae) and that the *si-to-ko-wo* on Av 104 are 'ceux qui s' occupent de' S., 'les desservants de sanctuaire de' S. (On this interpretation the second element of the compound would involve the root of Gr. *koeō*, 'I watch over', not *kheō*, 'I pour'.) While, however, they may be right in suggesting that *si-to* on TH Ft 219, 220 is the name of a divinity, their proposal about *si-to*, *si-to-ko-wo* on the Av tablets is not convincing. Given the other indications of a rationing context for these records, it seems far more likely that e.g. *po-te-we si-to ku-na-ki-si *120*, etc. on Av 100 is 'to *Po-te-u* (a man's name probably also attested on TH Ug 41): grain for the women (or for the huntresses)' than that it records an offering of **120* to three recipients named in asyndeton, as Godart and Sacconi suggest: the human *Po-te-u*, *the divine Sītō* and the human women or huntresses.

Table 8.2. Linear B attestations of commodity *121. *Notes continued over the page*

Site	Category of record	List of records
Knossos	Rations	Am(2) 819
	Religious offerings	Fs series; F(1) 51
	uncertain	F(1) 193, F(3) 741, 8242
Pylos	Rations	An 7,[i] 128 *verso*(?)[ii]
	Festival issues	Fn series
	Banquet 'menus'	Ua 9(?), 25(?);[iii] Un 2, 47, 138
	uncertain	Fa 1195; Un 443, 1177(?)
Mycenae	Religious offerings	Fu 711[iv]

Notes

i Though Melena (1996–97: 171) has suggested that this record should be reclassified as Fn, following the join with Fn 1427, I prefer to retain the An prefix, since it is plainly concerned with secular workers (like An 128, which also contains ration figures).

ii For a very good discussion of this entry, and the plausible suggestion (assuming that HORD is the correct reading of the ideogram) that it records the same total amount, expressed in **121*, as is shown in the **120* and *NI*(?) entries on the *recto*, see Palmer (1992: 483).

iii Both these records are in the same hand and stylus (S138 H42) as the banquet 'menu' records Un 47, 138, and record similar commodities, and are likely therefore to have banquet connexions. Note, however, that Un 9 records larger amounts of **121* and OLIV than are recorded on any of Un 2, 47, 138, and that Ua 25 lists larger numbers of animals than are found on any of those texts. Are these perhaps notes of amounts of foodstuffs consumed, or available for use, at more than one banquet; and is this why neither contains a heading mentioning the location or occasion of a banquet?

iv For identification of this as a record of religious offerings see Palmer (1983: 283–87) and Godart and Sacconi (1996: 110-11).

Contextual distribution of **129* (FAR): 'flour' (Table 8.3)

FAR only appears on the following types of record:

- records of religious offerings (KN Fs series; PY Un 718, 853; MY Fu 711; TH Fq series),
- records of festival issues (PY Fn 187??),
- records of banquet 'menus' (PY Un 2).

It is likely that the banquet whose 'menu' is recorded on PY Un 2 has at least some religious component: its location is *pa-ki-ja-ne*, clearly the scene of much religious activity (though it is also mentioned in secular contexts); and if *mu-jo-me-no e-pi wa-na-ka-te* in the heading of the text is 'upon the initiation of the king into the mysteries', it will presumably have marked a religious ceremony. A religious component may well have characterized state-sponsored banquets in general in the Mycenaean world, and this will certainly have been the case if the killing of animals in the Mycenaean world followed the general pattern 'throughout antiquity' that 'there was an intimate connection between butchery and sacrifice, even for meat that was sold commercially in shops' (Robert and Robert 1970: 438, quoted in Bruit Zaidman and Schmitt Pantel 1992: 33); see, too, Appendix n.i below for the suggestion that *ka-pa* before OLIV on Un 138.5 is '(for the) offerings dish'. It would therefore seem probable that FAR only occurs in *religious* contexts on the records (Palmer 1983: 286; Killen 1999a: 218).

There is a noticeable tendency for FAR to appear on the same records as **121* (HORD). See the KN Fs series, PY Fn 187, Un 2, MY Fu 711; and note Aravantinos (1999: 71) on the Fq series at Thebes: 'Most refer to barley (sc. **121*) and to the product FAR...'. Note, too, that on PY Un 47.4 'HORD [is] over erasure, possibly [[F̣ẠṚ]]' (Bennett and Olivier 1973: 248). The pattern is not fully consistent, however: on PY Un 718 (*do-so-mo* to Poseidon in respect of land on Er tablets) FAR appears in conjunction with **120*, not **121*. (For the exceptional nature of the appearance of **120* on this text if – as seems certain – it is a record of religious offerings, see above, *Cereals on records of religious offerings*.)

Table 8.3. Linear B attestations of commodity *129 *(FAR): flour* vel sim.

Site	Category of record	List of records
Knossos	Religious offerings	Fs series
Pylos	Festival issues	Fn 187(??)[i]
	Religious offerings	Un 718, 853
	Banquet 'menus'	Un 2, 47(??)[ii]
Mycenae	Religious offerings	Fu 711
Thebes	Religious offerings	Fq series[iii]

Notes
i The reading of F̣ẠṚ here (see l.3) is far from certain.
ii See the *apparatus criticus* in Bennett and Olivier (1973: 248) on Un 47.4: 'HORD over erasure, possibly [[F̣ẠṚ]]'.
iii On the appearance of F̣ẠṚ in the Fq series, see Aravantinos (1999: 71).

Contextual distribution of **30* (*NI*): figs and **122* (OLIV): olives (Tables 8.4–5)

NI never occurs on 'harvest' records which contain *a-ma* (*e-pi-ke-re*) or on E(2) tablets. OLIV (often sub-divided as OLIV+*A*, OLIV+*TI*) is common on both. *NI* occurs on F(2) 5001 only in a subsidiary entry (l.4) listing relatively small quantities; its only other possible appearances in 'harvest' contexts are on F(2) 7343 (a two-line record, as many certain or probable 'harvest' texts are, which – again like the 'harvest' records – lists other commodities besides *NI*) and on F(2) 7346 (a single-line record listing the very large quantity of *NI* 61[2̣][ ).

NI always accompanies **120* (GRA) on Pylos Ab ration tablets (H21); it also does on PY Fg 253 (H1: totalling tablet for Ab rations), 368 (H1), 374 (H1), all of which were found in Room 8, the last two in the area of the Ab tablets. Both *NI* and OLIV sometimes accompany **121* (HORD) on PY Fn festival issue records (*NI* only found on Fn 187). OLIV only certainly occurs in a rations context on PY An 7, where it occurs in some entries only, possibly accompanying **121* (see below). On KN Ap 5077, the sign is both doubtful and erased.

It is usually assumed that the Ab tablets record a standard monthly allocation of rations viz. that the women and children in question always received both **120* (GRA) and *NI*. But is this certain? No figs are found on the KN Ai records of rations for women and children[1] or on Eu 654 at Mycenae, where the two men(?) listed on ll.2,3 receive rations of T2 and T1.5 of **120* respectively; and while Fg 368 at Pylos records an issue of **120* 5̣ *NI* 5 to *ke-sa-da-ra*, Fg 828, at the same site but by a different scribe (H1, not H21), lists an issue of **120* 5 alone to this individual. Is it possible that the Ab tablets relate to an *exceptional* month in which a supplementary issue of figs was made in addition to the standard issue of **120*? Note that in the ancient Near East, while barley rations were issued to

*Table 8.4. Linear B attestations of commodity *30 (NI): figs. Notes continued over the page.*

Site	Category of record	List of records
Knossos	Religious offerings	Fs series; F(2) 866(?)[i]
	Banquet 'menus'	Uc 161(?)
	'Harvests'	F(2) 5001(??), 7343(?), 7346(?)
Pylos	Rations	Ab series; Fg 253, 368, 374
	Festival issues	Fn 187
	Banquet 'menus'	Un 2, 47
	'Benefits'	An 35; Ua 158; Un 1322
	uncertain	Un 1426
Mycenae	Religious offerings	Fu 711
	Banquet 'menus'	Ue 661(?)[ii]
	uncertain	Ue 611, 652(?)
Tiryns	uncertain	Uh 12

Notes

i Though the amount recorded here (10 units) is much larger than normal in records of religious offerings, the allative *di-ka-ta-de*, 'to Dikte', is found elsewhere only in 'offerings' contexts and suggests a religious connexion for the text. Cf. KN G 7509, which probably records 6(+?) units of PYC+*O* going to the same destination.

ii The initial *jo-po-ro-te-ke*, evidently */hō protheke/*, suggests a banqueting context (Killen 1992: 375-76); it is not clear, however, whether the meal concerned is a special, sacrificial banquet like that whose 'menu' is recorded on e.g. PY Un 2 or a more ordinary, domestic one.

*Table 8.5. Linear B attestations of commodity *122 (OLIV): olives*

Site	Category of record	List of records
Knossos	Rations	Ap 5077(?)
	Religious offerings	E 842(?)[i]
	Banquet 'menus'	Uc 161(?)
	'Harvests'	E(1) 669(?), 670(?); F(2) 844(?), 845, 851, 852, 853(?), 854(?),
	uncertain	F 7337(?), F(2) 7357, F(1) 8437
Pylos	Rations	An 7
	Festival issues	Fn 41, 79, 918, 965, 975
	Banquet 'menus'	Ua 9(?), 25(??);[ii] Un 2, 138
Mycenae	uncertain	Ue 611, 652
Thebes	Religious offerings	Ft series (other than Ft 140 and perhaps Ft 182)[iii]

Notes

i Although this record certainly has religious connexions, the amount in the OLIV entry (24 T4) (and seemingly in the *ki-da-ro *120* entry on l.3) is very much larger than those normally found in 'offerings' contexts. See further above: *Cereals on records of religious offerings*.

ii For OLIV in the text written on this tablet before the present one, see Bennett and Olivier (1973: 238).

iii On Ft 140, see above: *Prolegomena to a contextual analysis*; on Ft 182, which lists the large quantity of 'at least 76 units', see Aravantinos (1999: 71).

fully dependent workers each month, all the year round, other foodstuffs (fish, dairy products, vegetables, fruits and beverages) were only 'distributed over and above the standard rations during festivals and on other special occasions' (Gelb 1965: 238). It is also worth noting in this connexion that, whereas OLIV appears in some entries on PY An 7, in one case at least perhaps additionally to **121* (if]2 OLIV T2 on l.1 is restored as **121* T]2 OLIV T2), other entries on this record seem clearly to have involved rations of **121* alone: see ll.3, 4, 11. This is exactly in accord with the evidence of Am(2) 819 at Knossos, where a group of men (as the recipients on An 7 are) receive a ration (a) of **121* alone and (b) at exactly the same rate as the men on An 7 viz. Z3 per person per day.[2] And note, finally, that the PY Fn tablets, where some but by no means all entries show *NI* or OLIV accompanying **121* (HORD) issues, are likely to have been records of special distributions made during religious festivals, which, as we have just seen, were sometimes the occasions for supplementary distributions of non-cereal products in the ancient Near East.

The identity of **120* and **121*

As we have noted above, the identification of the commodities denoted by signs nos. **120* and **121* remains the subject of controversy. Though the conventional transcription of **120* is GRA(NUM), wheat, and of **121* HORD(EUM), barley, R. Palmer has argued (Palmer 1992) that we should reverse these identifications: that **120* is barley and **121* wheat, probably emmer rather than bread wheat, which is less well attested in the archaeological record. Her arguments may be summarized as follows.

1. Land is measured in terms of **120* (sometimes ligatured with *PE*, where *PE* clearly stands for *pe-mo*, *pe-ma*, 'seed', a term which often appears before **120* in land-holding records). But, she argues, a grain used in seed-corn measurement should be an undemanding species capable of growing in both good and poor soils; and while this is true of barley, it is not the case with wheat.
2. **120* is given as rations to dependent women and children, whereas **121* is issued as handouts to middle level religious personnel (and, we might add, to male workers, who may well be of a less dependent status than the women and children – Killen 1979b), and it is regularly attested as an offering to the gods, though there are also occasional mentions of **120* in this context. (In addition, as we have seen, **121* regularly occurs in the 'menus' for sacrificial banquets, whereas **120* is not certainly attested in such lists.) This distribution of the two cereals fits best, she suggests, with an identification of **120* as barley and **121* as (emmer) wheat: the grain used in religious offerings and in handouts to middle level religious personnel should be of higher status than that issued as rations to dependent workers; and wheat was of higher status than barley in the Classical world.

These conclusions have, however, been questioned by Halstead (1995); though he agrees with Palmer that 'the identity of the ... ideograms cannot definitely be resolved without new evidence'. First, he argues that palatial interest in grain production was highly selective, and that the bureaucracy may therefore only have been dealing with land of relatively high quality. (It is certainly the case that the records of land-holding in the archives of both Pylos and Knossos probably relate to relatively small areas; and while some of the quantities of **120* on 'harvest' records at Knossos are certainly very substantial, such as the 10,300 (plus?) units recorded on KN F(2) 852 in connexion with the place *da-wo*, there is nothing to confirm that these represent anything like the entire cereal production of the areas concerned.) Moreover, he suggests, if **120* is emmer wheat or einkorn, which are 'tolerant cereals of poor breadmaking quality', it 'might have been deemed suitable for measuring the area of poor-quality land and for issuing as rations to persons of low status'. Second, he argues that the traditional identification of **121* as barley is 'consistent with possible (admittedly ambiguous) textual indications of religious connotations for this cereal'; here he is referring to R. Palmer's discussion (1992: 485–86) of tablets at Knossos (KN G 820, E 777) containing the terms *ki-ri-ta* and *ki-ri-te-wi-ja* (see further below). And, third and finally, he notes that 'a slight hint that the conventional identifications [viz. of **120* as wheat and **121* as barley] are at least partly correct is provided by the form of ideogram **121*, which strongly recalls the characteristic 'nodding' head of barley. As he observes, 'some wheats do droop when ripe, and this tendency is very clear in einkorn, but examinations of several dozen einkorn populations in southern France suggested that this drooping tendency does not approach the characteristic nodding form of barley'.

Is there anything that we can contribute to this discussion in the light of our findings above about the distribution of **120*, **121* in the records? It should be stressed at the outset that it is still not possible to arrive at any final conclusion about the identity of the two cereals; indeed, the evidence which I am about to mention does not all point in the same direction. I first note a point which appears to favour, or at least to be consistent with, the identification of **121* as barley; I then turn to others which perhaps favour Palmer's contention that **121* is wheat.

As we have seen, there is a marked tendency for **121* to appear in what may loosely be termed *religious* contexts. Not only is it regularly found in records of religious offerings (whereas **120* is very rare in that context): it is nearly always the cereal recorded in 'festival issue' texts (the one seeming exception being the Av records at Thebes), and it is the cereal of choice in 'menus' for sacrificial banquets. (Indeed, the occurrence of **120* in the latter context is on PY Ua 434, which may be a 'harvest' record – see above, *Cereals on records of banquet 'menus'*.) This evidence accords well with an identification of **121* as *barley*, since in Classical Greece at least, as C.J. Ruijgh (1967: 129) has put it, 'barley plays a more important rôle in cult than wheat'. Not only, as Palmer herself notes (1992: 485), is barley meal associated with sacrifices both in Homer and in later classical texts (it was standard practice to carry the sacrificial knife to the altar hidden in a basket of barley, some of which was scattered on the altar, as part of the offering of 'first fruits' which was an essential preliminary to the slaughter of the animal(s) (Bruit Zaidman and Schmitt Pantel 1992: 33, 35): barley as well as wheat is often mentioned in classical inscriptions listing 'menus' for the civic banquets which customarily followed the animal sacrifice at major religious festivals. The following are among the examples.

1. In the accounts of the Posidea (*Inscriptions de Délos*: 440A.63 [Durrbach 1929]), the reference to *alphita*, 'barley meal or groats', follows references to two types of wine. Accordingly, T. Linders (n.d.) suggests that this may have been barley which was mixed with wine. [It should be noted, however, that while this banquet 'menu' mentions barley and not wheat, others from the same source do mention the latter, which was evidently used to make bread. See *Inscriptions de Délos*: 440A.69, *re* the accounts of the Eileithyiaia (and the mention of a payment 'to the baker' in the following line).]
2. Offerings to Heracles on Cos included 112 *medimna* of barley and 34 *medimnon* of wheat (*SGDI* 3636–38, Schwyzer 1923: 251c [quoted in Ventris and Chadwick 1956: 281]). These large amounts of cereal were presumably for consumption, together with the honey, cheese and wine which are also mentioned in the list, at a meal which followed the sacrifice of the ox which is referred to at the beginning of this section of the inscription.

Thus far, then, the evidence is consistent with an identification of **121* as barley. On the other hand, some further data perhaps point in a different direction – though the 'perhaps' needs very heavy emphasis. These are as follows.

1. The text of the Knossos record G 820 is given beneath.

KN G 820 + *fr.* ASHM (1910.215)/HM (–)

.1] , [·]- ṇạ , e-ko-si , a-pi , ku-do-ni-ja / pa-sa 'ki-ri-ta' LUNA 1
.2 i-ja-]pu$_2$-wi-ja-qe , *56-ko-we-i-ja-qe LUNA 4
.3 da-]*22-ti-ja , ku-ta-ti-ja-qe , po-ti-ni-ja-we-ja , a-pu , ke-u-po-de-ja
.4] LUNA 4

The appearance of the ideogram LUNA, 'month', in ll.1, 2 and 4 is a clear indication that this is a rationing record (as far as we are aware, the sign is only attested in rationing contexts – see KN Am(1) 597.b, Am(2) 819.B, E 777.1.2.3, 847.1.2.2, 7350, 9178). It is attractive therefore to understand the ethnics and other epithets in *-ja* which are found in the body of the record as feminine plurals, and references to groups of female workers, perhaps in the textile industry (Godart *et al.* 1996: 34),[3] who are in receipt of the rations in question. And given this general context, it is immediately attractive to interpret the term *ki-ri-ta*, which stands before LUNA 1 at the end of l.1 of the record, as /*krīthā*/, 'barley', i.e. a reference to the cereal which is here being issued to these women.[4]

If *ki-ri-ta* here is */krīthā/*, however, and if *i-ja-]-pu$_2$-wi-ja*, *po-ti-ni-ja-we-ja*, etc. are references to female workgroups, a difficulty arises for the hypothesis that *121 is barley and *120 is wheat; for, as we have seen earlier, no other record, at any site, records the issue of *121 to women as a ration. (Contrast the great number of records, such as the Ab tablets at Pylos and the Ai records at Knossos, which list *120 in this context.) Indeed, as we have noted, only three records in total in the archives list *121 as a ration, and in all cases the recipients are men. It is true that (as Palmer emphasizes) G 820 is exceptional as a rationing record in that it does not mention the amounts of cereal being issued; despite this anomaly, however, its evidence will still be remarkable if *ki-ri-ta* is 'barley' and this is a record of the issue of *121 to women.[5]

2. Another possible indication that *120 may be barley and *121 wheat is provided by the Knossos record E 777, whose text reads as follows:

KN E 777				ASHM	(1910.214) (–)
.1	ko-no-si-ja/ki-ri-te-wi-ja-i	LUNA	1	GRA	100[
.2	a-mi-ni-si-ja	LUNA	1	GRA	100[
.3	pa-i-ti-ja	LUNA	1	GRA	100[
↓					
v.1	a-ze-ti-ri-ja			GRA	1̣0̣ [
	reliqua pars sine regulis				

Discussing the record, Ventris and Chadwick (1956: 214–15) suggest that the *recto* of the tablet records the issue of rations to women at Knossos, Amnisos and Phaistos; and it seems difficult to contest their conclusions, given (a) the difficulty of making the feminine or neuter ethnics at the beginning of each register agree with GRA and (b) the appearance of the feminine trade-name *a-ze-ti-ri-ja*, */askētria(i)/*, 'decorators [of cloth]' (Killen 1979a: 165–67) at the beginning of the entry on the *verso* of the tablet. There is, however, one puzzling feature of the record: the term *ki-ri-te-wi-ja-i* which follows *ko-no-si-ja* on l.1, and is written in smaller signs than it. This is in the dative plural; and it is usually taken as a gloss on the preceding *ko-no-si-ja* (e.g., Ventris and Chadwick 1956: 214) viz. as a clarification that the women of Knossos to whom this entry relates are *ki-ri-te-wi-ja*, who we know from the Pylos records are a class of women, possibly with cult connexions. (In particular, they are listed on Ep 704 in company with a 'servant of the god', the priestess *e-ri-ta* and *ka-pa-ti-ja* the key-bearer as holding a plot of *ke-ke-me-na* land.) If this is correct, however, it is surprising that the term is not in agreement with the preceding *ko-no-si-ja*, */Knōsiai/*: we would have expected either both words to have been given in the nominative or both to have appeared in the dative. Moreover, if the women of Knossos who are recorded as the recipients of rations are all *ki-ri-te-wi-ja*, and if these are 'paid' at anything like the rate at which the women on the Ab tablets at Pylos are rationed (T2 of *120 per woman), there will be a remarkably large number of them (and similar numbers at Amnisos and Phaistos, if *ki-ri-te-wi-ja-i* is also to be understood in the two following entries). As Ventris and Chadwick put it (1956: 215), 'either the rations are very generous or large numbers of women are concerned; 500 at each place on the Pylos ration scale…'. (Given that none of the figures in the GRA entries is certainly complete, this should be amended to 'at least 500'.)

The question comes to mind, therefore, whether *ki-ri-te-wi-ja-i* might have a different function. Though the etymology of the term remains controversial, one possibility is that it is connected with the term for barley, *ki-ri-ta* (C.J. Ruijgh [1967: 129], for instance, suggests that it might be a derivative of a theonym *Krītheus*, 'god of barley'). If this is correct, is it possible that E 777 records rations for the (dependent) women of Knossos, Amnisos, and Phaistos as a whole, or perhaps those involved in the textile industry, which would accord with the reference to cloth-workers, *a-ze-ti-ri-ja*, on the reverse of the tablet; and does *ki-ri-te-wi-ja-i* after *ko-no-si-ja* serve to indicate that before being distributed to these women the rations they required were put in the care of this priestly class: women in the service of the god of barley whose duty was to guard that commodity, just as the keybearer(s) mentioned in the heading of Jn 829 at Pylos is/are plausibly understood as having some rôle in guarding the bronze which is dealt with on that tablet? (One recalls, incidentally, that one of the land-holders mentioned in conjunction with the group of *ki-ri-te-wi-ja* on PY Ep 704 is *ka-pa-ti-ja* the key-bearer). And if that is the case, this will be a further possible indication that **120* is *ki-ri-ta*, since GRA is the cereal recorded on E 777: though it is perhaps not entirely inconceivable that the *ki-ri-te-wi-ja*, although they originally had a connexion only with barley, and owe their appellation to this, now deal with other cereals as well, including wheat.

3. Another possible, but still more uncertain, indication that **121* is wheat and **120* barley is provided by the evidence, set out above, for the regular association on the records of **121* with the commodity **129*, conventionally transcribed as FAR(INA). As we have seen, FAR only occurs in 'religious' records; and **121* is by far the most commonly attested cereal in such contexts, in many cases appearing on the same records as FAR. In addition, there is a case (on the Pylos banqueting 'menu' record Un 47) of HORD possibly standing over an erased FAR. What does this evidence signify?

Our principal clue to the identification of **129* is provided by PY Un 718, where the ideogram is preceded by the term *me-re-u-ro*. As Chadwick (1954: 14) was the first to point out, it is attractive to interpret this as */meleuron/*; compare the classical terms *aleuron* and the much less common *maleuron*, which it is tempting to suspect may be a conflation of *aleuron* with the Mycenaean term (Chantraine 1968–80). [As Chantraine notes, whereas *aleuron* is derived from the verb *aleō*, 'I grind', and is cognate with Armenian *alewr*, 'flour', *meleuron*, like the Mycenaean occupational term *me-re-ti-ri-ja*, */meletria/*, 'grain-grinder', is derived from the other Indo-European root meaning 'grind', viz. **mel-*$ə_1$ (the root found in Latin *molō*, 'I grind', English *molar*).] Moreover, if *meleuron* has the same meaning as *aleuron*, it will mean 'wheat flour' rather than 'barley meal', for which the standard classical term is *alphita*. (See Plato, *Republic* 372b: *ek men tōn krithōn alphita skeuazdomenoi, ek de tōn purōn aleura*, 'preparing barley-meal from barley, and flour from wheat'.)

If, then, **129* is wheaten flour, rather than barley meal,[6] its close association with **121* could be explained as these being two different forms of the same commodity, viz. **121* being wheat in the form of grains and **129* being the milled form of the same cereal, viz. flour. Slight support for this explanation might be seen in the fact that three of the five attestations of the term *a-to-po-qo*, */artopok^{w}os/*, 'baker', on the tablets (PY An 39.11, An 427.3 and Fn 50.7) are in a seemingly religious context, in the lists of what J.-P. Olivier (1960) has called 'desservants de sanctuaire'. In classical Greek at least, *artos* is normally 'wheaten bread', as distinct from *māzda*, 'barley cake' (or 'barley gruel'); and as we have stressed repeatedly, **121*, not **120*, is the cereal most commonly attested in religious contexts on the tablets.

It need hardly be emphasized, however, that this evidence for a link between **129* and **121* cannot be regarded as conclusive for the identity of the latter (though it is possible that the full publication of the Fq tablets from Thebes will help cast some further light on the matter). Though **129* may denote wheaten flour on Un 718, where it is preceded by *me-re-u-ro*, it could have been a sign used to denote any milled grain (note that on 718 it is accompanied by **120*, not as normally by **121*); and even if it does always denote wheaten flour, its appearance on tablets like the Fs 'offerings' records at Knossos in conjunction with **121* could simply reflect a practice whereby barley was usually offered in the form of grain, while wheat was offered in the form of flour.

Conclusions

There are a number of trends visible in the contextual distribution of the five foodstuffs examined in the preceding discussion. In particular:

1. **120* is the only cereal listed in the 'harvest' records at Knossos: texts which appear to list crops in store and available for palace use at various centres in the island.
2. The cereal issued as rations to women workers and their children is normally **120*, and will exclusively be so if *ki-ri-ta* on KN G 820 is 'barley' and if **120* denotes that commodity.
3. **121* is issued as rations to male workers, who also occasionally receive **120*, and as allowances to male and female participants in religious festivals. It is

also by far the most common cereal recorded in other religious contexts: in the 'menus' for state-sponsored sacrificial banquets and in food offerings to divinities.

4. **129* (flour, meal or both) is found only in religious contexts: as a food offering to divinities; in 'menus' for sacrificial banquets; and once (perhaps) as an issue to a participant in a religious festival. It has a marked tendency to occur in the same contexts as **121*.

Appendix: **120* (GRA) as a measurement of land

Knossos	E 36(?), E(1) 71(?),[7] 288(?),[8] E 749(?),[9] 843(?),[10] 846(?),[11] 849,[12] 1569,[13] 7338(?),[14] 9295,[15] 9322,[16] F(2) 841,[17] 854.2.3(??)[18]
Pylos	E series
Thebes	Ft 140
Tiryns	Ef 2.

Endnotes

1 For discussion of the figures for women plus children and **120* on Ai(2) 7026, the most complete of these tablets, see Chadwick (1988: 68). Note that though the MUL and T figures are uncertain, the ration for this group appears to have been – at most – the same or very slightly more than the **120* ration for a group of the same size and make-up at Pylos: not double that amount. Note, too, that if the readings 3̣ and Ṭ on *Ai(2)* 752 are correct, the group here will have received a maximum ration of T9 of **120*, while a group of the same size and make-up at Pylos would have received T8 of both **120* and *NI*.

2 For the demonstration that the ration figure on the tablet is best explained on the assumption that men and boys alike received a ration of Z3 per day, see Chadwick (1976: 118); for confirmation that Z3 on An 7.3.4 is a daily ration (as suggested by Chadwick 1976: 118), see Melena (1996–97: 171–76).

3 As Olivier notes (in Godart *et al.* 1986: 34), it is difficult to believe that the women of *i-ja-pu*$_2$ here can be a different group from the women of *i-ja-pu*$_2$ mentioned on the textile records Lc(1) 541 and Lc 646.

4 We cannot perhaps entirely exclude the possibility that it refers only to the rations given to the women on the first line. Since, however, it would be unparalleled for a single rationing (or festival issue) tablet to record the issue of different types of cereal to different recipients, this does not seem at all likely.

5 It can hardly be argued that the appearance on the record of *po-ti-ni-ja-we-ja* workers (l.3), viz. women 'of' the goddess Potnia, has led to a change from the normal foodstuff given to dependent females. It is true, as we have seen, that there is a particular association of **121* with religious activity; but not only does the tablet record a number of other workgroups with no connexion with Potnia (and with nothing to suggest that they have any other religious connexion): all our evidence elsewhere suggests that the (few) workgroups (and animals) attributed to divinities were treated by the administration in precisely the same way as their secular counterparts: in the case of sheep, for instance, set

precisely the same targets for their wool and lamb yields as other flocks of the same make-up.

6 R. Palmer (1992: 488) suggests that *me-re-u-ro* on Un 718 might not be the name of the commodity which *129 represents, but a qualification of it: that the ideogram might denote a type of cereal (bread wheat?), which it is here being noted is in the form of flour. This seems unlikely, however, at least if the *me-re-u-ro* entry follows the pattern of others on the same record, where the term standing before the ideogram gives the name of the commodity. See *tu-ro*$_2$, 'cheese', preceding *TURO*$_2$ on l.4, *ko-wo*, 'fleece', preceding **153* on the same line, and *a-re-ro* (clearly an error for *a-re-pa*) preceding *AREPA* on l.8.

7 The interpretation of the term *ka-pa* at the beginning of the tablet remains uncertain. A. Sacconi (1998) argues that in all the contexts in which it appears, including E(1) 71, *ka-pa* has the same value, and refers to a container for offerings (/*skaphā*/). While, however, this is an attractive interpretation of *ka-pa* on PY Ua 9 (if it is complete there), Un 138 and TH Ft 141, 143, 217, 219, 220, 234, 268 (for the texts of these Thebes tablets see Sacconi 1998: 282), on all of which, with the possible exception of PY Ua 9, it is followed immediately or closely by a reference to olives, it is less certain to be /*skaphā*/ on E(1) 71, which contains **120*. For an alternative possibility, that it is here a place-name *ka-pa* (also attested by way of the ethnic *ka-pa-jo* on KN B(3) 5752), see Killen and Olivier (1966: 83 [Olivier]). And if *ka-pa* is here a place-name, the tablet might clearly be a reference to land in this area (or to **120* produced on it).

8 For the attractive suggestion that *ra-wa-si-jo* before **120* here is an error for *ra-wa-ke-si-jo* (cf.]*ra-wa-e-si-jo*,]*ra-wa-ke-si-jo* on E 846, E 1569 below), see Ruijgh (1967: 118). If it is, this will be a reference either to land held by the *ra-wa-ke-ta*, /*lāwāgetās*/, as]*ra-wa-ke-si-jo *120* clearly is on E 1569, or to **120* produced on this land.

9 For the suggestion that this is a record of land used for growing coriander, etc. (Melena), see Foster (1977: 47–49).

10 For the suggestion that this is a record of land held by the 'collector' *e-me-si-jo* in various localities (or of wheat grown on this land), see Driessen *et al.* (1988: 68 [Killen]) and Killen (1998: 22).

11 See notes on E(1) 288 above, E 1569 below. For the very plausible suggestion that *ra-wa-e-si-jo* here is an error for *ra-wa-ke-si-jo* see Ventris and Chadwick (1956: 407).

12 A record of *pu-ta-ri-ja*, /*phutalia(i)*/, 'orchard(s), vineyard(s)'. Since the classical Greek *phutalia* is the opposite of *aroura* 'corn-land', the **120* totalling entry on l.2 of the record is presumably a measurement of land, not a reference to a crop.

13 As J.-P. Olivier has stressed (Bennett *et al.* 1989: 208), the appearance of *pe-ma* after **120* 48 on line 1 indicates that the latter, and hence presumably the **120* entry following]*ra-wa-ke-si-jo* on l.2, is a measurement of land.

14 On the connexion between this tablet and E 843, see Driessen *et al.* (1988: 67).

15 Contains **120+PE(-ma)*, on which see n. 17 below.

16 Contains *120+*PE*(*-ma*), on which see n. 17 below.

17 For interpretation of this as a record of land-holdings viz. that **120+PE* on ll.2, 3 is a measurement of land, see Killen (1987: 174–77).

18 Though the entry on line 5 of the record (**120* 402 OLIV+*A* 52) appears to concern a 'harvest', one wonders whether the entries on ll.2–3, which involve much smaller amounts of **120* (5 and 8 units respectively), may have another purpose. They might record issues:]*-do-we-i* and *ma-so(-qe)* before **120* on line 3 could be datives of personal names (Landau 1958: 46, 81; Ruijgh 1967: 294); alternatively, however, they might be locatives of place-names (with *ma-so*, compare the Cretan place-name *ma-sa* ???), and the **120* entry a measurement of land in these places.

Bibliography

Aravantinos, V.

1999 Mycenaean texts and contexts at Thebes. In S. Deger-Jalkotzy, S. Hiller and O. Panagl (eds.), *Floreant Studia Mycenaea. Akten des X Internationalen Mykenologischen Colloqiums*: 45–102. Salzburg: Österreichische Akademie der Wissenschaften.

Bennett, E.L and J.P. Olivier

1973 *The Pylos Tablets Transcribed, 1: Texts and Notes.* Rome: Edizioni dell' Ateneo.

Bennett, E.L., J.M. Driessen, L. Godart, J.T. Killen, C. Kopaka, J.L. Melena, J.-P. Olivier and M. Perna

1989 436 raccords et quasi-raccords de fragments inédits dans *KT5. Minos* 24, 199–242.

Bruit Zaidman, L. and P. Schmitt Pantel

1992 *Religion in the Ancient Greek City.* Cambridge: Cambridge University Press.

Burkert, W.

1977 *Griechische Religion der Archaïschen und Klassischen Epoche.* Stuttgart: Kohlhammer.

Chadwick, J.

1954 Mycenaean: a newly discovered Greek dialect. *Transactions of the Philological Society*: 1–17.

1976 *The Mycenaean World*. Cambridge: Cambridge University Press.

1988 The women of Pylos. In J.-P. Olivier and T.G. Palaima (eds.), *Texts, Tablets and Scribes. Studies in Mycenaean Epigraphy and Economy Offered to Emmett L. Bennett, Jr.* (Minos Supplement 10): 43–96. Salamanca: Salamanca University.

Chantraine, P.

1968–80 *Dictionnaire étymologique de la langue grecque: histoire des mots.* Paris: Klincksieck.

Driessen, J., L. Godart, J.T. Killen, C. Kopaka, J.L. Melena, J.-P. Olivier and M. Perna

1988 107 raccords et quasi-raccords de fragments dans *COMIK I et II. BCH* 112: 59–82.

Duhoux, Y.

1976 *Aspects du vocabulaire économique mycénien (cadastre – artisanat – fiscalité).* Amsterdam: Hakkert.

Durrbach, F.

1929 *Inscriptions de Délos (372–509).* Paris: Académie des Inscriptions et Belles-Lettres.

Foster, E.D.

1977 An administrative department at Knossos concerned with perfumery and offerings. *Minos* 16: 19–51.

Gelb, I.J.

1965 The ancient Mesopotamian ration system. *Journal of Near Eastern Studies* 24: 230–43.

Godart, L. and A. Sacconi

1996 Les dieux thébains dans les archives mycéniennes. *Comptes rendus de l' Académie des inscriptions et belles lettres* 1996: 99–111.

1998 Les archives de Thèbes et le monde mycénien. *Comptes rendus de l' Académie des inscriptions et belles lettres* 1997: 889–906.

Godart, L., J.T. Killen, K. Kopaka and J.-P. Olivier

1986 43 raccords et quasi-raccords de fragments inédits dans le volume I du 'Corpus of Mycenaean inscriptions from Knossos'. *BCH* 110: 21–39.

Halstead, P.

1995 Late Bronze Age grain crops and Linear B ideograms **65, *120* and **121. BSA* 90: 229–34.

Killen, J.T.

1979a The Knossos Ld(1) tablets. In E. Risch and H. Mühlestein (eds.), *Colloquium*

Mycenaeum. Actes du sixième colloque international sur les texts mycéniens: 151–81. Neuchâtel, Geneva: University of Neuchâtel.

1979b The Linear B tablets and economic history: some problems. *BICS* 26: 133–34.

1987 Piety begins at home: place names on Knossos records of religious offerings. In P.H. Ilievski, L. Crepajac (eds.), *Tractata Mycenaea. Proceedings of the Eighth International Colloquium on Mycenaean Studies:* 163–77. Skopje: Macedonian Academy of Sciences and Arts.

1992 Observations on the Thebes sealings. In J.-P. Olivier (ed.), *Mykenaïka. Actes du IXe Colloque international sur les textes mycéniens et égéens* (BCH Supplement 25): 364–80. Athens, Paris: École française d' Athènes.

1994 Thebes sealings, Knossos tablets and Mycenaean state banquets. *BICS*: 67–84.

1995 A-ma e-pi-ke-re. *Minos* 29–30: 329–33.

1998 The rôle of the state in wheat and olive production in Mycenaean Crete. *Aevum* 72: 19–23.

1999a Some observations on the new Thebes tablets. *BICS* 43: 217–19.

1999b New readings and interpretations in the Pylos tablets. In S. Deger-Jalkotzy, S. Hiller and O. Panagl (eds.), *Floreant Studia Mycenaea. Akten des X Internationalen Mykenologischen Colloquiums:* 343–53. Salzburg: Österreichische Akademie der Wissenschaften.

2001 Religion at Pylos: the evidence of the Fn tablets. In R. Laffineur and R. Hägg (eds.), *Potnia. Deities and Religion in the Aegean Bronze Age* (Aegaeum 22): 435–43. Liège: Liège University.

in press The language of religious texts: some fresh thoughts on old problems. In Proceedings of the 11th International Mycenological Colloquium (Austin, Texas, 2000).

Killen, J.T. and J.-P. Olivier

1966 388 raccords de fragments dans les tablettes de Cnossos. In L.R. Palmer and J. Chadwick (eds.), *Proceedings of the Cambridge Colloquium on Mycenaean Studies:* 47–92. Cambridge: Cambridge University Press.

Landau, O.

1958 *Mykenisch-Griechische Personennamen.* Göteborg: Almqvist and Wiksell.

Linders, T.

n.d. Sacred menus on Delos.

Melena, J.

1996–97 13 joins and quasi-joins of fragments in the Linear B tablets from Pylos. *Minos* 31–32: 171–78.

Olivier, J.-P.

1960 *A propos d' une 'liste' de desservants de sanctuaire dans les documents en linéaire B de Pylos.* Brussels: Presses universitaires.

Palmer, L.R.

1983 Studies in Mycenaean religion. In P. Händel and W. Meid (eds), *Festschrift für Robert Muth*: 283–96. Innsbruck: Amoe.

Palmer, R.

1992 Wheat and barley in Mycenaean society. In J.-P. Olivier (ed.), *Mykenaïka. Actes du IX colloque international sur les textes mycéniens et égéens* (BCH Supplement 25): 475–97. Athens, Paris: École française d' Athènes.

Piteros, C., J.-P. Olivier and J.L. Melena

1990 Les inscriptions en linéaire B des nodules de Thèbes (1982): la fouille, les documents, les possibilités d' interprétation. *BCH* 114: 103–84.

Robert, J. and L. Robert

1970 Bulletin épigraphique. *Révue des études grecques* 83: 362–488.

Ruijgh, C.J.
1967 *Études sur la grammaire et le vocabulaire du grec mycénien*. Amsterdam: Hakkert.
Sacconi, A.
1998 I nuovi testi tebani ed il significato del termine *ka-pa*. *Rivista di Cultura Classica e Medioevale* 40: 281–88.
Schwyzer, E.
1923 *Dialectorum Graecarum Exempla Epigraphica Potiora*. Leipzig: Hirzel.
Ventris, M. and J. Chadwick
1956 *Documents in Mycenaean Greek*. Cambridge: Cambridge University Press.

9

Social Meanings of Food and Drink Consumption at LMIII Phaistos

Elisabetta Borgna

This paper introduces evidence for conspicuous consumption of food and drink from two partly contemporary sites within LMIIIC Phaistos: the 'Acropoli Mediana' and the 'Casa a ovest del Piazzale I'. The evidence from these two sites hints at contrasting roles and ideological meanings for ritual drinking and eating within the social framework of the community. Given the slight chronological difference between the sites, these contrasts may indicate evolution and transformation of ceremonial practices, anticipating later institutions such as the *symposion*, ritual meals and sacrifice (Borgna 1997a; 2000).

The Acropoli Mediana

The Acropoli Mediana was so named by Luigi Pernier for its eminent central position among the hills of Phaistos (Pernier 1902) (Figure 9.1). Rescue excavations in 1955 on the top of this hill, in advance of construction of the Stratigraphical Museum (Levi 1956; Borgna 1997b; 1999a; 2003), brought to light a heterogeneous group of ceramics belonging, typologically, to different phases within LMIII. A substantial group of sherds, however, dating to the end of LMIIIB and early LMIIIC, seems more homogeneous and most probably represents a secondary

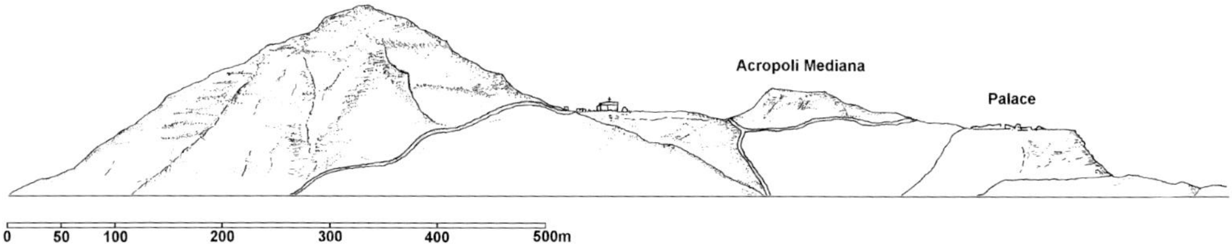

Figure 9.1. Profile of the Phaistos hills (after Pernier 1902: pl. 1).

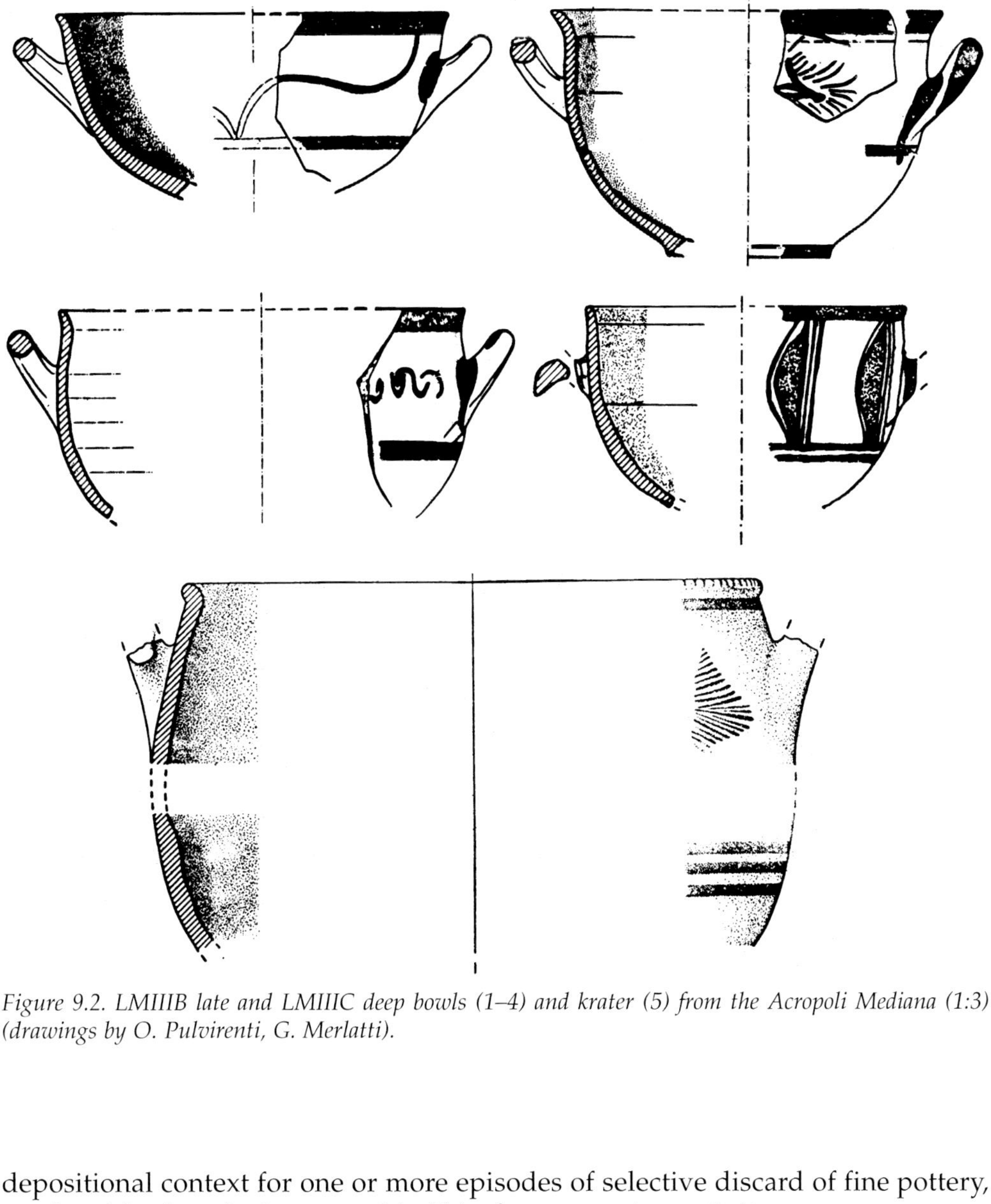

Figure 9.2. LMIIIB late and LMIIIC deep bowls (1–4) and krater (5) from the Acropoli Mediana (1:3) (drawings by O. Pulvirenti, G. Merlatti).

depositional context for one or more episodes of selective discard of fine pottery, used and broken during some kind(s) of consumption activity.

Functional analysis of the pottery (Borgna 2003) indicated that this latter group was a dinner set dominated by deep bowls and kraters (Figures 9.2–3), but also including vessels suited to the manipulation of liquids (dippers, jugs and juglets) and a smaller number of cups and kylikes. Some particular shapes, such as dishes, kalathoi and (among the few closed vessels) fine small-sized stirrup jars, pyxides and isolated specimens of alabastra and flasks (Figure 9.4), as well

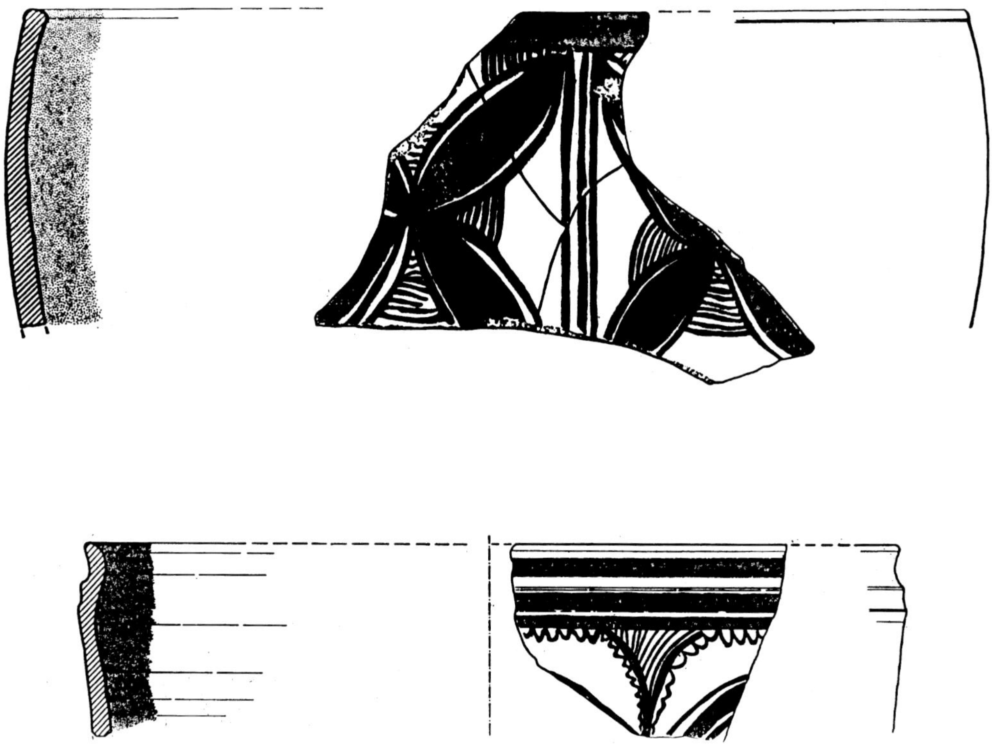

Figure 9.3. LMIIIC kraters with elaborate decoration from the Acropoli Mediana (1:3) (drawings by O.Pulvirenti, G.Merlatti).

as figurines of Mycenaean type, imply that ritual offerings also played a role in social consumption (cf. Morgan 1999: 315).

The highly visible location of this site, at the highest point of the settlement, will have been ideal for attention-focusing strategies (cf. Renfrew 1985; see Borgna 1999a, for an attempt to interpret the evidence of the Acropoli Mediana as a kind of sanctuary). Coupled with the lack of domestic material, this seems to point to an important locus for public meetings, perhaps relevant to the socio-political administration of the settlement and surrounding area towards the end of the Bronze Age. Study of the use of ceramic style (Borgna 2003) has helped to clarify the kind of consumption activity performed on the site during LMIIIC.

The redundancy and elaboration of the decorative style point to an important role for deep bowls and kraters in social communication among participants in the convivial gatherings (Figures 9.3, 9.5). Under the influence of a mainland functional model, the deep bowl was widespread in Crete and, especially as regards decoration, displaced the cup, that had been exclusively selected for the dinner set in earlier LM times. In the Acropoli Mediana assemblage, cups and

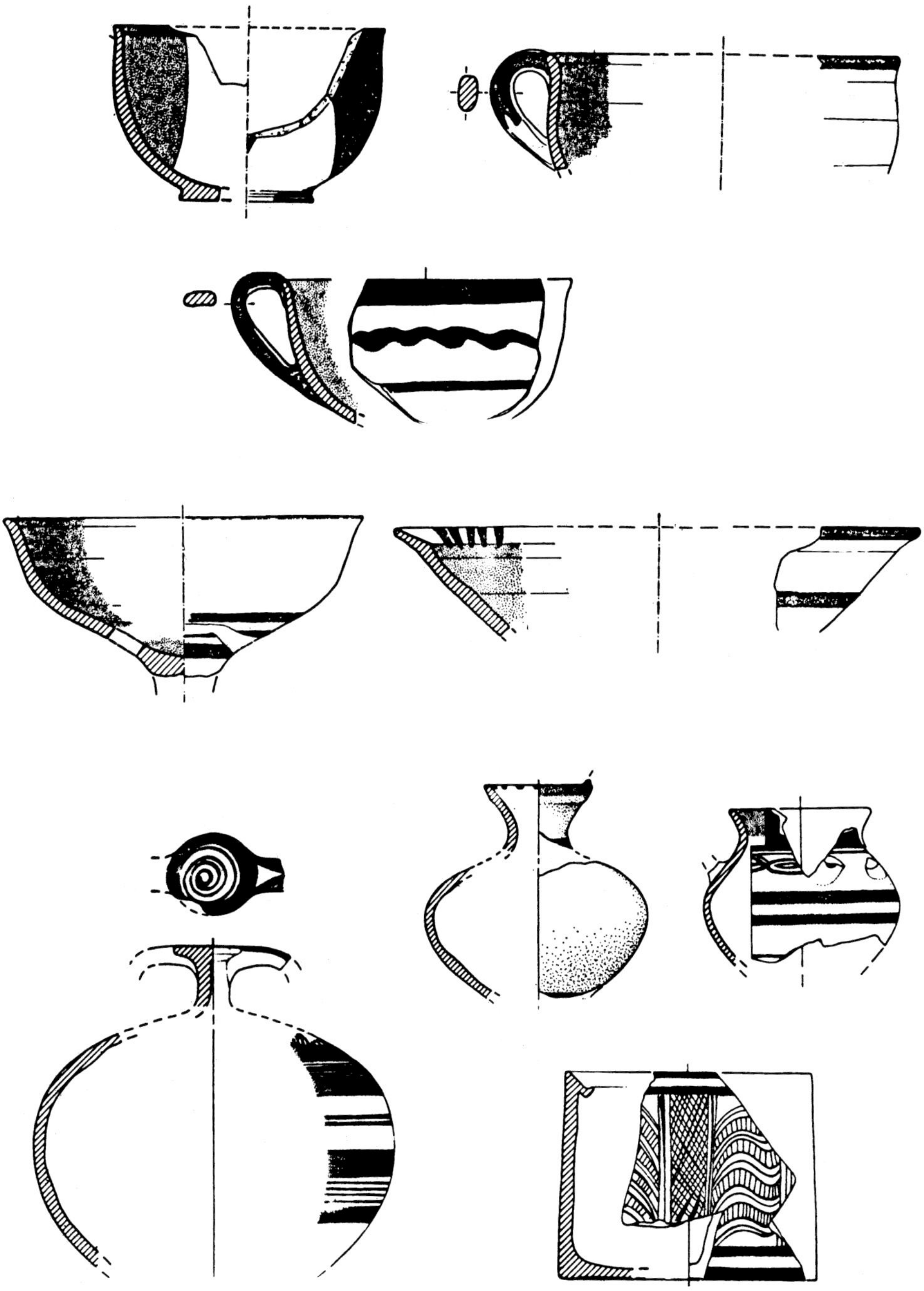

Figure 9.4. LMIIIB and LMIIIC pottery from the Acropoli Mediana: cups (1–3), kylix (4), dish (5), stirrup jar (6), juglet (7), alabastron (8) and pyxis (9) (1:3) (drawings by O.Pulvirenti, G.Merlatti).

Figure 9.5. Fragments of LMIIIC krater from the Acropoli Mediana (Archivio SAIA).

kylikes are mostly undecorated or treated with very simple surface techniques; the deep bowl, by contrast, is normally highly decorated, with simple or, more often, complex motifs and configurations. The double horizontal handles of the deep bowl are well suited to a vessel to be circulated among several people (cf. Sherratt 1987), while the continuous decorative compositions lend themselves to being viewed from changing angles within a circular movement (Figures 9.2:3–4, 9.12:3). Conversely, the cup and kylix are more suited, morphologically, to individual drinking or to 'bipolar' or 'bidirectional' circulation between only two people, as suggested by the Knossos and Pylos fresco representations of palatial banquets (Cameron 1987; Immerwahr 1990: 95, 176, Kn 26; McCallum 1991; Wright 1995a: 303, fig. 18.16; Shelmerdine 1999: 20).

Following the discussion of style in archaeology and anthropology (e.g. Conkey and Hastorf 1990; Plog 1995), the vessels selected for drinking occasions can be considered vehicles of a kind of 'symbolic style', variability in which is linked to the dynamics of identity negotiation among social groups. Decoding the decorative syntax of pottery within the Acropoli Mediana sample (cf. Pollock

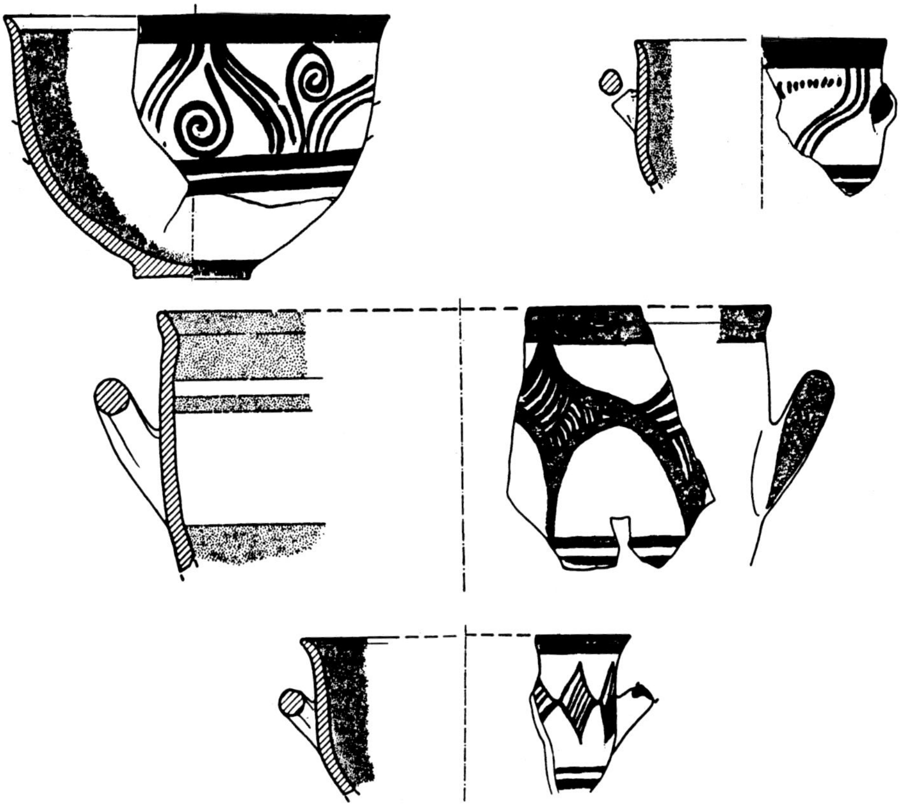

Figure 9.6. LMIIIB-C deep bowls (1–2, 4) and krater (3) from the Acropoli Mediana showing horizontal or qualitative decorative variability (1:3) (drawings by O.Pulvirenti, G.Merlatti).

1983), it can be argued that, in LMIII Crete, 'qualitative' variability in decorative configurations, involving substitution and alternation of the units of the ornamental set (Figure 9.6), characterized the products of communities subjected to limited social pressure and competition and open to integration with external elements. The LMIIIB products of the Acropoli, for example, may mirror a horizontal, perhaps balanced, confrontation between two artisan groups using respectively Mycenaean (Figure 9.7) and local stylistic languages (Figure 9.2:3) to claim cultural and ethnic affiliations rather than social status. In contrast, 'additive' variability, involving accumulation and redundancy of elements (Figure 9.8:1–3), may reflect vertical competition between social groups. The elaborate effects of decorative styles resulting from this kind of variation may point to periods of intense transformation and social competition (cf. Broodbank 1992 on Neolithic Knossos). In LH/LMIIIC, in general, cycles of production, circulation and consumption of elaborate pottery seem to be connected with the development

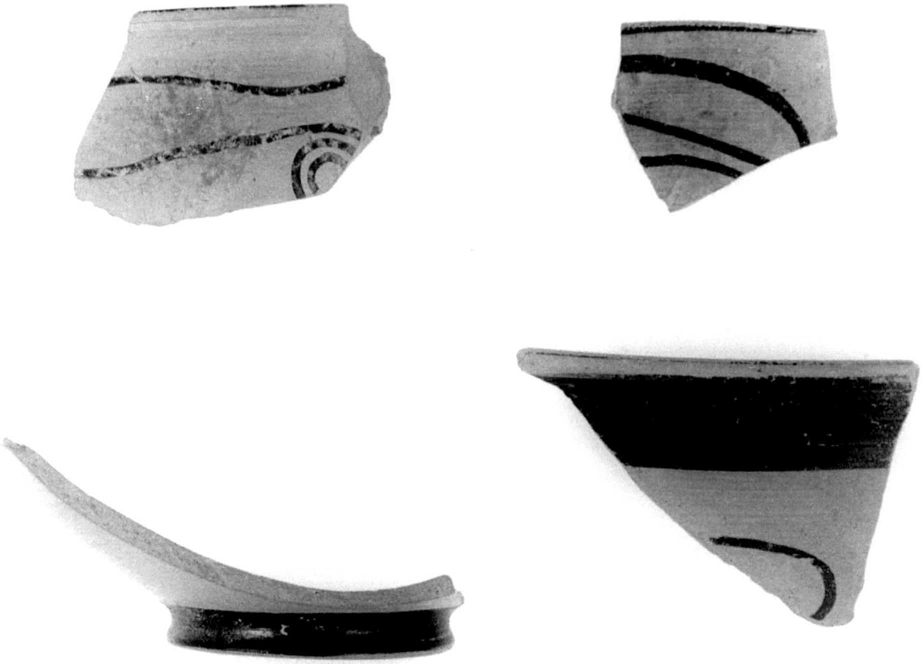

Figure 9.7. Sherds from the Acropoli Mediana with Mycenaean motifs (Archivio SAIA).

of larger and more powerful settlements and with a struggle to manipulate social and economic power following the collapse of the palaces.

Among the elaborate stylistic expressions of the Acropoli Mediana ceramics, pictorial pottery plays an important role (Figure 9.8:4–5) and may be interpreted as a kind of 'iconographic', 'élite' or 'mythic' style (Arnold 1985: 234; Plog 1995: 370; Earle 1990; cf. Morgan and Whitelaw 1991: 91–95), a special ideological means of self-representation in highly complex communities. The pictorial scenes of Aegean LBIIIC pottery point to a kind of formulaic communication including themes such as hunting, fighting, sailing and banqueting, selected by the emerging Aegean élites and related to values particular to a shared aristocratic ideology (cf. Deger-Jalkotzy 1994; 1995; 1998). The restricted use of the pictorial style for vessels, such as deep bowls and kraters, suited to specialized consumption and the uneven distribution of such evidence, which is concentrated at politically dominant centres, indicate the use of iconographic style as an instrument for mobilizing and legitimizing social and political power.

Both functional and stylistic analysis of the pottery from the Acropoli Mediana, therefore, indicate that consumption was bound to communal activities and provided the context for intense social and ideological exchange. The vessels used and discarded during these activities seem to underline the special social prestige of LMIIIC Phaistos, which may be compared to major Aegean LBIIIC

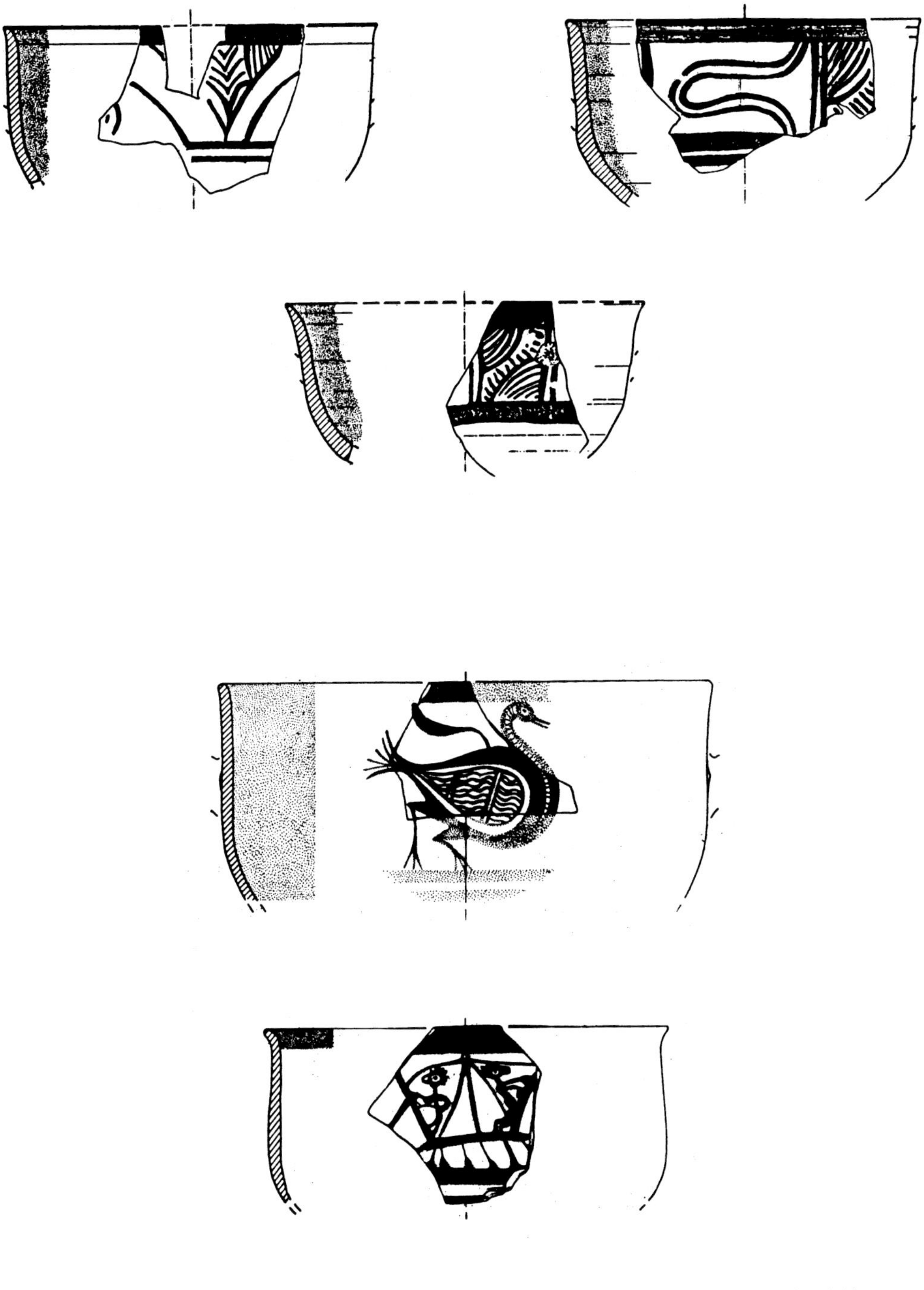

Figure 9.8. LMIIIC deep bowls (1–3) and stemmed bowls (4–5) from the Acropoli Mediana (1:3) (drawings by O.Pulvirenti, G.Merlatti).

Figure 9.9. Fragments of deep bowls from the Acropoli Mediana (Archivio SAIA).

centres with emphasis on elaborate pottery of the Close and related styles. Furthermore, the strong Mycenaean stylistic component detectable in local elaborate pottery (Figure 9.9) may point to an additional political meaning for ceremonial wine consumption in its use to claim prestige and social status (as a kind of 'international style', cf. Earle 1989; 1991: 9–10). Thus, Mycenaean stylistic influence on LMIIIC Cretan production should arguably be interpreted less in terms of aggressive acculturation and domination by Mycenaean culture and more in terms of selective adoption of mainland stylistic and functional models by local élites, using preferential access to external and distant domains in social competition for legitimization of authority (cf. Earle 1990; Helms 1992).

The social and ideological dynamics suggested here to have regulated pottery production and consumption at the LMIIIC Acropoli Mediana are paralleled in anthropological and ethnographic studies of the formation of chiefdoms (e.g. Pollock 1983; Brumfiel 1987; Spencer 1993; Clark and Blake 1994) and in some interpretations of Homeric and Dark Age Greek society (Donlan 1985; 1989; 1994; 1997; Whitley 1991; Van Wees 1995; Mazarakis Ainian 1997: 358–72). Such studies presuppose a decentralized and mostly pastoral population, composed of social groups founded on the extended family or Greek *oikos*; social relationships were governed by kinship and personal interactions, and stable hereditary institutions were lacking. Political power may thus have been attained by means of intense competition among equal social groups, involving the ideological mobilization of such values as generosity and group solidarity and of such activities as war, hospitality, marriage alliances, gift-exchange and indebtedness. Power was therefore founded on the personal ability to assume authority in both internal and external relationships (cf. Spencer 1993). Ties of male solidarity in war, based on kinship or ritual brotherhood and friendship, were probably sanctioned by means of feasts and banquets. Murray (1983a; 1983b; 1983c; 1990; 1994) was among the first scholars to detect the roots of the 'symposion' in the prehistory of Greek classical civilization, at the beginning of the first millennium BC, pointing to indications not so much of a general practice of communal drinking as of a ritual form of social control and political decision-making.

In short, wine consumption on the Acropoli Mediana of Phaistos is interpreted here as a forerunner of the later Greek *symposion*. From a diachronic perspective, this evidence falls between the Mycenaean banquets (Wright 1995a; 1995b) held in the closed space of the palace, as special and selective ritual occasions perhaps intended to consolidate élite relationships and to maintain the socio-political *status quo*, and the consumption practices of Dark Age and Archaic Greece (Mazarakis Ainian 1997; Morgan 1998); growing evidence for the latter includes, in Crete, the context of Building B at Kavousi-Vronda, interpreted by Whitley (1991; cf. Mazarakis Ainian 1997: 208–9) as the feasting-hall of a local big-man.

From a synchronic perspective, the 'protosymposion' of Phaistos seems to shed light on a critical point of connection between the local and Mycenaean ritual traditions (Borgna 1997a). Wine consumption within a defined social institution may be a primarily Mycenaean element, as suggested by the diffusion of the specialized set of deep bowls and kraters in LMIIIB-C Crete, as well as by prestige vessels such as kylikes and goblets in earlier LMII-IIIA contexts. At the same time, however, the more widespread participation and more intense social exchange proposed for Phaistos may be understood in terms not only of the new situation of postpalatial times, but also of the particular context of Crete; with a tradition of banqueting and ritual meals, especially in the field of cult and religious activity (e.g. Marinatos 1986: 37–39), Cretan society may have been especially open to collective participation.

The evidence from Phaistos would thus indicate that the social ritual of communal drinking moved from the closed space of the palace to an eminent position within a quasi-urban layout. Moreover, it would have developed from a behaviourally and socially static practice, playing no part in transformation of the socio-political order, into a dynamic means of defining authority and power relationships within a less homogeneous society subject to intense internal and external competition. During these ritual gatherings, the consumption of fine decorated pottery and the wide distribution of goods from the reconversion of 'surplus' farm produce – such as food and drink – were perhaps managed with the pretence of centralized mobilization and redistribution, thus disguising new concrete reciprocal relations founded on unstable equilibria of alliances, protection and obligation (Sahlins 1968; 1974: 229; van Wees 1998).

The Casa a Ovest del Piazzale I

The second conspicuous archaeological assemblage from LMIIIC Phaistos is provided by the Casa a ovest del Piazzale I. This building, comprising the incomplete layout of at least six or seven rooms, was excavated in 1965–66 under the direction of Doro Levi on the slope linking the Acropoli Mediana to the site of the palace (Levi 1965–66; Laviosa 1977; Borgna 2001) (Figure 9.10: A). The huge amount of kitchen ware found here led me, some years ago, to undertake a detailed analysis of the cooking vessels (Figure 9.11), which seemed to shed light on an important and articulated activity of food transformation, mostly devoted to ritual consumption (Borgna 1997a). On the basis of this study, cooking and consumption of meat and vegetables were identified as expressions of a complex ideology (cf. Goody 1982), well rooted in the aristocratic practices of Minoan Crete – and possibly contrasting with the simple and utilitarian mainland culinary tradition. In this preliminary analysis, however, the ritual meal was regarded as strictly connected, in the Cretan context, to religious cult and was not recognized as a special instrument of socio-political management and ideological communication; the Cretan ritual meals thus seemed to celebrate gatherings less restricted and selective than the Mycenaean 'symposion'.

On closer investigation, this provisional view may be modified or, at least, seen as more problematic and complex. The transformation of food may be related to a functionally diverse and perhaps self-sufficient unit, as suggested by traces of various production and consumption activities, such as textile manufacture, storage of foodstuffs, and perhaps metallurgy, together with evidence of prestige goods and symbolic and ritual connotations. The material culture of the Casa a ovest del Piazzale I may thus be related to the household or *oikos*, discussed by historians of Homeric Greece (Finley 1977; 1981; cf. Van Wees 1992: 27, 41–44; Rowlands 1980; Donlan 1985; Jones 1999; on possible archaeological evidence in LHIIIC, cf. Kilian 1985: 80; Deger Jalkotzy 1991: 59). Furthermore, the ritual performances in this context also seem to have involved drinking and so may be considered a parallel display, not merely complementary to but competing with those on the Acropoli Mediana. Deep bowls and kraters, similar in shapes and decoration to those of the Acropoli Mediana and related to them chronologically (Figure 9.12:1–2), are particularly associated with the floor of a room containing evidence of burning and unusual structures, such as a possible *trapeza*. Among other indications of ritual consumption, a bronze knife of 'barbarian', possibly Italian, type (Figure 9.12:4) could be interpreted in terms of a separate sphere of circulation, related to gift-exchange, and a bronze bowl may hint at the kinds of prestige goods which were kept in the *thalamoi* of the *oikoi*[1].

Provisional results of work still in progress suggest that ritual activity did not remain static during the life of the building and that changes probably involved an intensification of display. Furthermore, in late LMIIIC, the room with evidence of drinking activities was divided to give way to a smaller successor

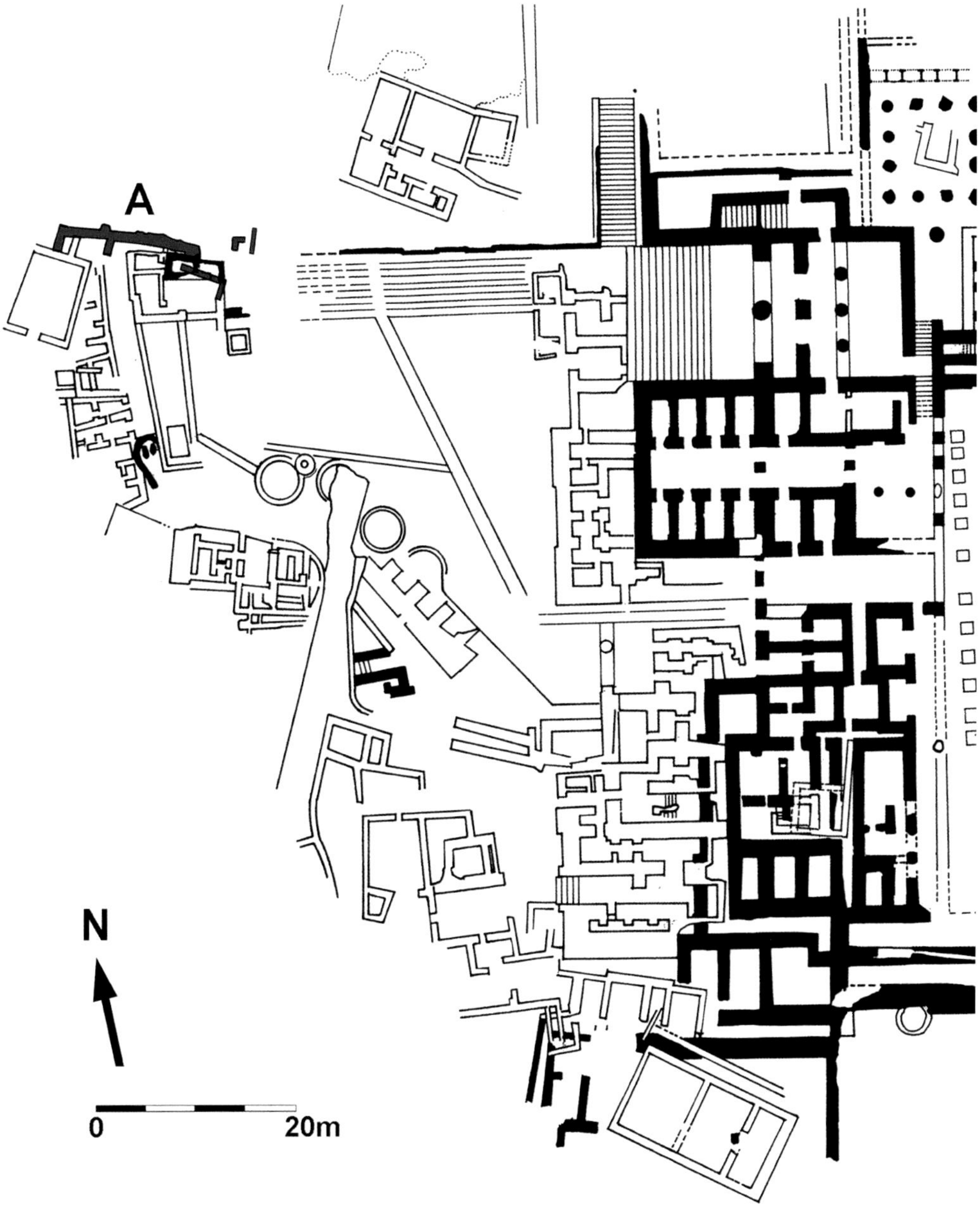

Figure 9.10. Plan of the western side of the palace site at Phaistos, showing location of the Casa a ovest del Piazzale I (A: walls shown in dark grey).

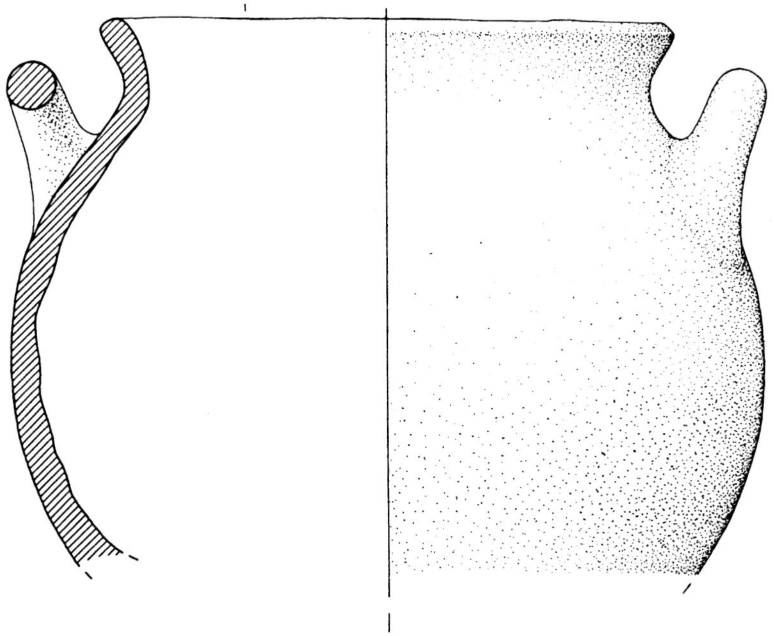

Figure 9.11. Cooking jar from the Casa a ovest del Piazzale I (1:2) (drawing by G. Merlatti).

(Borgna 2001). Only at this point does ritual activity appear to be of a religious nature – with funerary rites and offerings suggested by the burying of, respectively, a cooking jar with the bones of an infant and a pot filled with burnt seeds (Borgna 1997a: 210).

It is worth underlining the link between banqueting and funerary cult in Crete (for references, see Godart and Tzedakis 1993; and Borgna 1999a: 201; cf. Carter 1997) and also the restricted access to manipulation of food for ritual consumption, suggested in other important Cretan assemblages with evidence of banqueting, such as the exclusive LMIIIA warrior tombs with bronze vessels and cooking equipment (Matthäus 1983; Driessen and MacDonald 1984; Kilian-Dirlmeier 1985; Haskell 1989: 102–06, Popham 1994: 93–94; Löwe 1997: 52–60). Restricted participation in food consumption is also suggested by the ritual display explored in some neopalatial structures, particularly at Agia Triada in the Mesara plain, and interpreted by Koehl as an early stage of the historical Cretan *andreion* (Koehl 1997; Rehak and Younger 1998: 109–10). Marked by more limited access and by a stronger ideological and political grounding, ritual consumption of food in the closed space of aristocratic dwellings was possibly a parallel activity, related to but clearly different from the ritual meals connected with cult and sacrifice in sanctuaries, such as at Kato Syme (Lebessi and Muhly 1990; Kanta 1991: 482).

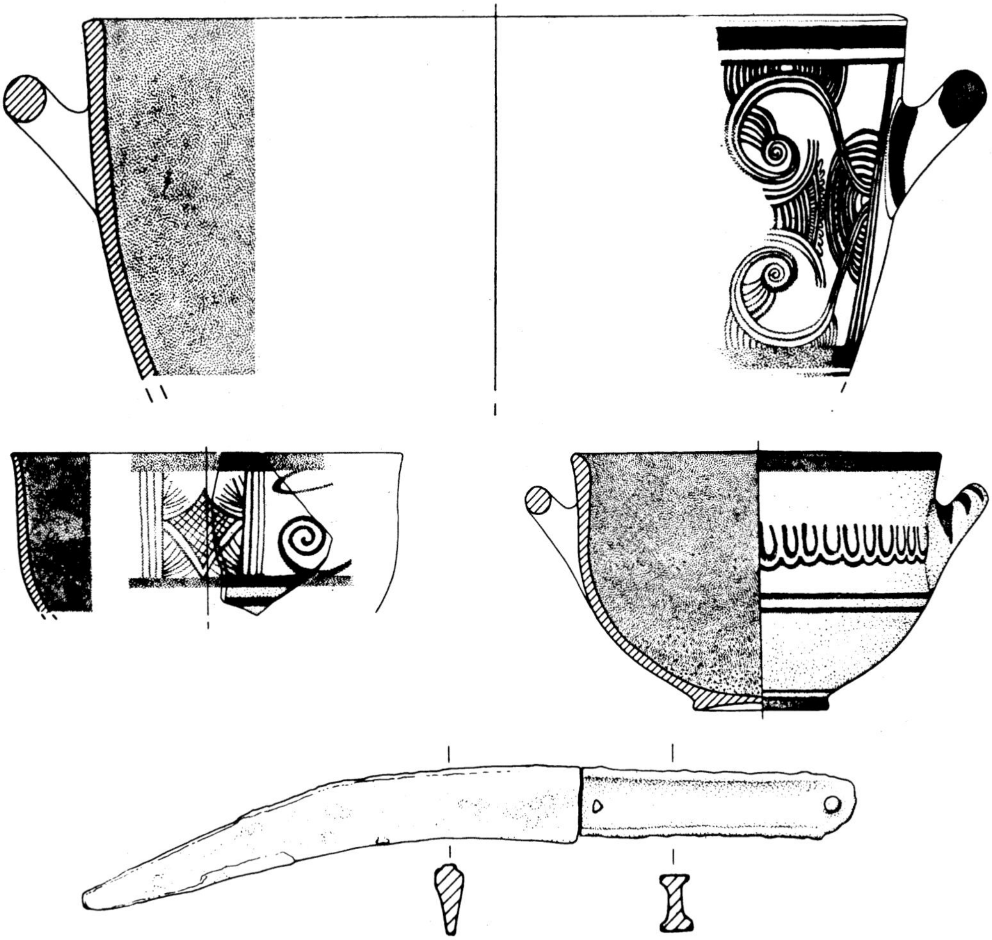

Figure 9.12. LMIIIC elaborate krater (1) and deep bowl (2), LMIIIB-C deep bowl (3) (1:3) and knife (1:2) from the Casa a ovest del Piazzale I (drawings by G.Merlatti).

Thus the Casa a ovest del Piazzale I at Phaistos, possibly heir to the secular side of the tradition of ritual consumption, may be interpreted as an aristocratic dwelling where economic and social power were maintained and exercised by means of ritual gatherings. These gatherings consisted of drinking activity with displays of pottery, of food transformation involving offerings and ritual meals, and perhaps, particularly in the more advanced phase of the life of the building, of cult activities. Finally, it is also worth noting that the ritual practices of the Casa a ovest del Piazzale I seem to have outlasted the 'protosymposion' of the Acropoli Mediana, which came to an end towards the middle of LMIIIC.

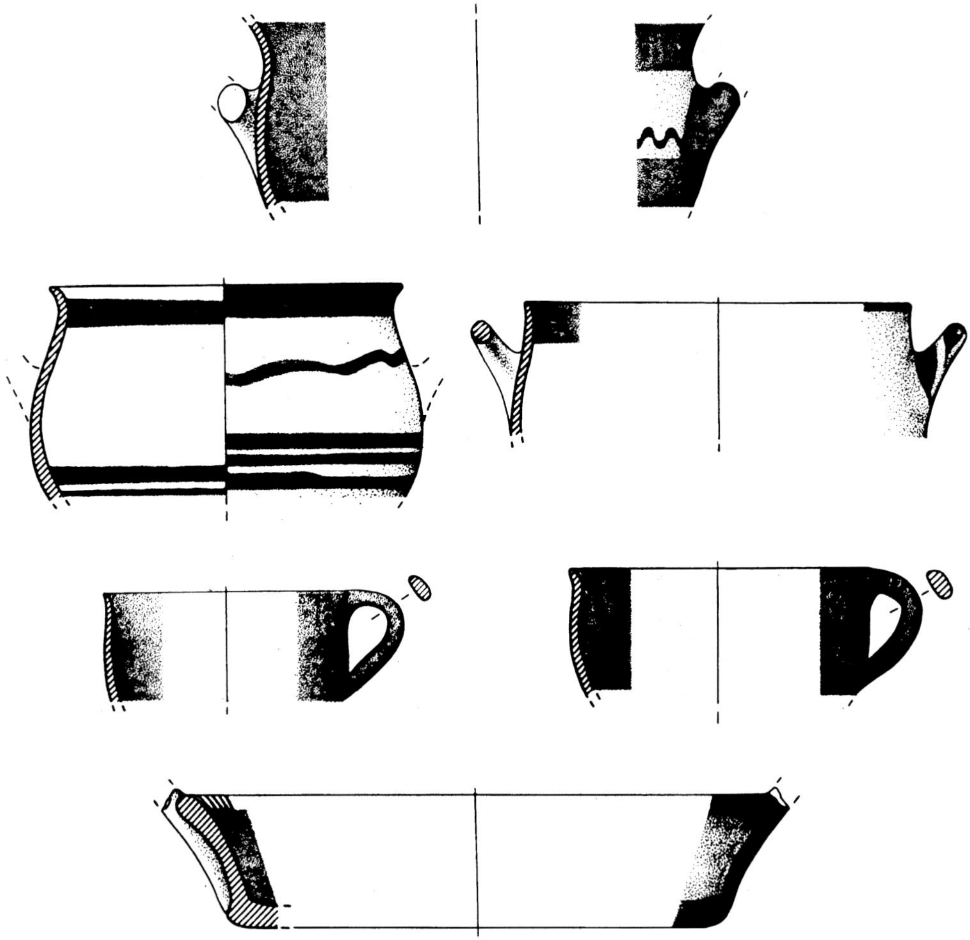

Figure 9.13. LMIIIC late pottery from the Casa a ovest del Piazzale I: deep bowls (1–3), cups (4–5) and tray (6) (1:3) (drawings by G.Merlatti).

Conclusion

Food transformation in the articulated and complex manner of the 'haute cuisine' (Levi-Strauss 1968) of local Minoan tradition, therefore, and food consumption on ritual occasions seem to have remained well rooted and to have played a dominant role in the dynamics controlling the structural management of social and economic power, as well as displays of political ideology, especially at the transition between the prehistoric and historical eras. To explore these ideas more thoroughly will require a systematic study of the archaeological topography of

LMIIIC and Dark Age Phaistos. In particular, such a study should clarify whether the Casa a ovest del Piazzale I was the pre-eminent building at Phaistos, or simply one of several important buildings, and whether it provides evidence of continuity from the Acropoli Mediana, or of confrontation and competition.

On the one hand, the hints of discontinuity towards the transition to late LMIIIC, noted in both assemblages, seem to favour competition between several small households, striving for supremacy by means of generosity, display and conspicuous consumption. On the other hand, if the differences between these two assemblages in layout and associations are not results of the nature of the archaeological deposits, then two different kinds of feasting may have confronted each other within the social framework of LMIIIC Phaistos: on the Acropoli Mediana, a kind of public banquet was more open to diverse social elements, but at the same time served to create hierarchical relationships and dependencies; in the Casa a ovest del Piazzale I, a banquet among equals, with restricted attendance, served to confirm and strengthen egalitarian relationships and social ties. The huge number of both unpainted fine pots and champagne cups and kylikes with simple dip-decoration, that is pottery excluded from social confrontation (cf. Hodder 1981), may support this hypothesis (on the use of fine plain pottery at late palatial Pylos, see Borgna 1999a: 202); some objects which could be interpreted as gifts – for example the knife and a fine stemmed bowl of Mycenaean provenance (Borgna 1999b: 200, fig.1) – may also have played an important role in creating ties. Consistent with the hypothesis of more restricted commensality and of an increase in restricted ritual and cult activity, especially during late LMIIIC, is the simple and severe decorative style of pottery (Figure 9.13), unsuited to the intense social communication inferred for the earlier period.

Acknowledgements

I would like to express my sincere thanks to Paul Halstead and John Barrett, who kindly invited me to participate in the Round Table, and the Sheffield Centre for Aegean Archaeology, which found financial support for my travel. I am also greatly indebted to Nong and Keith Branigan for their warm hospitality. Drawings are by Orazio Pulvirenti and Giuliano Merlatti and belong to the Archive of the Scuola Archeologica Italiana di Atene. I thank the Director of the Italian School, Emanuele Greco, for permitting their publication, and the Director of the excavations at Phaistos, Vincenzo La Rosa, who gave me the opportunity to study the LMIII pottery.

Endnote

1 The knife cannot be assigned to any precise type, but may be attributed to general classes

distinguished by Bouzek (1985: 145, 4.1.1 'Flange-hilted knives', B: 'Flanged hilt, curved blade like the Alpine types, but without stop-ridge') and Harding (1975: 197 'Late Types', 1. 'Knives with curved back'; cf. Harding 1984: 132–33); as regards Alpine knives of the Matrei type, it seems to be more similar to the later variant B than to the earlier variant A – Bianco Peroni 1976, 16–19; cf. also the Malhostovice type in central-eastern Europe: Ríhovsky 1972, no. 89; for technical features and in particular for the connection between the handle and the blade (the step on the back of the Phaistos knive is probably due to an incorrect modern restoration), see comparisons in the Aegean: Benzi 1992, table 179, h.T 15/26, ascribed to Class 1b of Sandars' classification (1955) and most probably of Aegean manufacture. For the symbolic value of knives in social exchange at the transition between Bronze and Iron Age, see Sherratt 1994.

Bibliography

Arnold, D.E.

1985 *Ceramic Theory and Cultural Process*. Cambridge: Cambridge University Press.

Benzi, M.

1992 *Rodi e la civiltà micenea*. Rome: Gruppo Editoriale Internazionale.

Bianco Peroni V.

1976 *I coltelli nell'Italia continentale* (Prähistorische Bronzefunde 7.2). Munich: C.H. Beck.

Borgna, E.

1997a Kitchen-ware from LM IIIC Phaistos. Cooking tradition and ritual activities in Late Bronze Age Cretan society. *SMEA* 39: 189–217.

1997b Some observations on deep bowls and kraters from the 'Acropoli Mediana' at Phaistos. In E. Hallager and B.P. Hallager (eds.), *Late Minoan Pottery. Chronology and Terminology*: 273–98. Aarhus: Aarhus University Press.

1999a Central Crete and the Mycenaeans at the close of the Late Bronze Age: the evidence of the 'Acropoli Mediana' at Phaistos. In *I Periferia tou Mykinaikou Kosmou, A' Diethnes Diepistimoniko Symposio, Lamia 1994. Praktika*: 353–70. Lamia.

1999b Circolazione della ceramica nello scambio cerimoniale tra mondo miceneo palaziale e Creta tardominoica: la prospettiva di Festòs nel TM III. In V. La Rosa, D. Palermo and L. Vagnetti (eds.), *Epi ponton plazomenoi. Simposio italiano di Studi Egei dedicato a L.Bernabò Brea e G. Pugliese Carratelli*: 199–205. Rome: Scuola archeologica italiana di Atene.

2000 Food preparation and ritual activity in LM III C Crete. *Pepragmena H' Diethnous Kritologikou Synedriou*: 147–59. Iraklio.

2001 Il periodo TM III B/C: la Casa a ovest del Piazzale I. In *I cento anni dello scavo di Festòs. Giornate Lincee, Roma, 13–14 dicembre 2000*: 273–98. Rome: Accademia Nazionale dei Lincei.

2003 *Il complesso di ceramica TM III dell'Acropoli Mediana di Festòs (Scavi 1955)*. Padova: Marsilio Editore.

Bouzek, I.

1985 *The Aegean, Anatolia and Europe. Cultural Interrelations in the Second Millennium B.C.* (SIMA 29). Göteborg: Paul Åström.

Broodbank, C.

1992 The Neolithic labyrinth: social change at Knossos before the Bronze Age. *JMA* 5: 39–75.

Brumfiel, E.M.
1987 Consumption and politics at Aztec Huexatla. *American Anthropologist* 89: 679–86.
Cameron, M.A.S.
1987 The 'palatial' thematic system in the Knossos murals. Last notes on Knossos frescoes. In R. Hägg and N. Marinatos (eds.), *The Function of the Minoan Palaces*: 321–28. Stockholm: Swedish Institute at Athens.
Carter, J.B.
1997 Thiasos and Marzeah. Ancestor cult in the age of Homer. In S. Langdon (ed.), *New Light on a Dark Age. Exploring the Culture of Geometric Greece*: 72–112. Columbia (Mo.): University of Missouri.
Clark, J.E. and M. Blake
1994 The power of prestige: competitive generosity and the emergence of rank societies in lowland Mesoamerica. In E.M. Brumfiel and J.W. Fox (eds.), *Factional Competition and Political Development in the New World*: 17–30. Cambridge: Cambridge University Press.
Conkey, M. and C. Hastorf (eds.)
1990 *The Uses of Style in Archaeology*. Cambridge: Cambridge University Press.
Deger-Jalkotzy, S.
1991 Diskontinuität und Kontinuität: Aspekte politischer und sozialer Organisation in mykenischer Zeit und in der Welt der Homerischen Epen. In D. Musti, A. Sacconi, L. Rocchetti, M. Rocchi, E. Scafa, L. Sportiello and M.E. Giannotta (eds.), *La transizione dal Miceneo all'Alto Arcaismo. Dal palazzo alla città*: 53–66. Rome: Consiglio nazionale delle ricerche.
1994 The post-palatial period of Greece: an Aegean prelude to the 11th century B.C. In V. Karageorghis (ed.), *Cyprus in the 11th Century B.C.*: 11–29. Nicosia: University of Cyprus.
1995 Mykenische Herrschafts-Formen ohne Paläste und die griechische Polis. In R. Laffineur and W.-D. Niemeier (eds.), *Politeia. Society and State in the Aegean Bronze Age* (Aegaeum 12): 367–77. Liège: University of Liège.
1998 The Aegaean islands and the breakdown of the Mycenaean palaces around 1200 B.C. In V. Karageorghis and N. Stampolidis (eds.), *Eastern Mediterranean. Cyprus – Dodecanese – Crete 16th – 6th Cent. B.C.*: 105–20. Athens: University of Crete.
Donlan, W.
1985 The social groups of Dark Age Greece. *CQ* 80: 293–308.
1989 The pre-state community in Greece. *Symbolae Osloenses* 64: 5–29.
1994 Chief and followers in pre-state Greece. In C.A.M. Duncan and D.W. Tandy (eds.), *From Political Economy to Anthropology. Situating Economic Life in Past Society*: 34–51. Montreal, New York: Black Rose Books.
1997 The relationship of power in the pre-state and early state polities. In L.G. Mitchell and P.J. Rhodes (eds.), *The Development of the Polis in Archaic Greece*: 39–48. London, New York: Routledge.
Driessen, J. and C. Macdonald
1984 Some military aspects of the Aegean in the late fifteenth and early fourteenth centuries B.C. *BSA* 79: 49–74.
Earle, T.K.
1989 The evolution of chiefdoms. *Current Anthropology* 30: 84–89.
1990 Style and iconography as legitimation in complex chiefdoms. In M. Conkey and C. Hastorf (eds.), *The Uses of Style in Archaeology*: 73–81. Cambridge: Cambridge University Press.

1991 The evolutions of chiefdoms. In T.K. Earle (ed.), *Chiefdoms: Power, Economy and Ideology*: 1–15. Cambridge: Cambridge University Press.

Finley, M.I.
1977 *The World of Odysseus*. London: Chatto and Windus.
1981 *Economy and Society in Ancient Greece*. London: Chatto and Windus.

Godart, L. and Y. Tzedakis
1993 La tombe à l'aède de la Canée et la peinture crétoise des XIVe et XIIIe siècles avant notre ère. *Comptes rendus de l'Académie des inscriptions et belles lettres*: 225–47.

Goody, J.
1982 *Cooking, Cuisine and Class*. Cambridge: Cambridge University Press.

Harding, A.F.
1975 Mycenaean Greece and Europe: the evidence of bronze tools and implements. *Proceedings of the Prehistoric Society* 41: 183–202.
1984 *The Mycenaeans and Europe*. London: Academic.

Haskell, H.W.
1989 LM III Knossos: evidence beyond the palace. *SMEA* 27: 81–110.

Helms, M.W.
1992 Long-distance contacts, elite aspirations and the age of discovery in cosmological context. In E.M. Schortman and P.A. Urban (eds.), *Resources, Power and Interregional Interaction*: 157–74. New York, London: Plenum.

Hodder, I.
1981 Pottery, production and use: a theoretical discussion. In H. Howard and E.L. Morris (eds.), *Production and Distribution: a Ceramic Viewpoint* (BAR International Series 120): 215–20. Oxford: British Archaeological Reports.

Immerwahr, S.A.
1990 *Aegean Painting in the Bronze Age*. University Park, London: Pennsylvania State University Press.

Jones, D.W.
1999 The archaeology and economy of Homeric gift exchange. *Opuscula Atheniensia* 24: 9–24.

Kanta, A.
1991 Cult, continuity and the evidence of pottery at the sanctuary of Syme Viannou, Crete. In D. Musti, A. Sacconi, L. Rocchetti, M. Rocchi, E. Scafa, L. Sportiello and M.E. Giannotta (eds.), *La transizione dal Miceneo all'Alto Arcaismo. Dal palazzo alla città*: 479–505. Rome: Consiglio nazionale delle ricerche.

Kilian, K.
1985 La caduta dei palazzi micenei continentali: aspetti archeologici. In D. Musti (ed.), *Le origini dei Greci. Dori e mondo egeo:* 73–115. Rome, Bari: Laterza.

Kilian-Dirlmeier, I.
1985 Noch einmal zu den 'Kriegergräbern' von Knossos. *Jahrbuch des Römisch-Germanischen Zentralmuseums Mainz* 32: 196–214.

Koehl, R.B.
1997 The villas at Ayia Triada and Nirou Chani and the origin of the Cretan andreion. In R. Hägg (ed.), *The Function of the 'Minoan Villas':* 137–49. Stockholm: Swedish Institute at Athens.

Laviosa, C.
1977 La casa TM III a Festòs: osservazioni sull' architettura cretese in età micenea. In *Antichità cretesi. Studi in onore di Doro Levi, 1* (Cronache di Archeologia 12): 79–88. Catania: Università di Catania, Istituto di archeologia.

Lebessi A. and P. Muhly

1990 Aspects of Minoan cult: sacred enclosures. The evidence from the Syme sanctuary (Crete). *Archäologischer Anzeiger*: 315–36.

Levi, D.

1956 Cronaca d' arte. Attività della Scuola Archeologica Italiana di Atene nell'anno 1955. *Bollettino d'Arte*: 238–71.

1966 La conclusione degli scavi a Festòs. *ASA* 27–28: 313–99.

Levi-Strauss, C.

1968 *L'origine des manières de table*. Paris: Plon.

Löwe, W.

1997 *Spätbronzezeitliche Bestattungen auf Kreta* (BAR International Series 642). Oxford: Tempus Reparatum.

Marinatos, N.

1986 *Minoan Sacrificial Ritual: Cult Practice and Symbolism*. Stockholm: Swedish Institute at Athens.

Matthäus, H.

1983 Minoische Kriegergräber. In O. Krzyszkowska and L. Nixon (eds.), *Minoan Society*: 203–15. Bristol: Bristol Classical Press.

Mazarakis Ainian, A.

1997 *From Rulers' Dwellings to Temples. Architecture, Religion and Society in Early Iron Age Greece (1100–700 B.C.)* (SIMA 121). Jonsered: Paul Åström.

McCallum, L.

1991 *Decorative Program in the Mycenaean Palace of Pylos: the Megaron Frescoes*. Ann Arbor: University Microfilms.

Morgan, C.

1998 Ritual and society in the Early Iron Age Corinthia. In R. Hägg (ed.), *Ancient Greek Cult Practice from the Archaeological Evidence*: 73–90. Stockholm: Swedish Institute at Athens.

1999 *The Late Bronze Age Settlement and Early Iron Age Sanctuary* (Isthmia 8). Princeton: American School of Classical Studies at Athens.

Morgan, C. and T. Whitelaw

1991 Pots and politics: ceramic evidence for the rise of the Argive state. *AJA* 95: 79–108.

Murray, O.

1983a Symposion and Männerbund. In P. Oliva (ed.), *Concilium Eirene 16*: 47–52. Prague.

1983b The Greek symposion in history. In E. Gabba (ed.), *Tria corda. Scritti in onore di A. Momigliano*: 257–72. Como: Edizioni New Press.

1983c The symposion as social organisation. In R. Hägg (ed.), *The Greek Renaissance of the Eighth Century B.C.: Tradition and Innovation*: 195–99. Stockholm: Swedish Institute in Athens.

1990 Sympotic history. In O. Murray (ed.), *Sympotica. A Symposium on the Symposion*: 3–13. Oxford: Clarendon Press.

1994 Nestor's cup and the origin of the Greek symposion. In B. d' Agostino and D. Ridgway (eds.), *Apoikia. I più antichi insediamenti greci in occidente: funzione e modi dell'organizzazione politica e sociale. Scritti in onore di Giorgio Buchner* (Annali di Archeologia e Storia antica, n.s. 1): 47–54. Naples: Istituto universitario orientale.

Pernier, L.

1902 Scavi della Missione italiana a Phaestos 1900–1901. Rapporto preliminare. *Monumenti Antichi* 12: 8–142.

Plog , S.
1995 Approaches to style. Complements and contrasts. In C. Carr and J.E. Neitzel (eds.), *Style, Society and Person. Archaeological and Ethnological Perspectives*: 369–86. New York, London: Plenum.

Pollock, S.
1983 Style and information: an analysis of Susiana ceramics. *Journal of Anthropological Archaeology* 2: 190–234.

Popham, M.R.
1994 Late Minoan II to the end of the Bronze Age. In D. Evely, H. Hughes-Brock and N. Momigliano (eds.), *Knossos. A Labyrinth of History. Papers in Honour of Sinclair Hood*: 89–102. London: British School at Athens.

Rehak, P. and J.G. Younger
1998 Review of Aegean prehistory 7: Neopalatial, Final Palatial, and Postpalatial Crete. *AJA* 102: 91–173.

Renfrew, C.
1985 Towards a framework for the archaeology of cult practice. In C. Renfrew (ed.), *The Archaeology of Cult. The Sanctuary at Phylakopi* (BSA Supplementary Volume 18): 11–26. London: British School at Athens.

Ríhovsky, J.
1972 *Die Messer in Mähren und dem Ostalpengebiet* (Prähistorische Bronzefunde 7.1). Munich: C.H. Beck.

Rowlands, M.J.
1980 Kinship, alliance and exchange in the European Bronze Age. In J. Barrett and R. Bradley (eds.), *The British Later Bronze Age* (BAR British Series 83): 15–55. Oxford: British Archaeological Reports.

Sahlins, M.D.
1968 On the sociology of primitive exchange. In M. Banton (ed.), *The Relevance of Models for Social Anthropology*: 139–236. London: Tavistock Publications.
1974 *Stone Age Economics*. London: Tavistock Publications.

Sandars, N.K.
1955 The antiquity of the one-edged bronze knife in the Aegean. *Proceedings of the Prehistoric Society* 21: 174–97.

Shelmerdine, C.W.
1999 Administration in the Mycenaean palaces. Where's the chief. In M.L. Galaty and W.A. Parkinson (eds.), *Rethinking Mycenaean Palaces. New Interpretations of an Old Idea*: 19–24. Los Angeles: Cotsen Institute of Archaeology, UCLA.

Sherratt, A.G.
1987 Cups that cheered. In W.H. Waldren and R.C. Kennard (eds.), *Bell Beakers of the Western Mediterranean. Definition, Interpretation, Theory and New Site Data* (BAR International Series 331): 81–103. Oxford: British Archaeological Reports.

Sherratt, S.
1994 Commerce, iron and ideology: metallurgical innovation in 12th–11th century Cyprus. In V. Karageorghis (ed.), *Cyprus in the 11th Century B.C.*: 59–106. Nicosia: University of Cyprus.

Spencer, C.S.
1993 Human agency, biased transmission and the cultural evolution of chiefly authority. *Journal of Anthropological Archaeology* 12: 41–74.

Van Wees, H.
1992 *Status Warrior. War, Violence and Society in Homer and History*. Amsterdam: J.C. Gieben.

1995 Princes at dinner. Social event and social structure in Homer. In J.P. Crielaard (ed.), *Homeric Questions. Essays in Philology, Ancient History and Archaeology*: 147–82. Amsterdam: J.C. Gieben.

1998 The law of gratitude: reciprocity in anthropological theory. In C. Gill, N. Postlethwaite and R. Seaford (eds.), *Reciprocity in Ancient Greece*: 13–49. Oxford: Oxford University Press.

Whitley, J.

1991 Social diversity in Dark Age Crete. *BSA* 86: 341–65.

Wright, J.C.

1995a Empty cups and empty jugs: the social role of wine in Minoan and Mycenaean societies. In P.E. McGovern, S.J. Fleming and S.H. Katz (eds.), *The Origins and Ancient History of Wine*: 287–309. Philadelphia: University of Pennsylvania.

1995b From chief to king in Mycenaean society. In P. Rehak (ed.), *The Role of the Ruler in the Prehistoric Aegean* (Aegaeum 11): 63–79. Liège: University of Liège.

10

Animal Husbandry Revisited: the Social Significance of Meat Consumption in a Highland Village of Mt Psiloritis, Central Crete

Elia A. Vardaki

Introduction

This chapter explores the social significance of livestock and the manipulation of consumption practice to define cultural identity. It questions the validity of the arguments put forward by researchers, who regard the consumption of food as an emulative aspect of human conduct. Instead, it is proposed that practices of identity management are conditioned by historically contingent ideological processes. People consume products, in the present context lamb-meat, not merely out of fashion or competitiveness. Such pursuits are indeed integral to, but not wholly determinant of, human conduct; people consume lamb-meat because they believe they will thus incorporate the social ideals that meat embodies. Meat consumption thus mediates cultural behaviour and so becomes the means by which people may express values, pursue individual and collective interests, and forge identities.

Ethnographic analyses offer useful insights into the forces shaping human conduct, providing the researcher with a better knowledge of the ideological framework of social groups. This chapter focusses on the way people incorporate meat consumption in practices that define social categories, forge personal and collective identities and signify changes. In the context of an ethnographic case study, I look at the way men and women manipulate consumption of food in general and lamb-meat in particular in order to construct themselves as persons, as gender categories, and as part of a social group. I then explore the archaeological implications of these ethnographic insights into food consumption, highlighting the importance of food preparation and consumption practices as factors generating social change and/or producing and reproducing social categories.

One aspect of meat consumption is political. This aspect is explored in the existing archaeological literature in the context of political competition for the establishment of an elite or for the negotiation of power, by groups in or aspiring to authority. The ways in which food may forge identities or in which culinary preferences may induce social change have not been thoroughly discussed, however, and an attempt is made here to remedy this with the help of ethnographic analysis.

Finally, the issue of change is approached from the viewpoint of the production and reproduction of knowledge. Knowledge is the collective values and skills transmitted from generation to generation in the form of practical know-how. Food preparation and culinary practices transmit and reproduce cultural knowledge in the form of tastes, food preferences and cooking techniques.

We Are What We Eat

People conceptualize their relationship to each other and formulate an identity through food consumption. The issues of agency and identity definition have attracted relatively close attention in the anthropological literature (Strathern 1988; Hoskins 1998; Hodder 2000; Dobres and Robb 2000; Sassaman 2000; Bell 1992). Hoskins, in her book *Biographical Objects,* demonstrates how personal possessions may be involved in the construction of identity: people's biographies are constructed through the objects they choose, and hence the perception of the self derives partly from objects (Hoskins 1998). Elaborating on this notion, food can be viewed as part of people's biographies since they remember events, places and people through a series of instances of feasting. Food involves the preparation and transformation of raw substances into a cultural object and transmits certain messages and taste preferences to consumers.

Viewed in such a theoretical framework, meat becomes a carrier of social signification intelligible by the social group. There is no single universal meaning which 'outsiders' are able to read, but there is an inside meaning, to use Mintz' term (1994: 114), which only people situated within the ideological framework are able to understand. Food is part of the strategies employed by people to express individual pursuits or the interests of historically constructed and conditioned social groups. It is precisely these individual pursuits prevalent in social groups that generate change. Each person relates differently to food, therefore, because it expresses his/her aims, reflects past pursuits and memories, and is identified with an event or place. People are also implicated in different stages of food production, preparation and consumption and so the perceptions of individuals are highly subjective and experiential.

For example, in the highlands of central Crete, a woman who prepares a lamb and consumes a small part of it has a different disposition from a man involved in rearing the lamb, in butchering it and finally in consuming the best part of it. Emotionally and psychologically, each stage of food preparation and consumption influences social practices. Thus, cooking the lamb may promote feelings of nurture and intimacy, while butchering creates emotions of virility and machismo. Social groups consume lamb for various reasons and lamb-meat mediates different emotions and ideological pursuits. The practices of cooking and butchering have ideological implications, apparent in the different ways that the genders manipulate meat preparation or consumption to construct their identity. As Herzfeld suggests, the role of men and women is not inherent but ideologically constructed, allowing people to produce and reproduce these categories, to challenge, modify or change them (1986: 217).

I do not wish to dismiss any objectivity in consumption practices or to claim a subjective and fragmentary view of social reality, whereby individuals have complete freedom of action. As Strathern suggests, society is comprised of *dividuals*, that is of persons embodying the values and relationships of the society in which each lives. Whereas individual is a singular term and implies that people act of their own free will and have their own rights and properties, dividuals are part of society since society is part of them. Strathern implies that thinking in terms of oppositions, like society:individuals, is a western misconception (1988: 12–13). The society of Axos, which I analyse in the following section of this chapter, does not think in these terms; people do not have an individualized identity, in the western sense. People perceive themselves as having freedom of choice to live their own way. They are products of a specific ideology which they reproduce, but also modify by their conduct.

A View from Ethnography

In order to investigate the cultural perspective of animals and how people manipulate the consumption of meat, and food in general, to construct themselves either as individuals or as part of a social group, I undertook an ethnographic case study of a highland village in central Crete. Axos, a village of 350 inhabitants, lies at the north foot of Mt Psiloritis, 65 km southeast of the town of Rethymnon. Until the 1960s, Axos was a mixed-farming village, specializing in herding. With the modernization and specialization of the Greek economy in the 1950s, however, the village turned to state-sponsored raisin production and herding declined. Nevertheless, many people continued to practise herding and most villagers still keep household animals today. For people in Axos, food and especially lamb is part of their social life as it creates, maintains and negotiates both social relationships and personal identity.

Participants in a meat consumption event often project to other people an ideal image of themselves. As Curtin and Heldke (1992) remarked, people are defined by what they eat and through food they express part of themselves, reflecting their gender or social status. Fieldwork provided an opportunity to look at the way men, and especially young men, manipulated meat consumption to create an image of virility and machismo. This is clearly illustrated by the following example.

I was often present at small talk between young men, and they always made sure that I heard about the feasting event they had recently attended, how much meat they had eaten or how much wine they had drunk. Nonetheless, Manolis made a striking impression on me. Manolis was one of the few young shepherds in the village and one day he was boasting to a friend about the amount of meat he had consumed a few days previously: 'We were only three men and in two days we ate 40 kilos of meat'. This account was expected to evoke the admiration and jealousy of the other young men, who were excluded from such an ostentatious feast. He wanted to show the other young men how privileged he was, as a herder, to be invited to such exclusive events. He also wanted to show that he was able to consume large quantities of meat, that the other young men could only have dreamed of and that, even if presented with the opportunity, they would have been physically incapable of eating. Manolis thus indulged the sense of superiority that his vocation secured for him, using an element of exaggeration to underscore how different he was: a man who exceeded normality, a macho man capable of consuming quantities of meat inconceivable for other people.

Rhetoric is usually employed by people to underline and amplify the effect of a specific activity, as Hertzfeld nicely demonstrated in his book, the *Poetics of Manhood* (1985). He showed that, in the village of Glendi at the foot of Mt Psiloritis, it is not enough to be born a man. A masculine identity is created through a series of practices including the way one acts, talks, eats and drinks. These activities are not equally performed by everyone. Herders project a strong machismo, a result of close contact with animals. It is the cultural rather than natural properties of meat that make it a masculine food; meat is identified with its source, the beast. Fiddes (1991) believes that meat can be viewed as a natural symbol, since it embodies nature in its untamed or wild form. Animals represent the fierce, the beastly, which must be tamed and manipulated for procurement purposes. Men, by virtue of being closer to procurement and the productive practices of herding, are identified with these cultural attributes of meat. Lamb-meat thus embodies herders' perceptions of themselves, of their animals, of their physical environment and of their lifestyle. By eating meat, therefore, herders believe they incorporate cultural properties of their lives such as machismo, toughness, vigilance and endurance. These cultural attributes of meat are amplified by a series of practices reserved traditionally for men: in marriage ceremonies, men butcher and handle raw meat, while women only wash it, and men eat conspicuous portions of cooked meat; and at the shearing feast or at Easter, it is men who cook the meat on bonfires.

Ideal images are historically constructed; the individual actor consumes products closely associated with the image which each has of her/himself and projects to other people. Campbell (1993) argued against a model that views consumption only as an emulative, competitive or cohesive activity. Instead, he proposed that consumption be viewed in its historical context in order to understand the consumption preferences of the time. For example, he viewed the increase in consumption in 18th century England as the result of an ideal image that was advocated in this period. People consumed objects that they thought embodied this image. Thus, ideological implications generated in a specific economic and political context create demand for certain products which in turn demonstrate power and superiority. Such products are not static but in constant flux, either changing or modifying their meaning in tune with a specific reality.

In the context of my own research, lamb consumption is viewed as serving different purposes in successive periods. In the period 1940–70, lamb was consumed to create solidarity or express patronage between members of the same kin group and to differentiate herding groups, who had access to the production of lamb, from other villagers. Lamb-meat, therefore, expressed exclusion and solidarity among members of the exclusive group. From the 1970s onwards, however, lamb-meat was consumed to project the affluence not only of herders but also of farmers and to underline the prestige not of the whole kin group but of the individual family, that is of the group which underpinned economic modernization and the improvement in village living standards. As a consequence the consumption of lamb-meat was intensified, as demonstrated by its abundance at public functions, marriages or name-day celebrations, and lamb-meat became a medium not of solidarity but of competition and negotiation of authority.

As suggested at the beginning of this chapter, through the preparation and cooking of food, individuals construct and define identities or induce changes not only in taste preferences but also in social structure. Food may also serve as the vehicle by which a social group becomes familiar with external influences and incorporates these into the social structure. This is most evident in the power exercised by women over the social group by virtue of their position in the kitchen of a household. Women in Axos can negotiate their own identity as capable and hospitable individuals through the preparation of lavish banquets. Women may also preserve cultural identity or act as a link between the commercial world of the towns and their community. New foods, such as crepes filled with mushrooms, meat dishes cooked in variety of white and red sauces, or soufflés, are very popular among young women. Such innovations assume great importance in the village and are quickly adopted even by reluctant, older housewives (Vardaki 2000).

These new foods familiarize villagers with economic and cultural developments in Greek society. Their adoption illustrates the capacity of women to transform external influences into common forms of social recognition, so familiarizing people with the new social and economic reality. Interest in this new cuisine is a matter of style. Contrary to Dietler's claim that use of an elaborate cuisine might demonstrate aspiration to or achievement of higher status (1996:

98), I believe that adoption of a specific food idiom is intended to differentiate a social group from its predecessors. Thus, young women appropriating the new cuisine believe that they incorporate the lifestyle and cultural properties of the towns; they incorporate the urban lifestyle in their cuisine because it expresses the way they see themselves – as emancipated women.

Food consumption in Axos is a practice of public interaction in which identities are recognized and forged. The manipulation of food practices and of the consumption of lamb-meat may be viewed, therefore, as strategic behaviour to challenge and negotiate the social reality. Moreover, the consumption of food in general, and of meat in particular, is in constant flux, signifying and even actively modifying existing structures.

Archaeological Implications

The preceding ethnographic example raised three main points:

1. The preparation and consumption of food are highly experiential and subjective, their meaning contingent on the ideological and historical structures of their time; it is thus difficult to discern, archaeologically, a single meaning for these practices. Nevertheless, their importance and values may be inferred through the use and manipulation of associated material culture.
2. Lamb-meat is regarded here as a luxury food of restricted and regulated availability. This does not necessarily imply the same importance in an archaeological context, although this possibility should be considered in the construction of archaeological theories concerning animal husbandry and food.
3. The fabrication of relationships, gender or status identity is moulded through the use and manipulation of meat consumption practices. In contrast to the suggestion (Lupton 1996) that food preferences and taste express hegemonic discourses, the preceding ethnographic example highlighted competition among individuals wishing to distinguish themselves temporally and spatially from others of the same gender, age, lineage or class. Although such competition demonstrates claims to the respect and honour of the wider social group, it does not necessarily indicate an aspiration to join the ruling elite, as is often assumed in the archaeological context.

How might archaeological investigation of animal husbandry, and of the preparation and consumption of animal products, be informed and enriched by viewing these as socially meaningful practices that forge individual or group identity? Hitherto, archaeological debate has regarded food either within a nationalistic framework, as establishing continuity between past and present food habits (Tzedakis and Martlew 1999), or as emulative behaviour, employed to signify social status and prestige (Hamilakis 1996). Such approaches view food one-sidedly, however, minimizing the dynamic properties of food. Instead of treating food as a mere reflection of people's intentions, the approach advocated here is to look at the way food and meat are implicated in the social reality to define relationships and to transmit cultural and social knowledge. Food and taste preferences are in constant flux, incorporated in social practices and expressing social interests. Food is viewed not as a denominator of cultural perceptions but as a dynamic element in social reality, appropriated by individuals or groups to express historically constituted interests.

The preparation of food, and of meat in particular, has not attracted enough attention as a powerful medium for controlling change or as a major input of knowledge within a social group. The transformation of food from raw to cooked, in other words from a natural into a cultural substance (Levi-Strauss 1970; Dubisch 1986), and the technical know-how involved, as well as the taste preferences that food mediates, make it a powerful means of shaping perceptions and cosmologies. People associated with preparation activities may be seen as mediating between two worlds (the natural and the constructed), while they are able to control access to social information transmitted through these practices. At the same time, people can manipulate such practices to restrict or facilitate access to groups. The consumption of products prepared under these conditions may convey values of exclusion, inclusion, or transmission of cultural and social knowledge to participants, as may be illustrated by an archaeological example.

Cooking utensils from the Old and New Palace periods in Crete consisted of trays for frying, large open-mouthed tripod cooking pots with flat-bases for baking foods using animal fats, and 'souvlaki trays' for grilling and roasting meats. Such an elaborate cuisine 'idiom' contrasts sharply with the later Mycenaean period, when cooking utensils included large rounded tripod cooking pots designed especially for large portions of boiled food (Borgna 1996). Elaboration of a cuisine idiom may denote increasing specialization and experimentation in food and tastes, in turn implying competitive relationships expressed in the form of food. Manipulation of food preparation techniques may lead to the regulation of related cultural information such as the construction of sexuality, in/equalities in gender relations or kin-group affiliation, elders' aspirations to social control, or even the integration into the group of ideals and values associated with distant times or places.

Experimentation and innovation in cooking techniques demonstrate social processes connected with the quest for identity formation. Elaborate cuisine can be developed as a response to competition among members of a group, either diachronically or synchronically. Through the control of culinary knowledge and of the complex preparation techniques suggested by an elaborate cuisine idiom, certain people may have posed within their group as authorities, claiming prestige and power. Moreover, appropriation of a stylish or complicated food idiom may have demonstrated the ability of a specific group to manipulate such mundane practices to negotiate cultural values and social relationships.

One final point is worth stressing: it may be misleading to think of social relationships in past societies in terms of elites or classes based on material wealth. Power and social differentiation may be based on gender, age, lineage or kin group affiliation. Groups of elders exercising control over social practices or the flow of knowledge, and thus controlling access to power, are often encountered in ethnographic studies (Meillassoux 1978; Barth 1975). Wealth has various forms of expression and, as shown above, cultural and social knowledge might be viewed as wealth. Individuals or groups that excel in performing certain tasks might claim access to and control over knowledge, its flow and the medium of its transmission. Access to food preparation and consumption practices, that mediate cultural information important for the social makeup of the group, could thus become a source of power in the social process.

Conclusion

This chapter has sought to demonstrate the complex way in which people express their identity and manipulate socially significant practices. Such an approach emphasizes social change, seeking to explain this on the basis of negotiation of values, ideologies and power relations between and within social groups. Accordingly, cultural systems are viewed as contingent and negotiable, and not as retaining equilibrium and solidarity. Humans are the active agents of changes within a social whole; humans are actively implicated in the creation of their own identity, manipulating social practices for their own benefit. Animals and their products, such as meat, are viewed as instruments for the definition of identity and transmission of knowledge, and as creating circumstances favouring change within a historically constituted social group.

The archaeological example set out here is both brief and speculative, but serves to argue that food preparation and cooking practices, as reflected in the cooking utensils of the Old and New Palace periods, should be considered important carriers of social information. Such culinary practices and knowledge have broad significance for understanding ideological and political structures of power. Lastly, although the ethnographic case study outlined here has highlighted the social and symbolic importance of lamb-meat, it is emphasized that the meaning of, and demand for, meat are contingent on the ideological structures and social strategies employed by different historically constituted groups.

Acknowledgements

I am grateful to John Barrett and Paul Halstead for inviting me to the Round Table, for thought-provoking discussion during its course, and for helpful comments during the preparation of this chapter. All shortcomings remain my own. My research was financially supported by the Ismene Fitch Scholarship of the British Council in Athens.

Bibliography

Bell, C.
1992 *Ritual Theory, Ritual Practice*. New York: Oxford University Press.

Borgna, E.
1996 Kitchen-ware from Late Minoan IIIC Phaistos: evidence for cooking traditions and ritual activity in Late Bronze Age Cretan society. In *8' Diethnes Kritologiko Sunedrio:* 1–21. Iraklio.

Campbell, C.
1993 Understanding traditional and modern patterns of consumption in 18th c. England: a character action approach. In J. Brewer and R. Porter (eds.), *Consumption and the World of Goods:* 40–57. London: Routledge.

Curtin, D.W. and L.M. Heldke
1992 Cooking, eating, thinking: transformative philosophies of food. In D.W. Curtin and L.M. Heldke (eds.), *Food, Body, Person*: 3–22. Bloomington: Indiana University Press.

Dietler, M.
1996 Feasts and commercial politics in the political economy: food, power and status in prehistoric Europe. In P. Wiesner and W. Schiefenhoevel (eds.), *Food and the Status Quest: an Interdisciplinary Perspective:* 87–125. Providence: Berghahn Books.

Dobres, M.-A. and J. Robb
2000 Agency in archaeology. In M.-A. Dobres and J. Robb (eds.), *Agency in Archaeology:* 3–17. London: Routledge.

Dubisch, J.
1986 Culture enters through the kitchen: women, food and social boundaries in rural Greece. In J. Dubisch (ed.), *Gender and Power in Rural Greece:* 195–214. Princeton: Princeton University Press.

Fiddes, N.
1991 *Meat: a Natural Symbol*. London: Routledge.

Hamilakis, Y.
1996 Wine, oil and the dialectics of power in Bronze Age Crete: a review of the evidence. *OJA* 1: 1–32.

Herzfeld, M.
1985 *The Poetics of Manhood*. Princeton: Princeton University Press.
1986 The category of 'female' in the ethnography of modern Greece. In J. Dubisch (ed.) *Gender and Power in Rural Greece:* 215–33. Princeton: Princeton University Press.

Hodder, I.
2000 Agency and individuals in long-term processes. In M.-A. Dobres and J. Robb (ed.), *Agency in Archaeology*: 21–33. London: Routledge.

Hoskins, J.
1998 *Biographical Objects: How Things Tell the Stories of Peoples' Lives*. New York: Routledge.

Levi-Strauss, C.
1970 *The Raw and the Cooked*. London: Jonathan Cape.

Lupton, D.
1996 *Food , the Body and the Self*. London: Sage.

Mintz, S.
1994 Eating and being: what food means. In B. Harriss-White and R. Hoffenberg (eds.), *Food: Multidisciplinary Perspectives:* 102–15. Oxford: Blackwell.

Sassaman, K.
2000 Agents of change in hunter-gatherer technology. In M.-A. Dobres and J. Robb (eds.), *Agency in Archaeology:* 148–68. London: Routledge.

Strathern, M.
1988 *The Gender of the Gift*. Berkeley: University of California Press.

Tzedakis,Y. and H. Martlew (eds.)
1999 *Minoans and Myceneans, Flavours of their Time*. Athens: Kapon Editions.

Vardaki, E.
2000 *Consuming Pastoralism: an Anthropological Insight in the Archaeology of Animal Husbandry*. DPhil dissertation, Oxford University.